MAKING
REPRESENTATIVE
DEMOCRACY
WORK

*This is Volume 17 in a series of studies
commissioned as part of the research program
of the Royal Commission on Electoral Reform
and Party Financing*

MAKING
REPRESENTATIVE
DEMOCRACY
WORK
THE VIEWS
OF CANADIANS

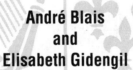

**André Blais
and
Elisabeth Gidengil**

Volume 17 of the Research Studies

ROYAL COMMISSION ON ELECTORAL REFORM
AND PARTY FINANCING
AND CANADA COMMUNICATION GROUP –
PUBLISHING, SUPPLY AND SERVICES CANADA

DUNDURN PRESS
TORONTO AND OXFORD

© Minister of Supply and Services Canada, 1991
Printed and bound in Canada
ISBN 1-55002-113-3
ISSN 1188-2743
Catalogue No. Z1-1989/2-41-17E

Published by Dundurn Press Limited in cooperation with the Royal
Commission on Electoral Reform and Party Financing and Canada
Communication Group – Publishing, Supply and Services Canada.

Canadian Cataloguing in Publication Data

Blais, André, 1947–
Making representative democracy work

(Research studies ; 17)
Issued also in French under title: La démocratie représentative.
ISBN 1-55002-113-3

1. Democracy – Canada. 2. Representative government and representation
– Canada. I. Gidengil, Elisabeth, 1947– . II. Canada. Royal Commission on
Electoral Reform and Party Financing. III. Title. IV. Series: Research studies
(Canada. Royal Commission on Electoral Reform and Party Financing) ; 17.

JC423.B53 1991   321.8′043′0971   C91-090529-0

#24.95

Dundurn Press Limited	Dundurn Distribution
2181 Queen Street East	73 Lime Walk
Suite 301	Headington
Toronto, Canada	Oxford, England
M4E 1E5	OX3 7AD

CONTENTS

TABLES

FOREWORD

THE ROYAL COMMISSION on Electoral Reform and Party Financing
was established in November 1989. Our mandate was to inquire into
and report on the appropriate principles and process that should govern the election of members of the House of Commons and the financing of political parties and candidates' campaigns. To conduct such a
comprehensive examination of Canada's electoral system, we held
extensive public consultations and developed a research program
designed to ensure that our recommendations would be guided by an
independent foundation of empirical inquiry and analysis.

The Commission's in-depth review of the electoral system was the
first of its kind in Canada's history of electoral democracy. It was dictated largely by the major constitutional, social and technological
changes of the past several decades, which have transformed Canadian
society, and their concomitant influence on Canadians' expectations
of the political process itself. In particular, the adoption in 1982 of the
Canadian Charter of Rights and Freedoms has heightened Canadians'
awareness of their democratic and political rights and of the way they
are served by the electoral system.

The importance of electoral reform cannot be overemphasized. As
the Commission's work proceeded, Canadians became increasingly
preoccupied with constitutional issues that have the potential to change
the nature of Confederation. No matter what their beliefs or political
allegiances in this continuing debate, Canadians agree that constitutional
change must be achieved in the context of fair and democratic processes. We cannot complacently assume that our current electoral
process will always meet this standard or that it leaves no room for
improvement. Parliament and the national government must be seen
as legitimate; electoral reform can both enhance the stature of national

political institutions and reinforce their ability to define the future of our country in ways that command Canadians' respect and confidence and promote the national interest.

In carrying out our mandate, we remained mindful of the importance of protecting our democratic heritage, while at the same time balancing it against the emerging values that are injecting a new dynamic into the electoral system. If our system is to reflect the realities of Canadian political life, then reform requires more than mere tinkering with electoral laws and practices.

Our broad mandate challenged us to explore a full range of options. We commissioned more than 100 research studies, to be published in a 23-volume collection. In the belief that our electoral laws must measure up to the very best contemporary practice, we examined election-related laws and processes in all of our provinces and territories and studied comparable legislation and processes in established democracies around the world. This unprecedented array of empirical study and expert opinion made a vital contribution to our deliberations. We made every effort to ensure that the research was both intellectually rigorous and of practical value. All studies were subjected to peer review, and many of the authors discussed their preliminary findings with members of the political and academic communities at national symposiums on major aspects of the electoral system.

The Commission placed the research program under the able and inspired direction of Dr. Peter Aucoin, Professor of Political Science and Public Administration at Dalhousie University. We are confident that the efforts of Dr. Aucoin, together with those of the research coordinators and scholars whose work appears in this and other volumes, will continue to be of value to historians, political scientists, parliamentarians and policy makers, as well as to thoughtful Canadians and the international community.

Along with the other Commissioners, I extend my sincere gratitude to the entire Commission staff for their dedication and commitment. I also wish to thank the many people who participated in our symposiums for their valuable contributions, as well as the members of the research and practitioners' advisory groups whose counsel significantly aided our undertaking.

Pierre Lortie
Chairman

INTRODUCTION

THE ROYAL COMMISSION'S research program constituted a comprehensive and detailed examination of the Canadian electoral process. The scope of the research, undertaken to assist Commissioners in their deliberations, was dictated by the broad mandate given to the Commission.

The objective of the research program was to provide Commissioners with a full account of the factors that have shaped our electoral democracy. This dictated, first and foremost, a focus on federal electoral law, but our inquiries also extended to the Canadian constitution, including the institutions of parliamentary government, the practices of political parties, the mass media and nonpartisan political organizations, as well as the decision-making role of the courts with respect to the constitutional rights of citizens. Throughout, our research sought to introduce a historical perspective in order to place the contemporary experience within the Canadian political tradition.

We recognized that neither our consideration of the factors shaping Canadian electoral democracy nor our assessment of reform proposals would be as complete as necessary if we failed to examine the experiences of Canadian provinces and territories and of other democracies. Our research program thus emphasized comparative dimensions in relation to the major subjects of inquiry.

Our research program involved, in addition to the work of the Commission's research coordinators, analysts and support staff, over 200 specialists from 28 universities in Canada, from the private sector and, in a number of cases, from abroad. Specialists in political science constituted the majority of our researchers, but specialists in law, economics, management, computer sciences, ethics, sociology and communications, among other disciplines, were also involved.

In addition to the preparation of research studies for the Commission, our research program included a series of research seminars, symposiums and workshops. These meetings brought together the Commissioners, researchers, representatives from the political parties, media personnel and others with practical experience in political parties, electoral politics and public affairs. These meetings provided not only a forum for discussion of the various subjects of the Commission's mandate, but also an opportunity for our research to be assessed by those with an intimate knowledge of the world of political practice.

These public reviews of our research were complemented by internal and external assessments of each research report by persons qualified in the area; such assessments were completed prior to our decision to publish any study in the series of research volumes.

The Research Branch of the Commission was divided into several areas, with the individual research projects in each area assigned to the research coordinators as follows:

F. Leslie Seidle	Political Party and Election Finance
Herman Bakvis	Political Parties
Kathy Megyery	Women, Ethno-cultural Groups and Youth
David Small	Redistribution; Electoral Boundaries; Voter Registration
Janet Hiebert	Party Ethics
Michael Cassidy	Democratic Rights; Election Administration
Robert A. Milen	Aboriginal Electoral Participation and Representation
Frederick J. Fletcher	Mass Media and Broadcasting in Elections
David Mac Donald (Assistant Research Coordinator)	Direct Democracy

These coordinators identified appropriate specialists to undertake research, managed the projects and prepared them for publication. They also organized the seminars, symposiums and workshops in their research areas and were responsible for preparing presentations and briefings to help the Commission in its deliberations and decision making. Finally, they participated in drafting the Final Report of the Commission.

On behalf of the Commission, I welcome the opportunity to thank the following for their generous assistance in producing these research studies – a project that required the talents of many individuals.

In performing their duties, the research coordinators made a notable contribution to the work of the Commission. Despite the pressures of tight deadlines, they worked with unfailing good humour and the utmost congeniality. I thank all of them for their consistent support and cooperation.

In particular, I wish to express my gratitude to Leslie Seidle, senior research coordinator, who supervised our research analysts and support staff in Ottawa. His diligence, commitment and professionalism not only set high standards, but also proved contagious. I am grateful to Kathy Megyery, who performed a similar function in Montreal with equal aplomb and skill. Her enthusiasm and dedication inspired us all.

On behalf of the research coordinators and myself, I wish to thank our research analysts: Daniel Arsenault, Eric Bertram, Cécile Boucher, Peter Constantinou, Yves Denoncourt, David Docherty, Luc Dumont, Jane Dunlop, Scott Evans, Véronique Garneau, Keith Heintzman, Paul Holmes, Hugh Mellon, Cheryl D. Mitchell, Donald Padget, Alain Pelletier, Dominique Tremblay and Lisa Young. The Research Branch was strengthened by their ability to carry out research in a wide variety of areas, their intellectual curiosity and their team spirit.

The work of the research coordinators and analysts was greatly facilitated by the professional skills and invaluable cooperation of Research Branch staff members: Paulette LeBlanc, who, as administrative assistant, managed the flow of research projects; Hélène Leroux, secretary to the research coordinators, who produced briefing material for the Commissioners and who, with Lori Nazar, assumed responsibility for monitoring the progress of research projects in the latter stages of our work; Kathleen McBride and her assistant Natalie Brose, who created and maintained the database of briefs and hearings transcripts; and Richard Herold and his assistant Susan Dancause, who were responsible for our research library. Jacinthe Séguin and Cathy Tucker also deserve thanks – in addition to their duties as receptionists, they assisted in a variety of ways to help us meet deadlines.

We were extremely fortunate to obtain the research services of first-class specialists from the academic and private sectors. Their contributions are found in this and the other 22 published research volumes. We thank them for the quality of their work and for their willingness to contribute and to meet our tight deadlines.

Our research program also benefited from the counsel of Jean-Marc Hamel, Special Adviser to the Chairman of the Commission and former

Chief Electoral Officer of Canada, whose knowledge and experience proved invaluable.

In addition, numerous specialists assessed our research studies. Their assessments not only improved the quality of our published studies, but also provided us with much-needed advice on many issues. In particular, we wish to single out professors Donald Blake, Janine Brodie, Alan Cairns, Kenneth Carty, John Courtney, Peter Desbarats, Jane Jenson, Richard Johnston, Vincent Lemieux, Terry Morley and Joseph Wearing, as well as Ms. Beth Symes.

Producing such a large number of studies in less than a year requires a mastery of the skills and logistics of publishing. We were fortunate to be able to count on the Commission's Director of Communications, Richard Rochefort, and Assistant Director, Hélène Papineau. They were ably supported by the Communications staff: Patricia Burden, Louise Dagenais, Caroline Field, Claudine Labelle, France Langlois, Lorraine Maheux, Ruth McVeigh, Chantal Morissette, Sylvie Patry, Jacques Poitras and Claudette Rouleau-O'Toole.

To bring the project to fruition, the Commission also called on specialized contractors. We are deeply grateful for the services of Ann McCoomb (references and fact checking); Marthe Lemery, Pierre Chagnon and the staff of Communications Com'ça (French quality control); Norman Bloom, Pamela Riseborough and associates of B&B Editorial Consulting (English adaptation and quality control); and Mado Reid (French production). Al Albania and his staff at Acart Graphics designed the studies and produced some 2 400 tables and figures.

The Commission's research reports constitute Canada's largest publishing project of 1991. Successful completion of the project required close cooperation between the public and private sectors. In the public sector, we especially acknowledge the excellent service of the Privy Council unit of the Translation Bureau, Department of the Secretary of State of Canada, under the direction of Michel Parent, and our contacts Ruth Steele and Terry Denovan of the Canada Communication Group, Department of Supply and Services.

The Commission's co-publisher for the research studies was Dundurn Press of Toronto, whose exceptional service is gratefully acknowledged. Wilson & Lafleur of Montreal, working with the Centre de Documentation Juridique du Québec, did equally admirable work in preparing the French version of the studies.

Teams of editors, copy editors and proofreaders worked diligently under stringent deadlines with the Commission and the publishers to prepare some 20 000 pages of manuscript for design, typesetting and printing. The work of these individuals, whose names are listed elsewhere in this volume, was greatly appreciated.

Our acknowledgements extend to the contributions of the Commission's Executive Director, Guy Goulard, and the administration and executive support teams: Maurice Lacasse, Denis Lafrance and Steve Tremblay (finance); Thérèse Lacasse and Mary Guy-Shea (personnel); Cécile Desforges (assistant to the Executive Director); Marie Dionne (administration); Anna Bevilacqua (records); and support staff members Michelle Bélanger, Roch Langlois, Michel Lauzon, Jean Mathieu, David McKay and Pierrette McMurtie, as well as Denise Miquelon and Christiane Séguin of the Montreal office.

A special debt of gratitude is owed to Marlène Girard, assistant to the Chairman. Her ability to supervise the logistics of the Commission's work amid the tight schedules of the Chairman and Commissioners contributed greatly to the completion of our task.

I also wish to express my deep gratitude to my own secretary, Liette Simard. Her superb administrative skills and great patience brought much-appreciated order to my penchant for the chaotic workstyle of academe. She also assumed responsibility for the administrative coordination of revisions to the final drafts of volumes 1 and 2 of the Commission's Final Report. I owe much to her efforts and assistance.

Finally, on behalf of the research coordinators and myself, I wish to thank the Chairman, Pierre Lortie, the members of the Commission, Pierre Fortier, Robert Gabor, William Knight and Lucie Pépin, and former members Elwood Cowley and Senator Donald Oliver. We are honoured to have worked with such an eminent and thoughtful group of Canadians, and we have benefited immensely from their knowledge and experience. In particular, we wish to acknowledge the creativity, intellectual rigour and energy our Chairman brought to our task. His unparalleled capacity to challenge, to bring out the best in us, was indeed inspiring.

Peter Aucoin
Director of Research

PREFACE

From its inception, the Royal Commission sought to take into account public concerns regarding the electoral process. To supplement what it heard at its public hearings and in written submissions, the Commission conducted a number of public opinion surveys to assess citizen attitudes regarding electoral reform. The most detailed of these surveys is the one on which the analysis presented in this volume is based. Indeed, it is the most comprehensive survey of citizen attitudes about electoral institutions ever conducted in Canada. Carried out by the Institute for Social Research (ISR) at York University under the supervision of Professors André Blais and Elisabeth Gidengil, the survey involved detailed interviews with 2 947 respondents in the fall of 1990. The survey provides comprehensive and reliable information on public attitudes and preferences relevant to electoral reform. The data are available from the ISR.

In this volume, the principal researchers present extensive analysis and interpretation of the survey data. They examine public opinion on a series of issues that are central to the democratic process, comparing the findings with previous surveys where data are available. They also analyse the findings in the light of democratic theory. Because many of the issues are abstract and have not been the subject of recent public debate, the analysis pays careful attention to the firmness with which opinions are held.

Citizens' attitudes toward electoral institutions are important because they form the basis for the legitimacy of the political system as a whole. The procedures through which representatives are chosen are at the heart of the democratic process and influence the responsiveness of the system. Thus, the survey asked citizens how well they understood the system and how satisfied they were with present arrangements.

In analysing the data, the authors tried to answer some central questions: How knowledgeable are Canadians about the rules and conventions that govern the electoral process? Are they seen as fair? Do they reflect the values and preferences of the electorate? What would citizens like to see changed?

The study examines the fundamental values of respondents, as they bear on the electoral system, and their opinions with respect to politicians, political parties and the role of money in the political process. It examines concerns about undue influence in political decision making and the level of confidence that electors have in politicians and parties. In particular, the study analyses public attitudes toward election financing, campaign communication (including advertising, televised leaders debates and news coverage) and the representative process.

The authors found overall satisfaction with the electoral process but pervasive frustration with electoral outcomes. While citizens regarded political parties as essential to the democratic process, they were unhappy with a perceived lack of responsiveness on the part of parties. More specifically, Professors Blais and Gidengil report that a strong majority of Canadians believe that (1) there should be strict limits on campaign spending; (2) parties should be obliged to reveal the names of financial contributors; (3) there should be no public funding of parties and candidates; (4) MPs should be more responsive to their constituents; and (5) selection of party leaders should be organized by the parties. No specific reforms were demanded but respondents favoured mandatory televised leaders debates and more media access for minor parties.

The study is particularly valuable because it uses earlier surveys and comparative data from other countries to assist in the interpretation of the findings and because it addresses both theoretical concerns and policy issues in the analysis.

This volume will be of interest not only to political scientists but also to election administrators, party strategists, journalists and, indeed, all citizens concerned about the electoral process and the values it expresses. Clearly written and presented, it will provide much food for thought for Canadians and others interested in the processes of representative democracy.

Our task as research coordinators for this volume has been to facilitate the work of the authors. We have had considerable assistance in this task. Pierre Lortie, chair of the Royal Commission, and Peter Aucoin, director of research, contributed to the design and focus of the study. The Commission staff have been of great assistance in preparing the study for publication. We are also grateful to the three conscientious peer reviewers and, in particular, to the authors, who brought a high level of competence and commitment to the work and who responded to our requests for revision with cheerfulness and despatch.

Herman Bakvis
Fred Fletcher
Research Coordinators

Making
Representative
Democracy
Work

1

INTRODUCTION

THIS STUDY EXAMINES citizens' attitudes about electoral procedures in Canada. Canada is one of approximately twenty countries that have had "democratic" elections over a fairly long period of time (Butler et al. 1981; Powell 1982). The recent dramatic push toward democratization in almost all parts of the world suggests that electoral democracy, whatever its shortcomings, must have – or must be perceived to have – considerable value, enough value that, in order to bring it about, people are willing to take serious personal risks. There is at least prima facie evidence that those who do not enjoy the benefits of electoral democracy feel that they are being deprived of something important.

Like any institution, electoral democracy must be assessed first and foremost on the basis of its own criteria. Since it is based fundamentally on the principle of representation, the procedure through which representatives are chosen is crucial in judging the quality of electoral democracy. We are interested in how Canadians themselves view the electoral process: how satisfied are they with the present arrangements, and what would they like to see changed?

Understanding citizens' attitudes about electoral institutions is important for two reasons. First, it provides us with an important yardstick for assessing the quality of electoral democracy in Canada. It is of the very essence of representative democracy that "the legitimacy of the government rests on a claim to represent the desires of its citizens" (Powell 1982, 3). The main benefit of the electoral process is that elected leaders are induced to be responsive to the needs and concerns of citizens. From that perspective, one sign of a healthy democracy is that electoral arrangements themselves correspond as much as possible to citizens' preferences. It would be very odd for a democracy which claims to be representative to adopt electoral rules that are completely at variance with the views of most of its citizens. Thus, one appropriate test of the democratic nature of an electoral system is to determine the extent to which the procedures do indeed reflect people's wishes. By examining Canadians' attitudes about the electoral process, this study provides a basis for evaluating the degree to which Canadian electoral institutions meet this important test of democracy.

The second reason that attitudes about the electoral process are important relates to the overall legitimacy of our political system. Elections are designed not only to represent but also to elicit consent. This point has been made forcefully by Ginsberg: "Permitting citizens the opportunity to participate in elections is conceived by governments to be a source of increased authority and stability. Expansion of the suffrage is often designed to control the potentially disruptive power of mass participation in politics and to convert it into support for the state" (1982, 19). From this perspective, elections constitute an institution of governance that is designed to ensure the legitimacy (and stability) of the political system. This function can only be performed successfully, however, if the electoral process itself is deemed to be fair. Understanding how fair the electoral process is considered to be, then, has important implications for assessing the legitimacy of our whole system of electoral democracy.

It is not enough, of course, simply to examine Canadians' attitudes about the electoral process. We also need to inquire into the sources of these attitudes and to explore the basic political values that underlie them. Democracy is essentially a question of values, and we must understand these values in order to make sense of how Canadians react to specific aspects of electoral law. This study begins with an analysis of those political values that are likely to shape Canadians' attitudes about electoral arrangements.

As Pennock (1979) argues persuasively, two values are fundamental to the democratic ideal: liberty and equality. Democracy is predicated on a belief in the supreme value of individual autonomy and dignity, and the democratic credo requires that autonomy and dignity be attributed to all individuals without distinction; everyone must count equally.

Liberty and equality may be mutually reinforcing, but they may also come into conflict. Much depends on how they are conceived. The more narrowly the two concepts are defined (in terms of negative liberty and formal equality, for example), the more they tend to complement one another. "When the two concepts are enlarged," however, "as they tend to be in order to embrace the full meaning of the democratic ideal, tensions and even contradictions emerge" (Pennock 1979, 45). Liberty is likely to create inequalities of condition and any attempt to restore some substantive equality (in terms of opportunities or outcomes) is bound to impinge upon liberty.

According to Pennock, there is an additional tension, which partially overlaps the first, between individualism and collectivism. As he notes, "historically ... democratic theory is associated with individualistic theory. Nor would it appear that the association is only historical and incidental. Its ideal of liberty relates to the individual; and the means taken to secure it, the franchise backed up by a series of individual rights, likewise reflects an individualistic philosophy" (1979, 62). At the same time, "democratic theorists at least as far back as Rousseau accommodated it to a much more collectivist outlook. Indeed ... just as man is both self-seeking and altruistic, so democracy has its collectivist aspect" (ibid., 63). As we will see, one issue that comes up again and again in the debate over electoral institutions concerns the extent of public regulation: should we devise rules to ensure that elections will be as fair as we would like them to be or should we try to let the players act as freely as possible?

We should not forget that Canada has a tradition of critical democratic thought. Historically, one important manifestation of this has been a strong populist strain (Laycock 1990). Populism can be a most ambiguous concept, but "its refusal to disappear, despite cycles of intellectual fashion, suggests it refers to a set of political phenomena inadequately encompassed by other concepts" (Richards 1981, 5). What is particularly interesting about populism is its heavy emphasis on grassroots politics and its profound unease with the principle of representation, which underlies the electoral process. It is thus important to see how populist values affect attitudes about electoral institutions.

As fundamental normative orientations, our values provide us with general standards or criteria that guide our more immediate attitudes on particular issues. Values do not, however, operate in a vacuum. They combine with beliefs about reality to shape evaluations. We will look at two types of beliefs about political reality: those that can be assumed to be relatively enduring and those that are more likely to respond to the unfolding events of Canadian political life. Chapter 2 deals with the first category by examining Canadians' basic beliefs about the democratic capabilities of their fellow citizens, as well as about the democratic necessity of having political parties. Chapter 3 moves on to an analysis of Canadians' empirical beliefs about three central elements in the electoral process: politicians, parties and money.

How much confidence do Canadians have in their politicians? Representative democracy poses a difficult dilemma for citizens. The "very notion of representation implies a division of political labour between 'the rulers' and 'the ruled'" (Kornberg et al. 1982, 66). To the extent that they accept that division of labour, citizens must put their trust in those whom they elect to be their leaders. At the same time, it is in the interest of the ruled not to trust their rulers completely; citizens need to keep a close eye on their elected representatives in order to ensure that those representatives are as responsive as possible to the electorate's wants and concerns. If citizens lose trust in their representatives, they may come to question the electoral procedures by which those persons were selected. We will therefore examine how much confidence Canadians have in their elected representatives and how this confidence (or lack of confidence) influences their views about the electoral process.

Next, we will turn our attention to Canadians' perceptions about what is, undoubtedly, the core political institution associated with representative democracy: the political party. The link between representative democracy and parties is so close, in fact, that freedom to form parties is typically deemed to be a necessary condition for democratic elections (Butler et al. 1981; Powell 1982; Dahl 1989). Sartori reflects the conventional wisdom of the discipline when he states that parties "appear to be a requirement of modern political systems in that they provide a channelling system for society" (1977, 27). Galeotti and Breton (1986) contend that parties enhance accountability because, as institutions, they have a longer time horizon than individual politicians and are therefore more dependent on the trust of citizens and more likely to fulfil their promises. Those views are not, however, necessarily shared by the general public. Dennis (1966) has shown that, in the United States at least, there is a deep ambivalence about the party system, arising in great part from the contradictory functions that parties must perform in a democracy – representing social cleavages on the one hand and building consensus on the other. Moreover, these roles may be performed more or less adequately. The centrality of parties and the importance of the functions they perform in democratic systems make it imperative that we examine Canadians' assessment of parties' overall performance and ascertain the extent to which attitudes about electoral institutions are affected by these assessments.

Finally, we will examine beliefs about the role of money in politics. Canadians' beliefs about money interest us because of the deep concern expressed in the literature on democracy regarding the implications for democracy of economic inequality. The question has been neatly summarized by Dahl (1989, 326): "But if income, wealth and economic position are also political resources, and if they are distributed unequally, then how can citizens be political equals? And if citizens cannot be political equals, how is democracy to exist?" These are difficult questions, for which there are no easy answers. The focus here is on beliefs about the amount of political influence that flows from money. We want to determine whether those who think that money buys a great deal of influence adopt positions on electoral procedures that are substantially different from those of people who perceive that money matters very little.

Once we have examined some major features of Canadians' values and empirical beliefs, we will be able to analyse attitudes about the electoral system per se. In our study, we distinguish three sets of attitudes: those about the representative process itself (Chapter 4), and those about two external factors that may affect the actual working of representative democracy – attitudes about electoral finances, examined in Chapter 5, and those about electoral communication, examined in Chapter 6. In each case, we will look first at the distribution of opinions on the various issues and, whenever possible, determine whether that distribution has changed over time. We will then examine the link between opinions and various socio-economic characteristics. We will also assess whether attitudes vary according to respondents' level of political information. Finally, and most importantly, we will relate Canadians' opinions to their political values and beliefs.

Chapter 7 adopts a broader perspective and assesses the overall level of satisfaction with the existing electoral institutions. We will examine how region, level of information, social background characteristics, and political values and beliefs affect the level of satisfaction. We will also attempt to pin down the sources of satisfaction or dissatisfaction, as spontaneously expressed by citizens, and to relate Canadians' overall evaluation of the system to their reactions to the specific issues surveyed in chapters 4, 5 and 6.

The Conclusion wraps up the major findings of the study and provides an overall assessment of the correspondence (or lack thereof) between the existing electoral institutions and Canadian public opinion – on the whole, do Canadians have the kind of institutions they would like to have? In the process, we will discuss what we believe to be the policy implications of our study. Do our findings suggest there is a need for a major overhaul of present arrangements? What kind of reform is more likely to enhance the perceived legitimacy of the electoral process and of the political system?

Throughout the study, we will relate Canadians' attitudes to their social background characteristics. We will focus on nine socio-economic characteristics: region, gender, age, education, income, occupation (blue-collar versus white-collar), unionization, language and religion. These are, we believe, the nine most important background characteristics to be taken into account when it comes to understanding Canadians' views about electoral democracy. These characteristics are among those that have been identified as being the most relevant to politics in general (Lipset 1983, 230–32) and to electoral behaviour in Canada in particular (LeDuc 1984).

Of these socio-economic factors, region of residence is the one to which we will pay the greatest attention. Region is the most obvious and extensively studied cleavage in Canada. It has been described as "one of the pre-eminent facts of Canadian life" (Elkins and Simeon 1980), and "a crucial – if not *the* crucial – variable in any serious study of the Canadian 'mosaic' system" (Chi 1972). From the very beginning, analyses of Canadian public opinion have focused on the regional cleavage (see, in particular, Schwartz 1967; 1974), and it still figures as the most prominent factor in more recent analyses (Johnston 1986). Regions have particular relevance to our study for two reasons. First, regions, as they are defined here (that is, as provinces or groups of provinces), correspond to political communities. Each province has its own arrangements for conducting elections for the provincial legislature, and it is quite possible that experiences with these procedures will affect attitudes about electoral arrangements at the federal level. More generally, these political communities have had differing historical experiences with the workings of representative democracy, both within their own political systems and as parts of the larger federal system. Second, from a public policy perspective, it is important to determine to what extent attitudes about representative democracy may be related to regional feelings of discontent. One source of such feelings is a sense of being inadequately represented within the institutions of the central government; in the province of Alberta, in particular, this sense has manifested itself in calls for an overhaul of our representative institutions.

The second most important social background characteristic for understanding attitudes toward electoral arrangements is, in our view, education. Converse's verdict that education is the top priority variable in comparative electoral research still holds: "It is almost unique in that while it is a prime predictor, and probably the prime predictor for the whole class of dependent variables reflecting political interest, participation, and mobilization, it also shows remarkable discriminating power as a status measure in predicting to variables on the other side of the watershed – ideology and party position" (1974, 730). The crucial role of education in the formation of political beliefs and attitudes is one of the major conclusions of *The Civic Culture* (Almond and Verba 1963). More recently, McClosky and Zaller (1984, 239) have shown that support for democratic norms is strongly related to level of education.

In McClosky and Zaller's model, education is a key to the process of social learning, which is required for the acquisition of political norms. In her critique of *The Civic Culture*, however, Pateman (1980) has pointed to a quite different type of social learning. She suggests that if citizens of lower socio-economic status appear to be less supportive of democratic norms, this may reflect their "scepticism that the system actually operates as it is held to" (ibid., 80). Socio-economic status has, in fact, proved to be strongly related to perceptions of government responsiveness and political trust in Canada (Simeon and Elkins 1980; Ornstein et al. 1980).

Income would seem to have a particular relevance to the attitudes about electoral finances that constitute a major concern of this study. We might expect those with a low income to be more cynical about the role of money in politics and to favour the imposition of strict regulations on parties' revenues and expenditures. We should note, however, that when Meisel and Van Loon (1966) examined Canadians' attitudes for the Advisory Committee on Election Expenses in 1965, the impact of income was found, at times, to be unclear, if not counterintuitive.

Occupation can be classified in many different ways. We will rely in this study on the simplest distinction of all, that between blue-collar and white-collar occupations. This distinction has been found to correspond with a marked discontinuity in subjective class identification. Those who are employed in blue-collar occupations are much more likely than those who are employed in lower white-collar occupations to think of themselves as working class (Gidengil 1989).

Actual membership in a particular class category does not, of course, automatically translate into a particular set of attitudes. One important vehicle for politicizing subordinate class sentiment has been the union. Union membership has, in fact, been found to have a substantial impact on political behaviour in Canada (Archer 1985). Given the role that unions play in Canadian politics, it is also useful, from a public policy perspective, to determine to what extent union members have distinct views on electoral institutions.

While the impact of socio-economic status and class on Canadians' attitudes has been the object of a great deal of attention in election literature, gender has only recently begun to receive attention from students of public opinion in Canada, with the emergence of a gender gap on many issues in a number of different countries (for Canada, see Wearing and Wearing 1991; for the United States and Britain, see Norris 1985a). Gender has particular relevance to many of our central concerns regarding representative democracy. As Pateman (1980) reminds us, if politics has tended to be the preserve of the middle class, it has been the *male* middle class. The underrepresentation of women in Parliament has been amply documented (Brodie 1991; Erickson 1991; Young 1991).

It is important, then, to examine whether patterns of exclusion and marginalization have affected the way that women evaluate our electoral system.

If gender is a relatively recently politicized cleavage, the linguistic cleavage has always been central to Canadian politics. For Gibbins (1985, 38), the two most crucial features of Canadian society in terms of their impact on political life are the existence of a French-speaking minority, and this minority's concentration in the province of Quebec. The linguistic cleavage is a fixture of Canadian politics that simply cannot be ignored. It is a cleavage that has become more complex as recent waves of immigration have increased Canada's multicultural character (Breton 1986). The representation of ethnic minorities has become a matter of concern (Pelletier 1991; Simard 1991; Stasiulis and Abu-Laban 1991) and we cannot obtain a full understanding of Canadians' opinions on questions of representative democracy without examining the views of those whose first language is neither French nor English.

We will also examine how age affects views about our electoral arrangements. Age may reflect life cycle and/or generational effects. While we will not be able to separate the two in this study, since this would require a longitudinal design, it is the latter effect that most interests us, because of its long-term impact. Inglehart (1977; 1990), in particular, has argued that the generation born after 1945 has come to adopt a new set of post-materialist values, which, among other things, have led to an emphasis on élite-directing, rather than élite-directed, politics (for Canada, see Nevitte et al. 1989). We will ascertain to what extent that generation has a distinct conception of representative democracy.

Finally, we will examine the impact of religion on opinion. We are particularly interested in relating religious attitudes to basic political values. Religion has been found to shape political values in important ways. For example, some writers have suggested a historical link between Protestant culture and the development of representative democracy (Bollen 1979; Inglehart 1990, 51). Such arguments suggest that there may well be differences in political values and attitudes toward electoral institutions among religious groups.

These are, in very broad terms, the questions to be addressed in this study. Our major data source will be a survey that we designed, in consultation with the Royal Commission, to tap Canadians' views about electoral institutions. To the best of our knowledge, this is the first survey that systematically measures public opinion on a wide array of questions related to the electoral process. This should enable us to enrich our understanding of the public's attitudes on these matters. Technical information on the survey, conducted by the Institute for Social Research at York University, is presented in appendix A. The questionnaire is presented in appendix B.

We would like to draw attention to some important features of the survey. First, we have a rather large sample size – 2 947 respondents. This allows us to document regional variations in attitudes. It should be stressed, however, that the sample is not large enough to allow us to document patterns that may be specific to either Manitoba or Saskatchewan alone or to any of the Atlantic provinces taken individually. The sample consists of approximately 600 respondents in each of Ontario and Quebec, 400 in each of Atlantic Canada, Alberta and British Columbia, and a combined total of 400 in Manitoba and Saskatchewan. Sample sizes of 400 and 600 yield margins of error of approximately five and four percentage points, respectively.

The interviews took place between 13 September and 30 October 1990. Interviews began one week after the Ontario provincial election, two days after the Manitoba provincial election, and one day after the prime minister nominated former Nova Scotia premier John Buchanan to the Senate. Eight additional nominations to the Senate were also announced in the second week of our field work. The acrimonious debate surrounding those nominations pervaded most of the interviewing period. To determine whether that particular aspect of the context made any difference to the responses, we compared the responses that we obtained during the various weeks of interviewing, and discovered no evidence of any significant effect. As well, we compared our findings, whenever possible, with those of previous studies. There is no indication that our results are systematically at odds with those of other surveys and there is, therefore, no reason to believe that our findings are biased in some systematic way.

Any study that examines opinions and attitudes must be concerned with the reliability of survey responses as indicators of people's beliefs. Converse (1964; 1970), in particular, has warned that some people may feel compelled to provide answers even when they do not really have opinions about particular topics. Such answers will be more or less random. The seriousness of the problem of non-attitudes is still being debated (for a useful review, see Kinder 1983). Given the topic at hand, the problem must be squarely confronted. We simply cannot dismiss the possibility that many people have not thought very much about some of the issues we will be considering.

It is therefore imperative to assess the firmness of opinions on these matters. This assessment will be based mostly on the results of experiments we have done with question wording and order. The experiments consist of supplying randomly selected groups of respondents with different versions of the same question, presenting the various options in a different order, or presenting the same questions in a different sequence. We will be able to compare responses in different experimental groups; to the extent that opinions are firmly held, different versions of the same question should yield similar results.

In the same vein, we will also determine whether those who are generally less informed about politics react differently from those who are better informed. We tapped respondents' level of political information by asking them to name the prime minister of Canada and the leaders of the Liberal party and the New Democratic Party – the percentages of correct answers were 95 percent, 57 percent and 33 percent, respectively. Respondents were given a score ranging from 0 to 1, depending on the proportion of correct answers.

In presenting our results, we have relied on cross-tabulations to indicate whether there is a relationship between two variables. The advantage of using these tables lies in their simplicity. If we are interested in the impact of, for example, region on attitudes toward some aspect of our electoral arrangements, we can construct a table that indicates how the distribution of opinions varies across the different regions of the country. The major drawback of this approach is that it does not allow us to sort out the specific impact of region – it could be that regional differences stem from variations in income across the different regions or differences in linguistic composition. We need to know whether region (or some other factor) has an independent impact, even after the effect of other factors such as income and language is controlled. The appropriate methodology for assessing the specific impact of a given variable on another is multivariate regression. In the process of making sense of the findings, we have relied to a great extent on regressions of this type, which enabled us to isolate the specific effect of each factor. Since regressions are more difficult to understand and explain than simple tables, however, we have not used them in the text. The multivariate regressions themselves are reported in appendix D and we would like to emphasize the fact that our interpretation is based on a systematic analysis of these regressions. Where the patterns presented in tabular form are substantially affected by the inclusion of control variables, this is noted in the text.

Unless otherwise indicated, percentages are computed on the basis of respondents who expressed an opinion (that is, after deleting "don't knows" and refusals). In the great majority of cases, the number of "no opinions" is quite small. When the number is sizable, however, it is reported.

2

CANADIANS' POLITICAL VALUES

THE PERFORMANCE OF electoral institutions will be evaluated, to some extent at least, in terms of consistency with deeply held political values; so, too, will proposals for improving performance. The term "values" has been variously defined, but two themes are common to most discussions: values shape people's evaluations, and are more general than other sorts of beliefs (Williams 1968; Searing 1979).

According to Williams (1968, 283), a person's values serve as "the criteria, or standards in terms of which evaluations are made." This implies that values are relatively enduring. It also implies that the number of values that a person possesses will be relatively small (Rokeach 1973, 3–4). Values transcend particular objects and situations and are thus more general than other sorts of beliefs. They embody judgements about what is good or preferable, rather than statements about what is (or what is believed to be) true or likely. In contrast to other sorts of beliefs, the truth or falsity of values cannot be demonstrated. This distinction between questions of value and questions of fact is at the heart of the difference between values and other sorts of beliefs.

Values, then, are normative orientations, deeply held beliefs that help us "to evaluate and judge, to heap praise and fix blame" (Rokeach 1973, 13). As enduring standards, values can impart some degree of coherence and meaningfulness to our more proximate judgements. Indeed, students of political belief systems have likened these values to "crowning postures" that might "serve as a sort of glue to bind together many more specific attitudes and beliefs" (Converse 1964, 211).

As Scheibe (1970, 121) reminds us, the types of values that shape political evaluations will be, to some extent, unique to that level of behaviour. In this chapter, we look at a number of fundamental political values that may structure Canadians' opinions about our electoral procedures: minoritarianism, populism, individualism, egalitarianism and statism. Since we are dealing with relatively enduring orientations, we must be particularly concerned with the stability of responses. The constraints of questionnaire length precluded the use of multiple indicators, so instead we checked for stability by comparing our results wherever possible with those obtained in the most extensive prior survey of Canadians' values, namely, the Attitudes Toward Civil Liberties and the Canadian Charter of Rights project, which was conducted in 1987. We have also sought to ensure the validity of our indicators by rooting them in a careful conceptual discussion of the political values they were chosen to reflect.

We begin by looking at certain assumptions or basic premises about our fellow citizens that are also at the core of political belief systems (Scarbrough 1984). Particularly germane to the issue of electoral democracy are beliefs about the ability of our fellow citizens to fulfil their democratic responsibilities. It is to these beliefs that we turn first.

BELIEFS ABOUT DEMOCRATIC CAPABILITIES

The question of beliefs about democratic capabilities leads us to two very different conceptions of democracy. On the one hand, those who aspire to a more participatory, less mediated, form of democracy share the optimism of classical democratic theory about the democratic potentialities of the ordinary citizen (see, for example, Bachrach 1967; Pateman 1970). Proponents of élitist democracy, on the other hand, resist broader participation on the grounds that too few citizens possess the requisite competence, knowledge and motivation to make rational and informed decisions about politically weighty matters (see, for example, Schumpeter 1943). Indeed, some proponents see inherent dangers in wide popular participation in politics, dangers to the stability, if not the very freedom, of the political system.

In revising democratic theory to fit the "realities" of political life, theorists of élitist democracy have significantly restricted the meaning of democracy. In place of "government by the people," they offer only "government approved by the people" (Schumpeter 1943, 246). Democracy becomes simply "that institutional arrangement for arriving at political decisions in which individuals acquire the power to decide by means of a competitive struggle for the people's vote" (ibid., 269). For the ordinary citizen, participation is limited to the act of voting. "Democracy means only that the people have the opportunity of accepting or refusing the men [sic] who are to rule them" (ibid., 285). This conception of democracy demands little of the average voter –

it requires merely the ability to render retrospective judgement on the performance of incumbents. According to Riker, this may be "a minimal kind of democracy; but this is the only kind of democracy actually attainable" (1982, 246).

For proponents of participatory democracy, however, participation is of the very essence, serving not merely as a method, but as an end in itself. To the élitists' scepticism about the quality of democratic citizenship, they retort that it is the lack of scope for genuine participation that has eroded democratic capabilities. As Pateman explains, "participation develops and fosters the very qualities necessary for it; the more individuals participate the better able they become to do so" (1970, 42–43). In this conception, apathy and ignorance on the part of ordinary citizens are taken as an indication of the need to improve democratic practice, rather than the need to recast democratic theory.

To examine Canadians' beliefs about their fellow citizens' democratic capabilities, we presented respondents with two statements: "The major issues of the day are too complicated for most voters" and "Most people have enough sense to tell whether a government is doing a good job." These two statements reflect the distinction between prospective and retrospective judgements (Fiorina 1981). Prospective judgements involve evaluations of future promises – in other words, the parties' proposals for dealing with the issues of the day. Retrospective judgements, on the other hand, involve appraisals of the government's record, its past performance and its past actions. The first of our two statements speaks to voters' competence when it comes to rendering prospective judgements on important questions of policy, while the second statement relates to evaluations of their ability to render retrospective judgements on the past performance of the incumbents.

It is evident that Canadians tend to have more confidence in the latter than in the former (table 2.1). Fully three-quarters of our sample believe that their fellow citizens have enough sense to be able to evaluate the government's performance, but fewer than half (44 percent) are sanguine about voters' capacity to come to grips with the major issues of the day. We should be open to the possibility, however, that some of this scepticism about voters' prospective capabilities may reflect as much on the parties and politicians – for obfuscating the issues – as it does on the perceived competence of the ordinary voter. In fact, 59 percent of those who agree that "the parties confuse the issues rather than provide a clear choice on them" (question p12) accept the suggestion that the major issues of the day are too complicated for most voters, compared to only 41 percent of those who deny that the parties fail to provide a clear choice (data not shown). We should also note that judgements of prospective and retrospective capabilities do not go hand in hand: only 31 percent of those who believe that the major issues of the day are too complicated for most voters question the ability of most people to know whether or not a government is doing a good job ($r = .16$).

Table 2.1
Canadians' political values and beliefs
(percentages)

Democratic capabilities — prospective (v1)	44
Democratic capabilities — retrospective (v2)	75
Minoritarianism (v15a/15b)	48
Anti-intellectualism (v5)	65
Grassroots populism (v6)	74
Belief in parties (p8)	74
Economic individualism (v3)	62
Statism (v4)	59
Egalitarianism (v8)	51

The wording of the questions was the following:

v1 Prospective capabilities: The major issues of the day are too complicated for most voters (% disagree).

v2 Retrospective capabilities: Most people have enough sense to tell whether a government is doing a good job (% agree).

v15a Minoritarianism: Which is more important in a democratic society: letting the majority decide or protecting the needs and rights of minorities?

v15b Minoritarianism: Which is more important in a democratic society: protecting the needs and rights of minorities or letting the majority decide?

Each respondent was (randomly) assigned one of 15a and 15b. The results are collapsed here.

v5 Anti-intellectualism: I'd rather put my trust in the down-to-earth thinking of ordinary people than the theories of experts and intellectuals (% agree).

v6 Grassroots populism: We would probably solve most of our big national problems if decisions could be brought back to the people at the grass roots (% agree).

p8 Belief in parties: Without political parties, there can't be true democracy (% agree).

v3 Economic individualism: Most people who don't get ahead should not blame the system; they have only themselves to blame (% agree).

v4 Statism: It's not up to the government to see to it that people have a job and a decent standard of living; the government should leave people to get ahead on their own (% disagree).

v8 Egalitarianism: This country would be better off if we worried less about how equal people are (% disagree).

MAJORITARIANISM VERSUS MINORITARIANISM

However we view the functions of elections and the competence of voters, the question arises as to how voters' individual decisions are to be aggregated. Our single-member plurality system can seriously distort the translation of votes into seats (see, especially, Cairns 1973, and Irvine 1979). Indeed, the defence of this system actually rests on one of its distorting effects, namely, its ability to translate a minority of votes into a majority of seats, and thereby produce the legislative majorities required for cabinet stability.

The notion of a system of aggregating votes that does not distort in some way may be a chimera. Indeed, Riker (1982) has sought to demonstrate by abstract argument and concrete example that no method of voting will necessarily yield a fair or even accurate reflection of voters' preferences. Simple majority voting on two alternatives might seem to provide an exception until we are reminded that binary choices are not naturally occurring and that their artificial generation will necessarily violate fundamental notions of fairness. "However democratic simple majority decision initially appears to be," Riker concludes, "it cannot in fact be so" (ibid., 65).

As the latter observation implies, the deceptively straightforward idea of letting the majority decide has a deeply rooted appeal for many people. For others, however, it raises the spectre of majority tyranny, fear of which is "a fear that the values of the 'majority' may be morally scarce and that enforcement of them will deprive the 'minority' of its values" (Riker 1982, 233). This notion of some inherent tension between democracy and liberty has received its most dramatic expression in Schumpeter's famous "mental experiment": "Let us transport ourselves into a hypothetical country that, in a democratic way, practices the persecution of Christians, the burning of witches, and the slaughtering of Jews" (Schumpeter 1943, 242). As Bachrach (1967, 21–22) responds, this scenario rests on the dubious assumption that systematic persecution could be carried out "in a democratic way" when it clearly violates the principle of freedom that is essential to democratic procedure. Nevertheless, the suspicion that democracy is inherently in danger of violating its own principles remains a powerful one.

There have been suggestions, of course, that the customary counter-posing of majority rule versus minority rights is too simplistic. From Dicey to Downs to Dahl, theorists have recognized that most majorities are themselves coalitions of minorities. "The making of governmental decisions is not a majestic march of great majorities united upon certain matters of basic policy. It is the steady appeasement of relatively small groups. Even when these groups add up to a numerical majority at election time it is usually not useful to construe that majority as more than an arithmetic expression" (Dahl 1956, 146). Dahl conceived of democracy as "polyarchy," as the rule of multiple minorities. The implication of this notion of coalitions of minorities is, of course, that these coalitions are necessarily in flux and therefore constitute no lasting threat of majority tyranny. In Canada, however, this notion of shifting coalitions may provide less reassurance when some citizens perceive themselves to be members of permanent minorities. These Canadians may share Cairns' view that "we have seen the ruthlessness of democratic politics when the stakes are high" (1988, 248).

We raised the issue of majority rule versus minority rights with our respondents in a very direct way. We asked them to decide which factor is more important in a democratic society: letting the majority decide or protecting the needs and rights of minorities. To guard against order effects, we randomized the order in which the two alternatives were presented. Eleven percent of our respondents insisted that both are equally important. Those who did make a choice were fairly evenly divided: 52 percent opted for letting the majority decide, while 48 percent gave priority to protecting the needs and rights of minorities. There was some evidence of an order effect, but it was modest: reversing the order in which the alternatives were presented made a difference of only 6 percent in the distribution of responses.

Cairns has written of the difficulty of devising institutional mechanisms that would allow for some rapprochement between the majoritarian and minoritarian elements in contemporary Canada (1991, 93). The very evenness of the split between majoritarian and minoritarian conceptions that we have found among our respondents lends considerable force to his argument. Canada has long had a strain of anti-majoritarianism – it is, in Cairns' words, "natural to peoples possessed of the federal condition" (ibid., 83). His point, however, is that contemporary anti-majoritarianism reflects more than the traditional apprehensions of territorially based minorities in a federal system. The heightened sense of the needs and rights of minorities can be linked in a direct way to the impact of the Charter. This phenomenon of "constitutional minoritarianism" reflects the new constitutional status and identities that the Charter has conferred on racial minorities, women, official language minorities and other minority groups. It is important to bear in mind, however, that this minoritarian strain is balanced by an equally widespread majoritarian impulse.

POPULISM AND BELIEF IN PARTIES

Cairns' perceptive analysis of "the kind of constitutional people Canadians are becoming under the influence of the Charter" (1991, 8) has broader implications for the aspects of electoral democracy we are addressing. With a more rights-conscious citizenry, he argues, comes a citizenry that aspires to greater participation in the direction of its affairs (Cairns 1988).

This democratizing impulse may find sustenance in an older populist tradition. Populism is increasingly appreciated as a significant indigenous strain of "practically oriented and critical democratic thought" (Laycock 1990, 3). Beyond Canada's borders, other scholars have also come to recognize populism as "fundamental to the shaping of the political mind" (Ionescu and Gellner 1967, 5). Populism has, however, proved to be a notoriously amorphous concept, and scholars here, as elsewhere, have struggled to elucidate its meaning.

"Elusive and protean" (Ionescu and Gellner 1967, 1) as the concept may be, scholars have nonetheless come to recognize that there is a basic core of meaning shared by the many manifestations of populism. Shils' work has proved particularly helpful in this respect. Writing about North American variants of populism, he has argued persuasively that populism subsumes two cardinal principles: the supremacy of the will of the people, and the desirability of a "direct" relationship between people and leadership, unmediated by political institutions (Shils 1956; see also Worsley 1967). These two principles imply, first, a desire that politics somehow be brought back to the people at the grass roots and, second, a distrust of "experts." This anti-intellectual strain in populism may, indeed, explain why "a certain shapelessness in ideas" seems to be inherent in populism – it tends to appeal to people who reject formal intellectual doctrine (see Stewart 1967, 180).

We attempted to gauge the prevalence of populist values by asking our respondents whether or not they agreed with the following two statements: "We would probably solve most of our big national problems if decisions could be brought back to the people at the grass roots" and "I'd rather put my trust in the down-to-earth thinking of ordinary people than the theories of experts and intellectuals" (cf. Blake 1985). The first statement reflects the notion that politics should be brought closer to the people, while the second captures the distrust of the "over-educated" and the corresponding confidence in the common sense of "the simple, ordinary untutored folk" (Worsley 1967, 242).

Almost two-thirds (65 percent) of our respondents exhibited this anti-intellectualism and fully three-quarters (74 percent) favoured bringing decisions closer to the grass roots. The Attitudes Toward Civil

Liberties and the Canadian Charter of Rights project conducted in 1987 included an item on anti-intellectualism (but not grass-roots populism). While the wording was not identical, the level of agreement was very similar to our results. Sixty percent of those with an opinion in the Civil Liberties project agreed that "In the long run, I'll put my trust in the simple down-to-earth thinking of ordinary people rather than the theories of experts and intellectuals."

As we would expect, the two populist values tend to go together: 75 percent of our respondents who agree with the notion of bringing decisions back to the people at the grass roots also express a preference for the down-to-earth thinking of ordinary people over the theories of experts and intellectuals. The fit, however, is far from perfect ($r = .33$) and the relative weight given to these two core beliefs has, in fact, helped to distinguish historical variants of populism (see Laycock 1990).

Indeed, if scholars agree on the defining principles of populism, they also have to agree that populism comes in many guises. For example, Laycock has identified no fewer than four historically distinct patterns of Prairie populism, which he labelled crypto-Liberalism, radical democratic populism, social democratic populism and plebiscitarian populism (Laycock 1990). One key dimension of variation in these Prairie populisms lay in the extent of their advocacy of popular democracy. While all four varieties were critical of the established federal political parties, only the radical democratic populists accepted the participatory implications of their critique. The crypto-Liberals and the social democratic populists, at least, rarely rejected party government as such and "generally expressed surprisingly few reservations about the adaptability of parliamentary forms to a system of effective popular democracy" (ibid.). Radical democratic populists, on the other hand, regarded political parties as "a failed form of popular-democratic action" and advocated new representational vehicles in their stead.

To tap this potential distinction among the different variants of populism, we presented our respondents with the statement that "Without political parties, there can't be true democracy." The fact that almost three-quarters (74 percent) of our respondents saw political parties as essential to democracy suggests that there are limits to radical democratic populism in Canada. In light of Laycock's observations on the historical reluctance of many Prairie populists to pursue their critique of party government to its seemingly logical conclusion, this should hardly surprise us. More surprising, perhaps, is the fact that, despite the centrality of political parties to our system of electoral democracy, fully one in four (26 percent) of our respondents could conceive of democracy without political parties. We have very little comparative data on this question with which to assess this finding. In 1965, the Norwegian National Election Study presented respondents with the statement, "Political parties are indispensable – they perform a useful and absolutely necessary task in society." This item was much more strongly worded than our question, yet it elicited much higher (92 percent) agreement.

As Laycock's labels imply, the various populist discourses could merge with other discourses, even while retaining their overall populist logic. Similarly, Worsley acknowledges that "a large part of the elements we find in populism will also be found to occur in other 'isms' " (Worsley 1967, 218). Particularly relevant for our purposes is Elkins' finding in British Columbia that populist orientations were to be found in the company of individualist and collectivist beliefs alike (Elkins 1985).

INDIVIDUALISM, STATISM AND EGALITARIANISM

Characterizations of Canada's ideological diversity have revolved around the two competing values of individualism and collectivism (see, especially, Horowitz 1966; Christian and Campbell 1990). Our strong collectivist strain is seen as setting Canada apart from the United States at the level of political ideas; liberal individualism failed to develop into the predominant political myth in Canada, as it did in the United States (see Horowitz 1966; Lipset 1990).

The individualist seeks to enhance personal liberty and believes that the rights of the individual should take primacy over the collectivity. Indeed, the collectivity is conceived of as being no more than the sum of the individuals who compose it. Collectivists, on the other hand, conceive of society as being something more than a mere agglomeration of competing individuals, and believe that there are some collective or community values that should take precedence over individual liberties. A corollary of collectivism is statism: the organized political power of the community – the state – should be used for the general welfare.

Individualism, in turn, might seem to include a presumption against government regulation, and certainly the liberal tendency is to distrust government as a potential source of unwarranted restrictions on the pursuit of individual ends. It is important, however, to distinguish the variants of liberalism in Canada. Particularly helpful in this respect is Christian and Campbell's distinction between what they term "business liberalism" and "welfare liberalism" (1990). Common to both is the conviction that the appropriate end of political activity is to ensure a society that maximizes individual liberty. Where they differ is in their perception of the nature of the threats to individual liberty and in their understanding of the most appropriate means of enhancing individual freedom. Business liberals cleave to a negative conception of liberty. This is the classical Lockean notion that liberty necessarily entails the minimization of restrictions on individual action, that liberty is threatened by the concentration of state power. Business liberalism typically accepts the inequality that results from the unrestricted pursuit of individual advantage.

Welfare liberals, on the other hand, are less ready to accept that individuals should be left to pursue their own ends in a self-regarding manner and are willing to endorse more restraints on individual liberty in order to maximize individual opportunity and initiative. For welfare liberals, the threat to individual liberty lies in the lack of resources – food, shelter, education – required for individuals to develop to their full potential, and to this end, they are ready to endorse action on the part of the state to give substance to formal liberty. This brand of liberalism received its classic expression in Canada in Mackenzie King's argument that "most effort to promote human welfare necessitates some interference with individual liberty. Where wisely applied and enforced, it is an immediate restriction, that a wider liberty in the end may be secured" (King 1918, 336).

The three core values of individualism, statism and egalitarianism were measured by posing the following statements to our respondents: "Most people who don't get ahead should not blame the system; they have only themselves to blame"; "It's not up to the government to see to it that people have a job and a decent standard of living; the government should leave people to get ahead on their own"; and "This country would be better off if we worried less about how equal people are."

The belief that people should get ahead on their own through hard work is at the core of economic individualism (see McClosky and Zaller 1984; Feldman 1988) and the first of our three statements directly taps this notion of the efficacy of the work ethic. Sixty-two percent of our respondents share the belief that most people who fail to get ahead have only themselves to blame. This individualism does not, however, necessarily translate into the anti-statist belief that the government should just let people get ahead on their own. In fact, fully 59 percent of our respondents support the statist idea of government intervention to help those who cannot help themselves, and almost as many (51 percent) reject the suggestion the country would be better off if there were less concern with equality. These latter figures are very similar to those obtained in the Attitudes Toward Civil Liberties and the Canadian Charter of Rights project conducted in 1987. When asked to choose between two propositions – that the government should see to it that everyone has a job and a decent standard of living, or that the government should let each person get ahead on his [sic] own – 54 percent of the respondents with an opinion in the Civil Liberties project chose the statist option of government intervention. Forty-eight percent of the respondents in the same survey rejected the notion that Canada would be better off if we worried less about how equal people are.

The finding that economic individualism does not necessarily go hand in hand with an acceptance of inequality and a desire to restrict government intervention in the economy is in line with Christian and Campbell's distinction between "business liberalism" and "welfare liberalism." Looking at those who believe that most people have only themselves to blame if they do not get ahead, only 50 percent also believe that the government should just leave people to get ahead on their own ($r = .25$) and only slightly more (55 percent) also agree that the country would be better off if we worried less about equality ($r = .14$). Research in the United States has also found that individualism and egalitarianism are relatively independent of one another (Feldman 1982).

THE PATTERNING OF POLITICAL VALUES AND BELIEFS

This brings us to a larger point. There are no a priori logical constraints on which values can stand together. How political values and beliefs stand together empirically, however, has potentially important implications for shaping more proximate political opinions. Taken alone, the prevalence of populist values would seem to point to a strong reformist impulse, but for many Canadians individualism and anti-statism may act as a brake when it comes to greater regulation of the electoral process. These same values may also temper a concern with the needs and rights of minorities if affirmative action is proposed to enhance minority representation.

There is, in short, a relative quality to values. As Rokeach reminds us, our proximate evaluations will "be a result of the relative importance of all the competing values that the situation has activated" (1973, 6). A value is not an absolute that operates in isolation. Rather than examining the impact of political values one by one, then, we need to focus on the patterning of basic political values and beliefs.

We used cluster analysis to identify the most important of these patterns. Cluster analysis offers an attractive method for this purpose because it does not require us to specify in advance which political values and beliefs will go together. Instead, the patterns are identified by empirical criteria alone. Cluster analysis identifies groups of respondents who share similar basic political values and beliefs. The cluster analysis was based on responses to the nine items tapping basic political values and beliefs that we have discussed in this chapter.

Technical details of the cluster analysis are described in appendix C.

The cluster analysis identified six groupings of respondents, each with its distinctive patterning of basic political values and beliefs. Not all respondents, of course, shared one of these patterns. There are many possible ways of combining the several items and some respondents had their own idiosyncratic ways of organizing them. There were also patterns that were common to only a handful of respondents. Fully 92 percent of the respondents did, however, meet the "goodness-of-fit" threshold, which was necessary in order to be included in one of the six groupings.

The resulting typology is presented in table 2.2. The different types are interpreted by examining the distribution of responses to each of the items included in the cluster analysis. The closer a given percentage is

Table 2.2
Canadians' political values and beliefs: a typology
(percentages)

	Technocratic liberals	Populist liberals	Minoritarian individualists	Majoritarian individualists	Radical collectivists	Party collectivists
Grassroots populism	26	89	90	90	83	87
Anti-intellectualism	2	85	86	93	70	76
Belief in parties	76	91	89	76	10	99
Economic individualism	76	62	87	81	21	49
Statism	75	65	0	21	93	100
Egalitarianism	60	93	30	9	53	60
Minoritarianism	17	60	100	0	78	64
Democratic capabilities: prospective	65	100	18	38	55	1
Democratic capabilities: retrospective	85	90	76	80	87	69
N	444	431	372	563	359	555
%	16	16	14	21	13	20

Note: The numbers in the table indicate the percentage within each grouping who hold the particular value or belief. For wording of questions, see table 2.1.

to 100 percent or to 0 percent, the more homogeneous the group is on that particular item.

We have labelled the first group "technocratic liberals." These respondents are almost unanimous in their rejection of the populist notion that they would rather put their trust in the down-to-earth thinking of ordinary people than the theories of experts and intellectuals. Most of these respondents also reject the other defining principle of populism, namely, that political decisions should be brought back to the people at the grass roots. For all their rejection of populist principles, however, members of this cluster are more confident than most of voters' ability to understand the major issues of the day and to pass judgement on the government's performance.

While three in four of these respondents subscribe to the individualistic belief that people who do not get ahead have only themselves to blame, this individualism does not preclude an egalitarian strain. More than half reject the idea that the country would be better off if we worried less about how equal people are, and fully three-quarters refuse to accept the anti-statist suggestion that the government should simply let people get ahead on their own. This combination of individualism with an acceptance of a positive role for the state and a confidence in technocratic solutions suggests the suitability of the label "technocratic liberals" for this grouping.

It should be emphasized that what really sets this grouping apart from the others is its rejection of populist values. All of the other groupings subsume populist beliefs, albeit with varying degrees of anti-intellectualism. If the extent to which populist orientations apparently permeate the value systems of Canadians seems surprising, we should perhaps recall that this is why scholars in Canada, as elsewhere, feel that we need the label – "populist" – "to describe this constantly-recurring style of politics – the eternal attempt of people to claim politics as something of theirs" (Worsley 1967, 248). It is a phenomenon of societies where people have a feeling of being peripheral to the centres of power (see Wiles 1967; Stewart 1967).

While sharing a populist strain, each of the remaining types combines this strain with other political values and beliefs in its own distinct way. Certainly, there is little to distinguish the populist liberals, the minoritarian individualists and the majoritarian individualists when it comes to populist beliefs. For most members of these three groupings, the desire to bring decisions back to the grass roots goes hand in hand with a scepticism about the theories of intellectuals and experts.

Looking at the populist liberals, however, we also see something of that same combination of individualism and statism that characterizes the technocratic liberals. This is also the most egalitarian of the groupings. The overwhelming majority of these respondents reject the notion that the country would be better off if we worried less about equality. This egalitarian strain may also reinforce their confidence in the capacity of their fellow citizens to perform their democratic role. Indeed, they are unanimous in their rejection of the notion that the major issues of the day are too complicated for most voters, and few have any doubt that most people have enough sense to tell whether a government is doing a good job. Interestingly, like all but one of the populist groupings, this grouping contains few respondents who can readily conceive of democracy without political parties. These populist liberals seem to bear some resemblance to Laycock's "crypto-Liberals," the Prairie populists who tended to believe that the Canadian federal state could be made more responsive to their interests without major institutional changes and saw the political party, in particular, as reformable (Laycock 1990).

The minoritarian and majoritarian individualists share not only populist beliefs but also a blend of individualism and anti-statism. The general consensus is that the system is not to blame if people do not get ahead and it is not up to the government to help; indeed, the minoritarian individualists unanimously agreed that people should get ahead on their own. Given this laissez-faire orientation, it is not surprising that members of both of these groupings tend to agree that the country would be better off if we worried less about equality.

More surprising, perhaps, is the tendency of many of these respondents to agree that the major issues of the day are too complicated for most voters. This scepticism about voters' capacity for rendering prospective judgements seems to run counter to populist principles: more direct democracy would seem to assume that citizens are informed. There is not necessarily a contradiction here, however; one theme in populist critiques of party politics – as currently practised – has been that it blocks the development of an informed citizenry capable of self-rule. In fact, over 90 percent of the members of both of these groupings agreed with the statement that "the parties confuse the issues rather than provide a clear choice on them" (data not shown). Certainly, only a minority of these respondents doubt that most people have enough sense to tell whether a government is doing a good job. Historically, however, one variant of populism in Canada – "plebiscitarian populism" – *was* associated with a certain scepticism about popular democratic capacity and promoted a very circumscribed form of mass movement activity (see Laycock 1990).

What really divides these two groupings are their views about the need to protect the rights of minorities. The majoritarian individualists unanimously agreed that it is more important in a democratic society to let the majority decide. For their part, the minoritarian individualists agreed as strongly that it is more important to protect the needs and rights of minorities. Both groupings, we should bear in mind, share a populist strain.

Turning to the final two groupings, the radical collectivists and the party collectivists, we find unanimous, or near unanimous, rejection of the notion that the government should let people get ahead on their own. Members of both groupings, and radical collectivists in particular, are also much more likely than the respondents at large to reject the individualist premise that most people who do not get ahead have only themselves to blame. These respondents seem readier to believe instead that the system is to blame and that the government should see to it that people have a job and a decent standard of living. For many of these respondents, this collectivist and statist stance is accompanied by an egalitarian strain. It is tempting to link their collectivist values with the priority that many members of both these groupings tend to accord to the needs and rights of minorities. In other words, this combination of values seems to suggest a recognition of a legitimate group basis to democratic politics, with democratic decisions requiring something more than the mere aggregation of individual wills.

Members of both groupings generally subscribe to the populist premise that we would probably solve most of our big national problems if decisions could be brought back to the people at the grass roots. There is less agreement, however, with the second defining principle of populism – that the down-to-earth thinking of ordinary people is to be trusted more than the theories of experts and intellectuals. There is some indication of the underlying tension that Laycock noted in social democratic populist thinking between technocratic and participatory democratic orientations, the social democratic predilection being to entrust public policy to planners (Laycock 1990).

Laycock also noted that while Prairie social democrats often attacked government by the established parties, they almost never rejected party government per se. Similarly, we see all but a handful of the party collectivists agreeing that there cannot be true democracy without political parties. The contrast with the radical collectivists could not be clearer. Only among the radical collectivists do we find a widespread ability to conceive of democracy without political parties. To this extent at least, members of this grouping resemble Laycock's radical democratic populists, who alone of Prairie populists accepted the implications of their critique of party government for participatory democracy (Laycock

1990). Add to this the widespread tendency for these respondents to hold the system responsible and to support government intervention to help those who cannot help themselves, and the label "radical collectivists" seems apt.

Conversely, the inability to conceive of democracy without political parties warrants the label "party collectivists" for the members of the final grouping. At the same time, their collectivist orientation sets them apart from the populist liberals and the minoritarian and majoritarian individualists. These party collectivists are also distinctive in the extent to which they accept the notion that the major issues of the day are too complicated for most voters.

As shown in table 2.2, party collectivists (20 percent) outnumber radical collectivists (13 percent), while majoritarian individualists (21 percent) are more numerous than their minoritarian counterparts (14 percent). Technocratic liberals and populist liberals appear in equal proportions (16 percent).

What sort of people are to be found in each of these groupings? We can see from table 2.3 that the different types do not fit neatly into socio-demographic characteristics. This is not to say, however, that each grouping contains a representative cross-section of the population.

Looking at regional differences first, we can see that residents of Manitoba and Saskatchewan are more likely to be radical collectivists and less likely to be party collectivists or technocratic liberals than residents of other regions. Albertans, too, are less likely to be party collectivists. Predictably, residents of Quebec are the least likely to be found among the majoritarian individualists: only 15 percent of Quebec residents are majoritarian individualists, compared with fully one in four Albertans. British Columbians, on the other hand, are the most likely to be populist liberals.

Perhaps more significant than the differences that we find are those that we do not find. First, populism is clearly not a phenomenon of western Canada alone. Fully 83 percent of the residents of Ontario, Quebec and the Atlantic provinces appear in one or another of the five groupings with a populist strain, rivalling the 84 percent of western Canadians to be found in these same groupings. If there is any East–West cleavage here, it lies more in the way that populist values combine with other values. Western Canadians in general are more likely to be populist liberals and less likely to be party collectivists than residents of eastern and central Canada. The second observation is that Quebeckers do not stand out as being significantly less individualistic than other Canadians. Where they differ, not surprisingly, is in being more likely to marry that individualism with minoritarianism.

Table 2.3
Distribution of typology membership
(percentages)

	Technocratic liberals	Populist liberals	Minoritarian individualists
Atlantic	17	13	13
Quebec	15	13	18
Ontario	20	13	12
Manitoba/Saskatchewan	12	18	13
Alberta	17	17	13
British Columbia	16	21	11
Men	18	14	13
Women	15	15	14
Under 45	18	17	12
45 and over	14	11	17
Low education	9	10	21
Medium education	16	17	11
High education	32	17	8
Low income	11	14	17
Medium income	18	17	12
High income	25	15	10
Blue collar	12	12	14
White collar	19	16	13
Union family	18	14	12
Nonunion family	16	15	14
English	18	16	12
French	15	13	16
Non-charter language	14	12	17
Catholic	15	14	15
Protestant	17	15	13
Canada	16	16	14

	Majoritarian individualists	Radical collectivists	Party collectivists
Atlantic	21	11	25
Quebec	15	14	25
Ontario	21	13	21
Manitoba/Saskatchewan	23	18	16
Alberta	25	12	15
British Columbia	22	12	18
Men	24	12	18
Women	15	14	25
Under 45	17	14	21
45 and over	24	12	22

Table 2.3 (cont'd)
Distribution of typology membership
(percentages)

	Majoritarian individualists	Radical collectivists	Party collectivists
Low education	24	11	25
Medium education	20	14	22
High education	12	16	15
Low income	21	12	26
Medium income	19	13	20
High income	20	12	18
Blue collar	24	13	26
White collar	18	14	20
Union family	18	16	22
Nonunion family	21	12	21
English	21	13	20
French	16	15	25
Non-charter language	21	13	22
Catholic	17	14	25
Protestant	24	12	19
Canada	21	13	20

Note: The numbers indicate the percentage of respondents within a group belonging to a given cluster. For instance, 17% of respondents from Atlantic Canada are technocratic liberals, 13% are populist liberals, and so on.

Turning to gender, we can see that women are significantly less likely than men to be majoritarian individualists and significantly more likely to be party collectivists. In fact, fully one woman in four (25 percent) is to be found among the party collectivists, while almost the same proportion of men (24 percent) qualify as majoritarian individualists. It is interesting to note that this contrast is not simply a function of differences in the material circumstances of men and women. The impact of gender remains significant even when controls are introduced for an array of socio-demographic characteristics (see table 1.D1). This finding lends some support to Conover's (1988) notion of a gender gap in basic political values.

Education and age, however, seem to be the more important determinants of typology membership. The higher the level of education, the more likely respondents are to be technocratic liberals: only 9 percent of non-high school graduates are technocratic liberals, compared with almost a third (32 percent) of those who have completed post-secondary education. We should hardly be surprised that university graduates are the most likely to want to put their trust in experts and intellectuals. What is perhaps surprising is that so many of them express greater confidence in the down-to-earth thinking of ordinary people. For their part, those with less education are more likely to be party collectivists or members of one of the two individualistic groupings and less likely to be populist liberals. Older respondents are also significantly more likely to be found in one of the two individualistic groupings. Indeed, only 29 percent of those under the age of 45 are minoritarian or majoritarian individualists, compared to 41 percent of older respondents. The converse does not hold true, however: those under 45 are not significantly more likely to be found in one of the two collectivist groupings.

While we can point to some differences in the kind of respondents who are more likely to be found in one or another category of our typology, we should not overstate the impact of respondents' background characteristics. Early socialization experiences are fundamental, but given the multiplicity of politically salient identities in Canada, we should not expect any simple one-to-one correspondence between belief systems and social categories. We should not forget, either, that tumultuous political events can affect deeply held beliefs. Indeed, for Cairns, significant normative shifts are one legacy of our "collective constitutional trauma." "The world of inner meanings and understandings we carry in our heads," he argues, "has been profoundly transformed by the experiences of the past dozen years" (1988, 245).

RECAPITULATION

We can characterize Canadians' basic political values and beliefs in the following ways:

1. There is a strong populist strain, which is to be found in every region of the country. Approximately two-thirds of our respondents value the down-to-earth thinking of ordinary Canadians over the theories of experts and intellectuals, and three-quarters endorse the notion of bringing decisions on big national problems closer to the grass roots.
2. Three-fifths of our respondents share a belief in economic individualism, but this individualism does not necessarily translate into a presumption against state intervention. Only half of these individualists also believe that the government should just let people get ahead on their own and only slightly more believe that we have been too concerned about the equality of individuals.
3. Our respondents are more or less evenly divided over the question of whether protecting the needs and rights of minorities or letting the majority decide is most important in a democratic society.
4. Three-quarters of our respondents believe that their fellow citizens

are competent enough to pass judgement on the government's performance, but they are less sanguine about citizens' ability to understand complex issues.

5. These basic political values – populism, individualism, statism, egalitarianism and minoritarianism – combine with one another and with beliefs about democratic capacities and the necessity of having political parties to form six distinct types. Over 90 percent of our respondents can be identified with one or another of these types. Five of the six types have a populist cast. The technocratic liberals and the populist liberals both tend to combine a belief in individualism with an acceptance of state regulation, but they differ fundamentally on the populist dimension. The more laissez-faire individualists, on the other hand, share a populist orientation, but are divided clearly along majoritarian/minoritarian lines. Both collectivist groupings are more concerned with protecting the needs and rights of minorities. They also tend to share populist values, albeit with a somewhat lesser presumption against experts and intellectuals. These two collectivist groupings differ fundamentally, however, in their beliefs about the necessity of having political parties. Among the populist groupings, only the radical collectivists can conceive of democracy without political parties.

6. This typology of basic political values and beliefs does not map neatly onto socio-demographic characteristics. There are some regional differences. Western Canadians are more likely to be populist liberals and less likely to be party collectivists than residents of eastern Canada. Although Quebeckers are not significantly less individualistic than other Canadians, they are more likely to combine individualism with minoritarianism.

7. While social background characteristics are, generally, only weakly related to these patterns of basic political values and beliefs, education and age do have a number of significant effects. In particular, younger respondents are less likely than older respondents to be found in either of the two individualistic groupings, while the better educated are the most likely to be technocratic liberals.

3

CANADIANS' BELIEFS ABOUT POLITICIANS, PARTIES AND MONEY

ALTHOUGH THEY ARE fundamental, values do not by themselves move opinions on specific issues. In order to have an impact, they need to be complemented by perceptions or beliefs about reality. People with exactly the same value systems may very well diverge on what should be done about a given problem, because they disagree on the seriousness or the sources of the problem. It is a combination of values and perceptions that nurtures opinions on various issues.

We examine three types of beliefs that are particularly salient to issues related to electoral institutions. First, how much confidence do Canadians have in politicians as a whole? This is clearly a central question when it comes to deciding on electoral arrangements. The less confidence one has in politicians, the more one may want to control their behaviour.

There is a widespread perception that Canadians are increasingly disenchanted with all politicians. This study measures the extent and depth of that cynicism and attempts to determine whether it has indeed increased over time and whether it is more prominent in Canada than in other countries. We pay particular attention to regional variations. There has been a great deal of talk about western alienation (Elton and Gibbins 1979), and we assess whether Westerners do indeed express greater cynicism toward politicians than other Canadians.

Second, we look at Canadians' perceptions of the existing party system. It is no exaggeration to say that our whole system is predicated on the view that parties are central players on the political stage. After an election, it is the leader of the party with the most seats who becomes the prime minister. The parliamentary system supposes that legislators form teams, with strong internal discipline. By reimbursing part of the expenditures incurred by parties during an election, the state indicates that the parties perform a public service. Individuals may, however, differ in their assessments of how well actual parties fulfil their roles. Moreover, and of more direct interest to us, individuals are likely to have different perspectives on electoral arrangements, depending on whether they view political parties in general positively or negatively.

As we write this report, polls show a strong sense of dissatisfaction with the established parties, which has been reflected in the rise of both the Reform Party and the Bloc québécois. It remains to be determined how this dissatisfaction translates into feelings about parties in general. Because parties are a central component of representative democracy, according to most theorists, it is essential to assess the extent to which Canadians attach importance to the existence of a strong party system. In particular, we want to test the hypothesis that better-educated respondents, who may be more likely to support the basic norms of the system – as McClosky and Zaller (1984) found in the United States – are more supportive of the party system.

Third, the influence that money is perceived to have in politics is examined. The question is of great importance for those who are concerned with the fairness of elections. People who feel that money has a great deal of influence in elections may feel that parties or candidates with less money will be at a great disadvantage when competing with wealthier opponents. Those who share that view may conclude that rules must be adopted to ensure fair competition; this concern is bound to be less serious among those who believe that money does not tend to buy influence.

Of particular concern here is the relationship between income and attitudes about the role of money in politics. To the extent that groups tend to underrate their own influence and overstate that of other groups, we would expect the rich to express relatively little, and the poor much greater, concern with the potential advantages or disadvantages flowing from access to financial resources. The legitimacy of elections requires that the poor do not feel that the cards are stacked against them.

Throughout the chapter, we examine how these attitudes relate to the political values and beliefs examined in Chapter 2. In particular, we consider the extent to which the strong populist strain documented in Chapter 2 is reflected in greater cynicism about politicians, parties and money.

ATTITUDES ABOUT POLITICIANS

Our survey included seven questions tapping various aspects of political cynicism in Canada. The distribution of answers to these questions is reported in table 3.1. The table documents a high level of cynicism

Table 3.1
Level of political cynicism in Canada
(percentage cynical)

1. Government does not care (p4)	70
2. Elected lose touch (p5)	79
3. No intention of fulfilling promises (p13)	82
4. MPs care (p14)	62
5. MPs misuse office (p15)	64
6. Politicians less honest (p16)	39
7. More corruption in government (p17)	30
8. Governments do not care	73
9. Governments in touch	69
10. Politicians tell the truth	79
11. Politicians intelligent and able	23
12. Politicians do their best	32

The first seven questions come from authors' survey.

The wording was the following:
BASICALLY do you AGREE or DISAGREE with each of the following statements.

p4 I don't think that the government cares much what people like me think.

p5 Generally, those elected to Parliament soon lose touch with the people.

p13 Most candidates in federal elections make campaign promises they have no intention of fulfilling.

p14 Most members of Parliament care deeply about the problems of ordinary people.

p15 Most members of Parliament make a lot of money misusing public office.

p16 On the whole, would you say that politicians are more honest, less honest or about as honest as the average person?

p17 Do you think there is more, less or the same amount of corruption in government as in business?

Questions 8 to 12 come from the *Globe and Mail*/CBC News poll (see the *Globe and Mail*, 29 October 1990). In items 8, 9, 11 and 12 respondents were asked whether they agreed with the following statements:

8. "I don't think governments care much what people like to think."
9. "Generally governments today seem to be pretty much in touch with the problems that most people have to face."
11. "Most of our politicians are intelligent and able people."
12. "Most politicians are just trying to do the best they can under difficult circumstances."

The wording of item 10 was the following: "On the whole how regularly do you think politicians tell the truth:
 – just about always.
 – most of the time.
 – only some of the time.
 – hardly ever."

about politicians in general. Approximately 80 percent of Canadians believe that those elected to Parliament soon lose touch with the people and that most candidates in federal elections make promises they have no intention of fulfilling. When the question refers explicitly to members of Parliament (MPs), cynicism is somewhat more subdued: approximately 60 percent think that most MPs do not care deeply about the problems of ordinary people and make a lot of money misusing public office. Two other questions indicate the limits of cynicism. Most Canadians do not trust politicians very much, but the majority of people still feel that politicians are about as honest as the average person and that there is as much corruption in business as in government. When reminded of the fact that politicians ought to be assessed not only according to an abstract perfect ideal but also according to the limits of human nature, Canadians prove to be much less cynical.

How much cynicism, then, do these data reveal? On the one hand, the main thrust of responses is perfectly clear. On each of the first five items, negative answers easily outnumber positive ones. In the two questions involving comparisons, the modal response, as mentioned previously, is that politicians are about as honest as the average person and that there is the same amount of corruption in government as in business, but among those who see differences, cynicism predominates: for every respondent who perceives politicians to be more honest than the average person, there are 30 who believe that the opposite is true. On the other hand, cynicism may not be as deep as a quick reading of the results may suggest. As we have just pointed out, the more abstract the object, the greater the cynicism; but as the object becomes more concrete (that is, when we refer to MPs or invite a comparison with business or ordinary people), that cynicism becomes more moderate. This disjunction between more general and more specific views emerges in other areas of politics (see Johnston 1986, 216). It indicates, we believe, that there is ambivalence among many Canadians. The prevailing mood is indeed one of cynicism, but that cynicism is somewhat restrained, especially when people are invited to think concretely.

A similar picture emerges from another survey undertaken at about the same time as ours – the *Globe and Mail*–CBC News poll conducted between 15 and 20 October 1990. In this survey, as in ours, a clear majority of Canadians expressed considerable scepticism about politicians. The item eliciting the greatest cynicism pertained to the perceived propensity of politicians not to tell the truth. The same pattern is found in our survey: the item with the greatest agreement is the one that asks about politicians not fulfilling campaign promises. This is particularly intriguing, given the finding in the literature that governments, in

Canada as in other countries, do fulfil the majority of their campaign pledges (Monière 1988; Rollings 1987; Krukones 1984; King 1981). This rather harsh judgement may indicate that Canadians attach great value to honesty in politics and become upset whenever politicians are perceived to fail on this criterion. Since politicians talk a great deal and about many different matters, it is possible to infer that they cannot really believe in everything that they say. It may seem to many, therefore, that politicians are not particularly concerned about meaning what they say – especially since they usually repeat the party line – and should therefore be listened to with great scepticism.

The *Globe and Mail*–CBC poll also shows the limits of cynicism. Three-fourths of Canadians believe that most politicians are intelligent and able people. Moreover, and most significantly, two-thirds acknowledge that most politicians do their best under difficult circumstances; again, when reminded of the severe constraints politicians are faced with, people expressed understanding and sympathy. There is no doubt that cynicism is the spontaneous, visceral reaction, but Canadians are willing to temper their judgements when asked to think concretely about politicians they know, and to consider the constraints of the job.

Has the level of political cynicism increased over time? It is possible to track the evolution of opinions on the first two indicators of political cynicism. On both of these indicators, there has been a marked increase in the level of cynicism, of about 20 percentage points, since 1965 (see table 3.2). Most of that increase has occurred over the last decade. Canadian National Election Studies have also included questions tapping feelings about "people running the government," questions that are part of the standard political trust scale. Unfortunately, these questions were not asked in 1974, and the wording was different in 1979 and 1984, so we can only compare 1988 answers with those of 1965 and 1968. The pattern, however, is similar; the evidence points to a substantial increase in political cynicism. It is interesting to note that the question eliciting the greatest cynicism pertains to the waste of tax money (for a more extensive discussion of public opinion about spending and taxing, see Johnston 1986; Blais and Dion 1987). The fact that a majority of Canadians, twice as many as in 1965, now believe that quite a few people running the government are a little "crooked" also testifies to the growing concern about politicians' perceived honesty. On the other hand, it is useful to keep in mind that even in 1988 half of Canadians surveyed indicated that we can trust the government to do what is right most of the time. On this most direct question, cynicism appears to be subdued.

Table 3.2
Evolution of political cynicism in Canada
(percentage cynical)

	1965	1968	1974	1979	1984	1988	1990
1. Government does not care (p4)	49	45	59	53	63	N/A	70
2. Elected lose touch (p5)	60	61	65	65	78	N/A	79
3. Government crooked	27	27	N/A	N/A	N/A	52	N/A
4. Government wastes	38	46	N/A	N/A	N/A	66	N/A
5. Trust government	39	39	N/A	N/A	N/A	49	N/A
6. Government smart	56	49	N/A	N/A	N/A	63	N/A

Sources: CNES (1965, 1968, 1974, 1979, 1984, 1988); Blais and Gidengil 1990.

N/A = not applicable. Questions not asked in 1974, 1988, 1990, and wording was different in 1979 and 1984.

For the wording for items 1 and 2, see table 3.1.

The wording for items 3 to 6 was the following:

3. Do you think that:
    1. Quite a few of the people running the government are a little bit crooked?
    2. Not very many are crooked?
    3. Hardly any of them are crooked?
    8. Don't know.
4. Do you think that people in the government:
    1. Waste a lot of the money we pay in taxes?
    2. Waste some of it?
    3. Don't waste very much of it?
    8. Don't know.
5. How much of the time do you think you can trust the government in Ottawa to do what is right?
    1. Just about always.
    2. Most of the time.
    3. Only some of the time.
    8. Don't know.
6. Do you feel that:
    1. Almost all of the people running the government are smart people who usually know what they are doing?
    2. Quite a few of them don't seem to know what they are doing.
    3. Don't know.

Are Canadians more or less distrustful of their politicians than citizens of other countries? The easiest comparison is with the United States, where similar questions have been asked over time. As indicated in table 3.3, Americans are somewhat less likely to believe that the people running the government are crooked, but also less likely to trust the government to do what is right. The overall level of political cynicism in Canada appears to match the level observed in the United States. In Canada, however, the rise of political cynicism seems to have taken place in the 1980s. In the United States, there is no clear trend except for the "trust government" question: distrust increased substantially in the 1970s, with the Watergate scandal undoubtedly playing a major role in the process.

Table 3.3
Evolution of political cynicism in the United States
(percentage cynical)

	1968	1972	1976	1980	1982	1984	1986
1. Government does not care	44	50	54	55	49	44	55
3. Government crooked	26	38	42	49	—	33	—
4. Government wastes	61	68	77	80	68	66	—
5. Trust government	38	46	66	74	67	55	62

Source: Adapted from Miller and Listhaug (1990, table 1, p. 360).

Note: For the wording of the questions, see tables 3.1 and 3.2. Note that, in the American survey, the wording of item 1 refers to "public officials" rather than "government."

As for other countries, the rather sparse evidence we have tends to suggest that political trust is lower in North America than in most other Western democracies. Miller and Listhaug (1990) note that although cynicism is of the same magnitude and has followed more or less the same path in Sweden as in the United States, political trust is considerably higher in Norway and has not dropped. Similarly, Kaase (1988, 126) reports that while political trust in the United States in the 1970s was higher than in Italy, it was lower than in six other European countries.

In short, a strong dose of political cynicism characterizes the Canadian public. That cynicism has increased substantially over the last decade and has reached or surpassed the level observed in the United States, by most indicators. It also tends to be higher than that found in most European countries. At the same time, however, it is important not to overstate the depth of that cynicism. When the issue is put in more concrete terms, Canadians express a modest amount of confidence in their politicians.

We have constructed a political cynicism scale based on the seven questions listed in table 3.1. Each of the seven indicators is correlated with the others (correlation coefficients range from 0.16 to 0.41). Respondents were given a score ranging from 0 to 1, depending on the proportion of "cynical" answers. The overall average on the scale for the full sample is 0.67, a reflection of the fact that there were many more negative than positive answers.

Cynicism reaches its peak in Alberta, where the average "cynicism" score is 0.74 (see table 3.4). It is lowest in Quebec, where the average score is 0.62. The fact that the chief political figure in Canada, the prime minister, is from Quebec may partly explain the higher level of confidence in that province. On the whole, however, regional variations are not large. In particular, the data do not support the view that cynicism is more widespread in the West; it is only Alberta that distinguishes itself from the rest of the country, and even there the difference is rather modest.

The most important determinant of cynicism is education (see table 3.4). Those with a university degree exhibit much greater confidence in politicians: their average score on political cynicism is 0.58, compared to 0.71 for those with little education (high school not completed) and 0.69 for those with a medium level of education (high school completed

Table 3.4
Distribution of political cynicism in Canada

	Mean score on political cynicism
Atlantic	.69
Quebec	.62
Ontario	.68
Manitoba/Saskatchewan	.70
Alberta	.74
British Columbia	.68
Men	.65
Women	.70
Under 45	.67
45 and over	.67
Low education	.71
Medium education	.69
High education	.58
Low income	.70
Medium income	.66
High income	.63
Blue collar	.71
White collar	.66
Unionized	.67
Nonunionized	.67
English	.62
French	.69
Non-charter language	.72
Catholic	.68
Protestant	.65
Canada	.67

Note: The political cynicism scale is based on the seven questions listed in table 3.1. Scores range from 0 to 1, depending on the proportion of "cynical" responses. The higher the score, the higher the level of political cynicism.

but no university degree). Women, those with blue-collar occupations and low incomes, as well as those whose mother tongue is neither French nor English, tend to be more cynical. Those groups that are underrepresented in government (Olsen 1980) are less likely to trust political élites; the reverse is, of course, also true. This is why having a university degree, which is so crucial an asset in reaching the top positions of bureaucratic as well as political power, makes such a large difference. It is easier for a university-educated person to have confidence in élites who come from the same milieu and are likely to share the same values and beliefs. By the same token, it is understandable that women, who know very well that the great majority of politicians are male, express some scepticism. There is an exception to this pattern, however. Younger Canadians are not more cynical about politicians than those who are older. It could be that younger citizens feel this way because they have been less exposed to politics and to the conventional description of it as a "dirty" world. (For an indication of a life-cycle effect on political trust in the United States, see Abramson 1983.)

Finally, attitudes about politicians are related to the political values and beliefs examined in Chapter 2. Particularly, we find that the technocratic liberals, the only group to reject populist values, are the least cynical, with an average score of 0.58, while average scores for the five other groups hover around 0.70 (data not shown). This confirms the view that populism and political cynicism tend to be mutually reinforcing.

ATTITUDES ABOUT PARTIES

In every federal election Canadians are invited to choose not only among a set of individual candidates but among a number of political parties. It is the parties' share of seats that determines the composition of government. Our system of election and government is very much a contest between parties. It is therefore appropriate to see how Canadians feel about parties and how satisfied they are with their behaviour.

We first asked our respondents whether, in their opinion, we would have better laws if MPs were allowed to vote freely rather than having to follow party lines (question p7). Do citizens have more confidence in individual politicians or organized teams of them? The response is unequivocal: 78 percent of Canadians have greater confidence in their MPs than their parties (table 3.5). The MP is a concrete individual, with whom a substantial minority of Canadians have direct contact, and who does not elicit as much cynicism as the party, an institution that may seem abstract to many citizens. This parallels the contrast found in the United States between strongly positive evaluations of one's own representative in Congress and equally strong negative feelings toward Congress as a whole (Fenno 1975).

Our survey also included questions about three standard criticisms that are often addressed to parties: that they are all the same and thus offer no real choice; that they squabble all the time and for no useful purpose; and that they always try to confuse the issues. Canadians overwhelmingly agree with the latter two assertions but are evenly divided on the first. The perception of useless squabbling is not surprising. When Canadians see representatives of different parties, they usually see them attacking one another. On the face of it, this looks most unproductive, even though a case can be made that in a democracy we need strong opposition parties that systematically challenge the government's positions and therefore provide a different perspective on the issues of the day. Obviously, this is not the view of most Canadians; parties should not always debate for the sake of it.

The other two questions deal with whether parties are perceived to offer a real choice to Canadians. When the focus is on what parties do, on whether they confuse the issues, responses are overwhelmingly cynical. When the question is about what they are, and whether they are all basically the same, opinion is more balanced. Even then, however, close to 50 percent of Canadians believe that parties do not offer a real choice. This is a harsh judgement, especially taking into account the fact that in the last federal election the parties took clearly different positions on the major issue of the election, free trade. It reflects a strong discontent with the traditional parties, all of which are felt to be wanting, and it is in that sense that "there isn't really a choice."

Table 3.5
Attitudes about parties in Canada
(percentage agree)

MPs should vote freely (p7)	78
Parties are the same (p9)	47
Too much party squabbling (p11)	81
Parties confuse the issues (p12)	87

The wording of the questions was the following:

BASICALLY, do you AGREE or DISAGREE with each of the following statements.

p7 We would have better laws if members of Parliament were allowed to vote freely rather than having to follow party lines.

p9 All federal parties are basically the same; there isn't really a choice.

p11 Our system of government would work a lot better if the parties weren't squabbling so much of the time.

p12 The parties confuse the issues rather than provide a clear choice on them.

These results show a deep sense of uneasiness about parties. While at least 50 percent of Canadians feel that they can distinguish between the different parties (see Nadeau and Blais 1990), there is great cynicism about parties' behaviour, their useless squabbling and their frequent attempts to dodge the issues. That cynicism emerges the most sharply in Canadians' overwhelming propensity to have greater confidence in their individual MPs than in organized parties.

The questions posed in our survey had not been asked previously and it is therefore impossible to compare responses over time. Most Canadian National Election Studies have, however, tapped overall feelings about parties by having people rate each party on a thermometer running from 0 to 100. Table 3.6 reports the average score given to each party at various points in time. This score dropped by nine points between 1968 and 1988. The same pattern is reported by Gallup. The percentage of Canadians who say that they have very little respect for and confidence in political parties went from 22 percent in 1979 to 33 percent in 1989 (Gallup Report 9 February 1989). Thus, at the same time as political trust waned, attitudes about parties became more negative.

Is this trend peculiar to Canada? Dennis (1966; 1975) provides the most systematic study of attitudes about parties in the United States. His conclusion is very clear: "The American party system has undergone a marked erosion of its legitimacy" (1975, 226). A similar evaluation is made by Wattenberg (1986), who suggests, however, that Americans are increasingly indifferent to parties, rather than alienated from them. The same pattern thus emerges in Canada and the United States. The question remains as to whether parties are more or less legitimate in Canada. This is much more difficult to assess; the scanty

Table 3.6
Evolution of feelings about parties in Canada*
(mean score)

Parties	1968	1974	1979	1980	1988
Liberal party	65	62	58	56	48
Progressive Conservative party	56	54	55	51	51
New Democratic Party	48	44	47	46	43
Average	56	53	53	51	47

Source: CNES (1968, 1974, 1979, 1980, 1988).

*In every Canadian National Election Study since 1968 respondents have been asked how much they liked or disliked specific parties by requesting that they indicate their feelings for each party by placing each one on a 100-point scale or "feeling thermometer."

evidence we have suggests that attitudes about parties in Canada are at least as, and perhaps more, negative. For instance, the average score given to the major parties on feeling thermometer questions in the United States hovers around 60 (ibid., 64), compared to around 50 in Canada (table 3.7).

It should be pointed out that responses to the four questions listed in table 3.5 are weakly correlated with each other. The main thrust of Canadians' reactions is inescapable: they mistrust parties. They feel ambivalent enough, however, that their responses vary according to

Table 3.7
Distribution of attitudes about parties in Canada
(percentage agreeing with the statement)

	MPs should vote freely (p7)	Parties are the same (p9)	Too much party squabbling (p11)	Parties confuse the issues (p12)
Atlantic	78	48	85	89
Quebec	80	60	74	80
Ontario	77	40	84	89
Manitoba/Saskatchewan	81	47	88	91
Alberta	80	43	82	90
British Columbia	77	39	81	88
Men	80	46	77	86
Women	77	48	86	88
Under 45	76	45	79	86
45 and over	82	50	84	88
Low education	79	54	89	90
Medium education	79	46	82	88
High education	76	37	68	78
Low income	81	51	86	89
Medium income	79	47	80	87
High income	78	39	75	83
Blue collar	79	52	86	90
White collar	78	45	79	85
Unionized	78	50	79	85
Nonunionized	79	46	83	88
English	76	41	82	89
French	82	61	77	82
Non-charter language	84	48	89	85
Catholic	81	54	80	86
Protestant	78	40	85	90
Canada	78	47	81	87

Note: For the wording of the questions, see table 3.5.

the specifics of the context. Particularly interesting is the low correlation between responses given to questions p9 and p12. Fifty percent of those who think that the parties confuse the issues rather than provide a choice still disagree with the statement that all federal parties are the same. Even though Canadians are quite willing to condemn parties for all kinds of shortcomings, they are more reluctant to jump to the conclusion that there is no real choice left.

On the whole, responses to these questions are only weakly related to background variables (see table 3.7), so that the pattern of reactions we have described characterizes most groups. The absence of regional variations with regard to views about parties is particularly striking. As in the case of political cynicism, the group that stands out as the most positive about parties is the one whose members have a university education; the proportion believing that there is too much party squabbling is a full 21 percentage points lower among university graduates than among those who have not completed high school.

At the other end of the scale, ethnic minorities, whose mother tongue is neither French nor English, are particularly critical of parties. This does not seem to stem from a lesser acquaintance with Canadian parties, since cynicism is not stronger among those born outside Canada (data not shown). It may reflect the perception that Canadian parties are not sensitive to the concerns of ethnic minorities. We also find that women are particularly annoyed with parties' squabbling. This could be related to women's greater concern for consensus building (Ferguson 1984).

One may wonder whether having direct experience with a party makes one less cynical about them. We would expect those who are or have been members of a party to form more positive attitudes about the party system, but this does not seem to be the case. The differences between party members (including former members) and non-members on most questions are very small, ranging from one to eight percentage points (data not shown). This is still another indication of the extent of the cynicism that prevails in Canada with respect to the party system; even those who participate in the system hold negative views about it.

Finally, we again find evidence of the pervasive role of populist values. The sole nonpopulist group, the technocratic liberals, comes out as having the least negative views about parties; for example, the percentage who believe that our system of government would work better if the parties were not squabbling so much is about 85 percent among the five groups with a populist strain, but drops to 72 percent among technocratic liberals (data not shown).

In short, support for the party system is quite weak in Canada. Cynicism about how parties conduct themselves is shared by almost all groups but is not without some limits. A slim majority disagrees with the view that parties are all basically the same. Canadians still feel they have some choice, even though the menu is not very appealing.

ATTITUDES ABOUT MONEY

Money plays a central role in our daily lives. It allows us to enter into all kinds of exchanges with other people. It is a crucial marker that tells us what we can and cannot afford to do. From early childhood we start thinking about the appropriate place of money in life. We may, therefore, expect most people to have formed strong opinions about the role of money in society; of course, it is Canadians' beliefs about the interconnection between money and politics that concern us here. How important a motivation is money in politics? How much power does money buy? How much impact does money have on electoral outcomes? These are fundamental and thorny questions that elicit different responses from different people, and that are bound to affect one's views about electoral institutions.

Our survey contained three questions about the role of money in politics. The first question pertains to motivations. Only 43 percent of our respondents agreed with the assertion that "anybody who gives money to a political party expects something in return" (table 3.8). This rather sanguine view of contributors is intriguing, especially when juxtaposed with the common perception that most politicians make a lot of money misusing public office. This suggests that Canadians' cynicism about politics does not stem from the perception that those involved in politics have bad motivations; politicians, after all, are seen to be about as honest as the average person. The majority simply does not subscribe

Table 3.8
Attitudes about money in Canada
(percentage agree)

Anybody who gives money expects something (f18)	43
People with money have a lot of influence (f19)	85
The party that spends the most wins the election (f20)	38

The wording of the questions was the following:

BASICALLY, do you AGREE or DISAGREE with each of the following statements.

f18 Anybody who gives money to a political party expects something in return, like a job or a contract.

f19 People with money have a lot of influence over the government.

f20 The party that spends the most during a campaign is almost sure to win the election.

to the sinister view that all contributions should be considered to be like any other financial investment – that is, as profit-motivated, and as having nothing to do with some conception of the public interest.

Perceptions about the general impact of money in politics are, however, much less sanguine. There is overwhelming agreement with the assertion that people with money have a lot of influence over government. Perhaps Canadians have come to the view that, since one can obtain so many things with money, it is difficult not to believe that having money helps obtain some degree of political influence.

Most Canadians do not, however, believe that money is the most crucial factor in an election, or that the party that spends the most in a campaign is almost certain to win. This attitude suggests that most people believe money is particularly powerful in "behind-the-scenes" politics, when it comes to making decisions on specific issues; the electoral arena is apparently seen to be less vulnerable to the influence of money. It should be stressed that this optimistic view is not shared by 38 percent of our respondents. The last federal election, in which the pro-free trade group greatly outspent the anti-free trade group and was seen to have helped re-elect the Conservative government, may have induced quite a few Canadians to form cynical views about the role of money in politics.

All in all, Canadians are not overly cynical in their assessment of the place of money in politics. They are certainly not naive and do recognize that money can buy a great deal of influence, but a majority disagrees that all contributions are motivated by some kind of personal reward and that electoral outcomes are, basically, shaped by financial resources. Even if a substantial minority holds pessimistic views about these matters, the majority believes that money plays an important but not overwhelming role in politics.

Furthermore, opinions about the role of money in politics are not closely linked to each other. The correlations between the three questions are all quite modest, ranging from 0.16 to 0.21. This means that those who are cynical about motivations, for instance, are not necessarily cynical when it comes to assessing the impact of money on elections. Indeed, the majority (53 percent) of those who believe that contributors expect something in return disagree with the assertion that the party that spends the most in an election is almost sure to win. These relatively weak correlations do not mean that people are inconsistent, since there is no logical necessity for opinions to be interconnected. Rather, they indicate the absence of an underlying sanguineness or cynicism about money that pervades responses to the three questions.

We do not have any data that would enable us to track the views of Canadians regarding the role of money in politics over time, or to compare them with people in other countries. Sorauf (1988, 326), however, cites circumstantial evidence that Americans may be even more cynical than Canadians in this regard. He indicates, for example, that it is now conventional wisdom in the United States that money buys elections. According to him, the burden of proof has shifted to those who hold less cynical views; it is up to them to demonstrate that in some cases this perception is not true.

Opinions about the role of money in politics do not vary substantially among subgroups. As far as region is concerned, the most interesting result pertains to perceptions of the impact of money in elections; on this question, Ontarians are much more sanguine than residents of all other regions. Only 32 percent believe that the party that spends the most will win the election, compared to 41 percent of Canadians elsewhere. The New Democratic Party (NDP) victory in the provincial election that was held just before our survey was conducted must have conveyed the message that indeed money is not enough to win an election.

It is also interesting to look at the relationship between attitudes about the role of money and income. We could expect cynicism on this matter to be more widespread among the poor, but do not find this to be the case, with one exception: those with a low level of income agree, to a greater degree than other groups, that money can help "buy" an election (see table 3.9). Even among this group, however, the majority rejects the idea. In particular, we do not see the expected propensity for groups to understate their own influence and to overstate that of others: those with a high level of income are just as likely as others to subscribe to the view that those with money have a lot of influence.

We noted in the previous section that party members evaluate the party system in the same way as non-members. What about those who have themselves given money to a party or candidate? Do they view the place of money in politics any differently? The answer is yes, in one respect. Unsurprisingly perhaps, contributors (who represent 19 percent of our sample) are more charitable toward those who give money; 66 percent of them disagree with the assertion that contributors always expect something in return, compared with only 55 percent in the rest of the population. Contributors and non-contributors, however, do not differ in their perceptions of the impact of money on politics in general and on elections in particular (data not shown).

On the whole, attitudes about the role of money in politics do not

Table 3.9
Distribution of attitudes about money in Canada
(percentage agreeing with the statement)

	Anybody who gives money expects something (f18)	People with money have a lot of influence (f19)	Party that spends most wins (f20)
Atlantic	49	84	41
Quebec	39	82	44
Ontario	45	84	32
Manitoba/Saskatchewan	43	90	37
Alberta	43	89	42
British Columbia	44	88	38
Men	43	85	38
Women	43	84	38
Under 45	42	86	36
45 and over	44	83	41
Low education	43	80	40
Medium education	45	88	37
High education	37	84	38
Low income	45	83	44
Medium income	42	86	35
High income	43	85	36
Blue collar	46	84	40
White collar	42	86	37
Unionized	44	86	40
Nonunionized	43	84	37
English	45	87	36
French	39	82	43
Non-charter language	44	79	40
Catholic	41	83	42
Protestant	44	87	34
Canada	43	85	38

Note: For the wording of the questions, see table 3.8.

vary substantially among socio-economic groups. Canadians from all backgrounds believe that money buys a great deal of influence; they are, however, somewhat less concerned about its impact on electoral outcomes and about the motivations that lead people to contribute to parties. The majority does not hold the view that all contributions are motivated by narrow personal interests. This does not, however, imply the absence of cynicism. Close to 40 percent believe that the party that spends the most usually wins the election.

RECAPITULATION

We can characterize Canadians' beliefs about politicians, parties and money in the following ways.

1. On the whole, Canadians are highly cynical about politicians, parties and the role of money in politics. That cynicism, however, is not as deep as it may first appear. When Canadians think about actual politicians and take into account the constraints of the job, their judgements are more moderate.
2. Canadians express the most negative views about parties, and are upset about how parties behave in the real world. Respondents were somewhat more sanguine about the role of money in politics: a majority of Canadians reject the assertion that the party that spends the most wins the election.
3. Cynicism has increased over time.
4. The degree of cynicism in Canada is similar to that found in the United States and generally greater than that in Europe.
5. Attitudes about politicians, parties and money are weakly related to socio-economic variables. Furthermore, party members or contributors hold views that are not substantially different from those of the rest of Canadians.
6. Regional variations are modest. The most significant exceptions are that Quebeckers are less cynical about politicians and Ontarians are less likely to believe that the party that spends the most wins the election. The latter belief might be explained by the election of an NDP government in that province just before our survey was conducted. This indicates that beliefs are affected by political conjuncture and are not immutable.
7. The better educated tend to be less cynical about parties and politicians.
8. Attitudes about the role of money in politics do not vary substantially across income groups.
9. Cynicism and populist feelings tend to reinforce each other.

4

ATTITUDES ABOUT THE REPRESENTATIVE PROCESS

Iₙ THIS CHAPTER, we focus on Canadians' opinions regarding various aspects of the representative process. We examine their views about our electoral system, the role of MPs, the representation of women and visible minorities, and internal processes of party democracy. Each of these issues relates in its own way to a more profound concern, namely, perceptions of the representativeness of our institutions of electoral democracy. Electoral democracy rests fundamentally on the principle of representation: it is democratic only to the extent that it is representative. However, what exactly does "representative" mean? The notion is more complex than it may appear to be at first glance.

Pitkin (1967) has distinguished several ways of understanding representation. Three, in particular, seem germane to the issues discussed in this chapter: the "formalistic," "descriptive" and "acting for" approaches. The "formalistic" approach to representation focuses on the formal procedures: those that precede and initiate representation and those that follow and terminate it. From a formalistic perspective, a system is representative to the extent that its institutions both grant authority to those who govern and also enable the public to hold those who govern accountable. Elections perform a crucial role in ensuring representativeness in this sense, by simultaneously granting authority and holding that authority accountable. The presumption here is that these formal arrangements will ensure responsiveness, if only for the pragmatic reason that those who govern seek re-election.

The "descriptive" approach to representation, on the other hand, seeks its assurance of responsiveness in the characteristics of those who are elected. Where the formalistic approach focuses on the electoral

process, the descriptive approach is more concerned with the composition of the resulting legislative assembly. In this conception, representation is understood as a matter of "standing for" others, and
representatives are considered to do this by virtue of some resemblance
to those whom they represent. Descriptive representation, then, directs
our attention to the question of what representatives must be like in
order to represent; the answer is that collectively they must constitute
a mirror – or a miniature replica – of the electorate at large. This concept
of representation, in other words, is essentially microcosmic (see Birch
1971). One practical expression of this approach to representation is
the concern with improving the gender balance in the House of
Commons and increasing the proportion of MPs who are members
of visible minorities.

While "descriptive," or "standing for," representation is preoccupied with *who* governs, "acting for" representation focuses on *what*
governments do. "Acting for" representation looks beyond the formalities of representation to its substantive content. This approach links
representation with actions: representation in this sense means acting
in the interest of the represented, in a manner that is responsive to them.
As Pitkin (1967, 118) notes, this view of representation is by far the most
difficult to specify of the three she distinguishes. The difficulty lies in
the ambiguity of the notion of "acting for" others: does it require representatives to do what their constituents want or should representatives
be free to do what they believe to be best for their constituents? The
tension between wishes and welfare has been a classic focus of contro-
versy among theorists of political representation.

One of the questions that we examine in this chapter is how Canadian
electors view the proper role of the representative. We also examine a
number of aspects of the representative process that have particular
relevance for descriptive representation: the way that votes translate
into seats; the representation of women and members of visible minorities in the House of Commons; and the selection of party leaders. In
examining Canadians' opinions on these questions, we are particularly
interested in the role of fundamental political values. A number of writers
have noted the affinity between populist values and descriptive conceptions of representation (see Pitkin 1967). From a populist perspective,
descriptively accurate representation seems to offer the best assurance
that the representatives will do what the people themselves would do
if they could act directly. If representatives are to stand for the people,
they should at least approximate the whole people, as far as it is possible
to do so. Conversely, there seems to be an affinity between technocratic
values and formalistic conceptions of representation. If government is

the proper preserve of those with the requisite knowledge and competence to lead, it is enough that they be properly authorized and periodically held to account.

Neither type of value operates in isolation, however. Any individual will hold a number of values which combine – or compete – to help shape opinion. In particular, we can expect individualism and anti-statism to constrain the populist impulse. A concern with minimizing restrictions on individual autonomy and limiting the role of the state may render proposals for improving descriptive representation less attractive. We also expect opinions on these issues to reflect beliefs about reality. Particularly relevant to questions of descriptive representation are beliefs about discrimination. Finally, we look at the impact of respondents' own social characteristics. We could expect women, members of ethnic minorities and other groups that have been numerically underrepresented in the House of Commons to have distinct views on questions of descriptive representation.

THE ELECTORAL SYSTEM

We began our examination of opinions about the various aspects of representative democracy in Canada by asking our respondents for their views on the formalities of representation. Do they find our present arrangements for translating votes into seats acceptable? Would they favour a system that allowed them to separate the questions of choosing a party to form the government and choosing an MP to represent their constituency?

Our "first-past-the-post," single-member plurality system can cause serious distortions in the way that seats translate into votes (see, especially, Cairns 1973; Irvine 1979). Typically, the party with the most votes is rewarded with significantly more seats than its share of the popular vote would warrant; so, too, is a minor party with regionally concentrated support. A minor party with diffuse national support, on the other hand, will rarely receive as many seats as its share of the popular vote would seem to warrant. These distortions in the translation of votes into seats can weaken elections as mechanisms of descriptive representation; after all, the hallmark of a representative body is "accurate correspondence or resemblance to what it represents, by reflecting without distortion" (Pitkin 1967, 60).

Criticism has indeed focused on "the tendency of the electoral system to make the parliamentary parties grossly inaccurate reflections of the sectional distribution of party support" (Cairns 1973, 138). The "winner-take-all" nature of our electoral system has worked, historically, to shut major parties out of particular provinces. In Alberta, for example, the federal Liberal party has on occasion won as much as 25 percent of the vote and not been rewarded with a single seat.

We began our sequence of questions tapping views on the electoral system by asking our respondents whether or not they found it acceptable that under our present system a party can win a majority of seats and form the government without winning a majority of votes. We then asked those with an opinion whether they found this completely or only somewhat (un)acceptable. Fully a third of our sample (34 percent) replied that they did not have an opinion about this issue. (Parenthetically, it is encouraging that respondents were so ready to admit that they did *not* have an opinion, rather than feeling constrained to affect one.) This should not surprise us. The workings of the electoral system can be hard for some electors to grasp, and, for others, the complex mix of pros and cons associated with our first-past-the-post plurality system (see Blais 1991) makes it difficult to arrive at a clear opinion on one side or the other. Of those who do have an opinion, we can see (table 4.1) that fewer than half (42 percent) find this aspect of the present system acceptable.

We can also see from this table that there is a significant regional division in views about the electoral system. Residents of Alberta and Quebec are significantly less likely to find the present system acceptable, at least with respect to the way that votes translate into seats. Alberta and Quebec, of course, are the two provinces where the distorting effects of the electoral system have been most striking at the federal level. Moreover, Quebec is a province where the possibility of an alternative system, incorporating an element of proportional representation, has received the most serious public consideration. In no province in the recent past, however, have the distorting effects of the first-past-the-post system been more dramatic than in the last provincial election in New Brunswick; yet, perhaps surprisingly, New Brunswickers turn out to be as accepting (51 percent) of the workings of the electoral system as other residents of the Atlantic provinces.

The electoral system is often perceived to be an obstacle to new parties; in fact, it was the discrepancy between the proportion of votes (30 percent) and the proportion of seats (5 percent) won by the Parti québécois (PQ) in the 1973 provincial election that put the issue on the public agenda in Quebec. Similarly, we find acceptance of the present system to be lowest among supporters of the Reform Party (30 percent), the Bloc québécois (27 percent) and the Green Party (29 percent). Perceptions of how easy or difficult it is for new parties in general to get their candidates elected (question p3), however, have only a very modest impact on opinion on this question (data not shown).

Table 4.1
Distribution of opinions about electoral arrangements

	% finding system acceptable	% in favour
Atlantic	51	70
Quebec	33	85
Ontario	47	73
Manitoba/Saskatchewan	42	66
Alberta	39	78
British Columbia	41	70
Men	46	72
Women	36	80
Under 45	42	80
45 and over	41	68
Low education	38	77
Medium education	40	78
High education	49	66
Low income	40	75
Medium income	43	77
High income	43	72
Blue collar	43	77
White collar	41	75
Unionized	43	76
Nonunionized	42	75
English	44	73
French	35	81
Non-charter language	44	78
Catholic	41	79
Protestant	44	72
Canada	42	76

The questions were the following:

d1 Now we would like to get your views on the electoral system. Under our present system, a party can win a majority of seats and form the government without winning a majority of votes. Do you find this ACCEPTABLE or UNACCEPTABLE or DON'T YOU HAVE AN OPINION on this?

d5 How about a system where you would have TWO votes, ONE to choose your local MP, and ONE to choose which party forms the government? Would you be in FAVOUR of or OPPOSED to such a system?

As we can see, gender does have significant effects: women are less likely than men to find the present system for translating votes into seats acceptable. Indeed, we shall see throughout this chapter that there are significant gender differences on the issues discussed. Women are more likely than men to see problems with the existing electoral system in general and to endorse action on these questions. While we are not able to probe the underlying motivations, this pattern of responses would seem to reflect a reaction against power structures, shaped by men, that are perceived to have worked to marginalize women and their concerns. On the specific issue of the electoral system, it is worth noting that a number of studies have found a relationship between the type of electoral system and the legislative representation of women. Systems of proportional representation – especially party list systems – seem to favour the election of women much more than do single-member plurality systems (see, for example, Castles 1981; Norris 1985b; Rule 1987).

Education is another factor that consistently affects opinions about various aspects of representative democracy. University graduates are generally more likely to be satisfied with the present arrangements and less likely to favour changes. As shown in table 4.1, for example, those with a university education are more likely to find the workings of the present electoral system acceptable. Respondents' level of information per se, however, does not seem to affect responses (see table 1.D5).

Political values also do not affect responses. The issue of representativeness does not divide respondents along populist–nonpopulist lines; the technocratic liberals are not appreciably more likely than those with populist leanings to find the present system acceptable (see table 4.2). There is, in fact, no obviously superior method for translating votes into seats from a populist perspective. A concern with achieving descriptively accurate representation might mean that some system of proportional representation is more desirable. At the same time, however, this

Table 4.2
Political values and opinions about electoral arrangements

	Electoral system (% acceptable)	Two-vote system (% in favour)
Technocratic liberals	45	69
Populist liberals	40	77
Minoritarian individualists	39	76
Majoritarian individualists	43	74
Radical collectivists	40	78
Party collectivists	40	84

For the wording of the questions, see table 4.1.

type of system can result in further removing government from the grass roots if no party emerges a clear winner and party élites have to enter into coalitions.

The relevance of populist values is clearer when we turn to respondents' views on the question of having two votes: one to choose their local MP and the other to choose the party that will form the government. It is a system that would, arguably, make MPs more responsive to grassroots concerns. As we can see in table 4.2, all five of the groupings that share this populist desire to bring decisions closer to the people at the grass roots show enhanced support for a two-vote system. Interestingly, support for such a system is highest among the party collectivists, who combine a strong populist strain with an even more pervasive commitment to the notion that there cannot be true democracy without political parties. This is a system that seems to promise greater grassroots control over the local MP while retaining the system of party government; whether that is indeed possible is an open question (see Katz 1980).

The lesser enthusiasm of the technocratic liberals is also easy to understand. From a formalistic perspective, a two-vote system could be seen as actually posing a threat to responsiveness. What makes for responsive government from this perspective is accountability, but lines of accountability would be less clear with a party system with weaker or partial party discipline. A two-vote system could also imply a threat to traditional responsible government. One of the virtues of what Birch (1971) terms party representation is that it facilitates responsibility; the idea is that political leaders should enjoy sufficient support and scope "to accept a broader responsibility than that of responding to day-to-day pressures" (ibid., 115). To this end, the model of responsible party government assumes "first, that the parties are able to bring forth programmes to which they commit themselves and, second, that the parties possess sufficient internal cohesion to carry out these programmes" (American Political Science Association 1950, 17–18). A weakening of party discipline, therefore, would imply a weakening of responsible government.

Overall, fully three-quarters of our sample (76 percent) were ready to endorse a two-vote system (see table 4.1). We can also see that women are more likely than men to favour having two votes; so, too, are Quebeckers and those with neither French nor English as their mother tongue. The only other significant regional effect is residence in Manitoba or Saskatchewan. Residents of these two provinces are significantly less likely to favour a two-vote system. Only 66 percent favour such a system, compared with fully 85 percent of Quebeckers. Support is also less likely to be found among older respondents, the better informed (see table 1.D6) and the better educated. Those with more experience with the existing system, or more knowledge of its workings, have, it seems, more reservations about a change that could dramatically affect its operation, perhaps because they have a better grasp of the ramifications. Even among these groups, however, fully two-thirds of respondents favoured a two-vote system.

Not surprisingly, those who are (or have been) party members are somewhat less likely to favour a system that might work to diminish parties' control over their MPs (see table 1.D6). Conversely, respondents who believe that, in general, those elected to Parliament soon lose touch with the people are more likely to favour this type of reform (data not shown).

MPs AND REPRESENTATIVE DEMOCRACY

One way of helping to ensure that MPs keep in touch with their constituents might be to limit their term in office. In the United States, where the issue has been publicly debated (and where limited terms have become a reality in three state legislatures, including California), term limitation has been advocated in classic populist language. "Careerist monopoly in government squeezes out the popular element which can give realism and overview to policy decisions ... To introduce, therefore, a more democratic class of representatives who stay in touch with the simplicity and lucidity of popular vision would counterbalance the narrow and sometimes tunnel vision of the experts" (Struble and Jahre 1991, 36). The technocratic response, of course, is to point to the benefits of the experience that long-serving representatives can bring to their task. A number of observers have, in fact, bemoaned the rapid rate of turnover in the House of Commons, arguing that its effectiveness may be jeopardized if there are too many inexperienced members (see Franks 1987). Objections to term limitation could also be raised from the standpoint of formalistic representation: freed from the need to face re-election, representatives would actually have less incentive to be responsive during their final term.

To tap Canadians' opinions on this question, we asked our respondents whether or not they thought it would be a good idea to prohibit MPs from running again if they have been in Parliament for more than 12 years. Fully 13 percent did not have an opinion on this question. We can see from table 4.3 that, among those who did respond, only 38 percent were ready to endorse the proposal. A further 3 percent agreed with the idea but not with the suggested number of years.

There are some regional differences in opinions on this question

Table 4.3
Distribution of opinions about MPs and their role

	Limiting MPs' terms (% a good idea)	MPs' role (% follow public interest)	Allowing MPs to change parties (% in favour)
Atlantic	41	39	28
Quebec	39	45	34
Ontario	34	36	27
Manitoba/Saskatchewan	41	29	23
Alberta	47	25	32
British Columbia	38	32	30
Men	37	35	32
Women	40	39	26
Under 45	36	37	30
45 and over	41	36	28
Low education	43	40	27
Medium education	40	37	28
High education	27	30	38
Low income	40	39	27
Medium income	38	33	30
High income	35	34	28
Blue collar	40	38	29
White collar	37	36	30
Unionized	37	37	31
Nonunionized	39	36	29
English	38	33	28
French	39	46	34
Non-charter language	37	34	28
Catholic	37	42	30
Protestant	39	28	28
Canada	38	37	29

The questions were the following:

d6 Some say that MPs who have been in Parliament for more than 12 years should not be allowed to run for Parliament again. Do you think this is a GOOD idea, or a POOR idea, or DON'T YOU HAVE AN OPINION on this?

d7 When MPs vote on a controversial issue in Parliament such as the death penalty, should they follow what THEY BELIEVE to be THE PUBLIC INTEREST or should they follow THE VIEWS OF THE PEOPLE IN THEIR RIDING?

d7a What about MPs who want to change their party between elections: should they be ALLOWED TO CHANGE parties or should they be REQUIRED TO RESIGN their seat in Parliament?

(see table 4.3). Almost one-half of Albertans favour a limit on MPs' terms, compared with only one-third of Ontarians. Interestingly, older respondents are somewhat more likely than younger respondents to approve of the idea of limiting MPs' terms. Again, those with a higher level of education are more reluctant to endorse a change in existing arrangements, with only 27 percent declaring themselves in favour of limiting MPs' terms. How informed respondents are, however, appears to have little impact independent of education. Party members are little different from non-members on this question (see table 1.D7).

The similarity in the opinions of men and women on this question is particularly interesting. The privileged place of incumbents has been identified as a significant barrier to women's candidacies in competitive ridings and hence to greater gender balance in the House of Commons (Erickson 1991). A recent study by Young (1991), however, suggests that, in contrast to the United States, this constraint is of limited importance in Canada.

As shown in table 4.4, all of the groupings with a populist strain are, predictably, more favourable to term limitation. Only 29 percent of the technocratic liberals, however, favour limiting MPs' terms. These are the respondents who reject the notion that decisions need to be brought closer to the grass roots, and prefer to place their trust in experts. The fact that both the minoritarian and majoritarian individualists are more supportive of limiting MPs' terms than the radical and party collectivists is interesting – individualism in itself is apparently no bar to enhanced support. The belief that MPs generally lose touch with the people has an independent impact on response to this question; so, too, does political cynicism, increasing the likelihood that respondents will favour limited terms for MPs (data not shown).

These sorts of concerns necessarily raise questions about the appropriate role of elected representatives. The role of the representative

Table 4.4
Political values and opinions about MPs and their role

	Limiting MPs' terms (% a good idea)	MPs' role (% follow public interest)	Allowing MPs to change parties (% in favour)
Technocratic liberals	29	34	31
Populist liberals	39	31	30
Minoritarian individualists	44	35	24
Majoritarian individualists	44	35	30
Radical collectivists	37	43	33
Party collectivists	40	41	28

For the wording of the questions, see table 4.3.

has been a central preoccupation of the "acting for" approach to representation discussed above (see Pitkin 1967). In this approach, representation means acting in the interest of the represented. This seemingly straightforward belief, however, begs the question of what it means to act in the interest of others. What is the proper relationship between representatives and those for whom they act? Should representatives feel bound by the wishes and opinions of their constituents or should they do what they consider to be in the best interests of those whom they represent? Whether the representative should act as a delegate or as a trustee is one of the classic conundrums of political representation.

Underpinning the arguments for one role over the other are very different assumptions about the democratic capabilities of the average citizen. The notion of the representative as agent, or delegate, assumes that citizens are fully competent – and, indeed, the best qualified – to determine what is in their best interests. The notion of the representative as trustee, however, often reflects a scepticism about the capacity of the ordinary citizen, or at least a belief in the superior wisdom of the élite.

The notion of trusteeship does not necessarily imply, however, that representatives should not be responsive to their constituents. The debate turns not on whether representatives should be responsive but on what responsiveness means: responsiveness to the expressed demands and opinions of constituents or responsiveness to their real needs (see Birch 1971, 109–12). As Pennock explains, "The distinction I am intending to make between 'desire' and 'interest' is the distinction between what is immediately demanded and what in the long run, with the benefit of hindsight, would have been preferred" (1968, 13).

Should MPs act as trustees or as delegates? We raised this issue with our respondents by asking them what representatives should do when they vote on a controversial issue in Parliament, such as the death penalty: should MPs follow what they believe to be the public interest or should they follow the views of the people in their riding? In selecting a hypothetical issue for this question, we needed an issue where there could, plausibly, be a free vote in Parliament. We chose the death penalty issue over abortion as being less emotive.

As table 4.3 shows, only 37 percent of our respondents thought that MPs should follow what they believe to be the public interest, compared with fully 63 percent who replied that MPs should follow the views of the people in their riding. Quebeckers are more likely, and Albertans less likely, than residents of the other provinces to think that MPs should be guided by what they believe to be the public interest;

a full 20 percentage points separate residents of Quebec and Alberta on this question. Protestants, the more informed and those with more education are also less likely to think that MPs should follow what they believe to be the public interest (see table 1.D8). It may be tempting to see some sort of collectivist versus individualist dichotomy underlying the Quebec–Alberta contrast and the opinions of Protestants. While members of the two collectivist groupings, the radical collectivists and the party collectivists, are somewhat more likely to think that MPs should be guided by what they believe to be the public interest, we can see that these effects are rather modest.

This question also did not appear to divide respondents along populist–nonpopulist lines. This may be because both conceptions of the MP's role – delegate and trustee – reflect the idea of representing "the people." How "the people" should be understood and how popular democracy should be achieved are two of the dimensions that serve to distinguish historical variants of Prairie populism (Laycock 1990). While the radical democratic populists advocated forms of delegate democracy and favoured close relations between citizens and their delegates, plebiscitarian populist discourse revolved around the notion of the general will, "the objectively correct common interest of the incorporated citizens" (Riker 1982, 11).

What is noteworthy about the regressions (see table 1.D8), in fact, is the paucity of statistically significant effects, which may indicate a relative lack of deeply grounded opinions on the question. The same lack of significant determinants is apparent when we turn to the question of allowing MPs to change parties (see table 1.D9). We asked our respondents whether MPs who want to change party affiliation between elections should be allowed to make the switch or whether they should be required to resign their seat in Parliament. Fewer than one in three of our respondents (29 percent) believed that MPs should be allowed to change parties between elections (see table 4.3). The majority view is clearly in favour of requiring representatives to resign in such circumstances.

Albertans, Quebeckers and those with a higher level of education are all more likely to favour allowing MPs to change parties. It is possible that the views of these Albertans and Quebeckers are linked to prior experience with MPs who have crossed the floor and to the growth of the Reform Party and the Bloc québécois, respectively. In fact, fully 60 percent of prospective Bloc québécois voters and 39 percent of prospective Reform Party voters believe that MPs should be allowed to change parties between elections (data not shown). There is some evidence of a gender gap, with women being less likely than men to consider that MPs should be allowed to switch. Neither level of information nor, surprisingly, party membership had a significant effect on opinions on this question (see table 1.D9). Views were also relatively unaffected by differences in basic political values (see table 4.4).

THE REPRESENTATION OF WOMEN AND VISIBLE MINORITIES

We turn now to the central preoccupation of "descriptive" or "standing for" approaches to representation: the composition of the House of Commons. Allowing that a perfect replica of society is an unattainable ideal, the question for proponents of descriptive representation becomes: which societal characteristics should be reproduced (see Pitkin 1967, 87)? Attention in Canada has focused on two groups, in particular: women and members of visible minorities.

Patterns of exclusion and inclusion have been similar for women and members of visible minorities alike and analogous explanations have been offered for these similarities (for women, see Bashevkin 1990; Brodie 1991; Erickson 1991; Young 1991; for visible minorities, see Pelletier 1991; Simard 1991; Stasiulis and Abu-Laban 1991). Access to elected office has been easiest for both women and members of visible minorities at the municipal level, where the financial costs of running for election are considerably lower and party structures less entrenched. Party control over recruitment has been cited as a critical barrier to both women and minority candidacies at the federal level; if not excluding them, it relegates them to unwinnable ridings. In a recent study, however, Erickson (1991) has suggested that, at least in the case of women, the problem may be due more to supply than to demand. While she identifies barriers to women's candidacies in competitive ridings, she argues that the fundamental problem lies with the lack of women who are willing to run for politics in the first place (see Young (1991) on the same point). She attributes this reluctance to seek office to the nature of the personal sacrifices required of national politicians, sacrifices that can be particularly heavy for women given the dominant pattern of family relationships. Other authors, however, have pointed to the role of socialization, citing differences in women's motivations and expectations, to explain their underrepresentation among candidates and elected members (see, for example, Clarke and Kornberg 1979).

How concerned are Canadians about the underrepresentation of these two sectors of the population? How ready are they to endorse affirmative action to enhance descriptive representation? What role do beliefs about discrimination and gender roles play? In order to examine Canadians' views about the underrepresentation of women and visible minorities in the House of Commons, we first randomly divided our sample into two subsamples of equal size. One subsample was asked for their opinions regarding the representation of women, while the other was queried about members of visible minorities. The advantage of doing this was that responses on one issue could not influence responses on the other.

We will look first at the issue of the underrepresentation of women. We started by asking our respondents whether or not they considered the relative lack of women in the House of Commons to be a serious problem. Fully one-third (33 percent) felt that the gender imbalance is not a problem, and a further 35 percent considered it to be not a very serious problem. Only 8 percent went so far as to describe the under-representation of women as a very serious problem.

The gender of the interviewer had a significant effect on responses (see table 1.D10). People who were interviewed by a female interviewer were more likely to claim that there was a problem than those who were interviewed by a male. This effect was much more evident for male respondents than for female respondents. Only 20 percent of men interviewed by a male replied that there was a problem, compared with 30 percent of the men interviewed by a woman. Interestingly, women who were interviewed by a male were twice as likely (16 percent) as women interviewed by a female (8 percent) to characterize the under-representation of women as a very serious problem (data not shown). Irrespective of the gender of the interviewer, however, we find that the respondent's gender has an important effect. As we can see from table 4.5, women are more likely to perceive a problem with the lack of members of their own sex in the House of Commons than are men.

Education also has an impact, as does level of information (see table 1.D10). The more education respondents have, and the more informed they are about politics, the more likely they are to feel that there is a problem with the underrepresentation of women among MPs.

Views on the underrepresentation of women also reflect under-lying political values, as shown in table 4.6. What seems to be the oper-ative factor is laissez-faire individualism, rather than any populist strain. It is the minoritarian and the majoritarian individualists who are the least likely to characterize the underrepresentation of women as a serious problem. Members of these two groupings generally agree that people who do not get ahead have only themselves to blame, that it is not up to the government to help them, and that the country would be better off in fact if we were less concerned about equality. Conversely, those who marry a concern about equality with an acceptance of collective responsibility – the party and especially the radical collectivists – are more likely to be concerned about the lack of women in the House of

Table 4.5
Distribution of opinions about the representation of women in the House of Commons
(percentages)

	Serious or very serious problem	Better or much better government	Favouring requirement
Atlantic	29	33	46
Quebec	37	42	56
Ontario	33	39	35
Manitoba/Saskatchewan	23	32	37
Alberta	26	34	36
British Columbia	27	32	28
Men	26	32	35
Women	37	43	48
Under 45	32	36	41
45 and over	30	39	41
Low education	25	35	55
Medium education	31	36	40
High education	41	44	26
Low income	32	40	50
Medium income	31	36	41
High income	31	37	30
Blue collar	31	36	52
White collar	32	38	37
Unionized	31	40	45
Nonunionized	32	36	39
English	30	37	34
French	37	41	56
Non-charter language	32	32	48
Catholic	32	38	51
Protestant	28	38	31
Canada	32	37	41

The wording of the questions was the following:

d8 As you may know, there are many more men than women in the House of Commons. In your view is this a VERY SERIOUS problem, a SERIOUS problem, NOT A VERY SERIOUS problem or NOT A PROBLEM at all?

d9 If there were as many women as men in the House of Commons do you think we would have MUCH BETTER government, BETTER, WORSE or MUCH WORSE government or do you think it WOULDN'T REALLY MAKE A DIFFERENCE?

d10 Would you FAVOUR or OPPOSE [quotas] requiring the parties to choose as many female as male candidates?

Commons. So, too, are the populist liberals, who almost unanimously reject any suggestion that the country would be better off if equality were less of a concern.

Empirical beliefs about discrimination also play an important role.

Table 4.6
Political values and opinions about the representation of women in the House of Commons
(percentages)

	Serious or very serious problem	Better or much better government	Favouring requirement
Technocratic liberals	30	33	26
Populist liberals	36	44	42
Minoritarian individualists	23	38	47
Majoritarian individualists	24	29	39
Radical collectivists	42	43	51
Party collectivists	37	39	50

For the wording of the questions, see table 4.5.

Regardless of gender, those who agree with the statement that discrimination makes it extremely difficult for women to get jobs equal to their abilities are much more likely (39 percent) to perceive a problem with the lack of women in the House of Commons than are those who do not perceive discrimination (15 percent). It may well be that these respondents attribute the underrepresentation of women to structural factors that impede female candidacies. Conversely, those who believe that everyone would be better off if more women were satisfied to stay home and raise their children are less likely (22 percent) to be troubled by this issue than are those who reject this traditional conception of gender roles (35 percent).

Proponents of descriptive representation tend to presume that the composition of a legislature will determine its actions. Others, however, may question whether "standing for" translates so readily into "acting for" a particular element in the population. Descriptively accurate representation, in other words, does not guarantee responsive government (and conversely, of course, descriptively inaccurate representation may not necessarily mean unresponsive government).

Accordingly, we followed up our question about the relative lack of women in the House of Commons with a question asking whether or not we would have better government if there were as many women as men in the House of Commons. Fully three-fifths (60 percent) of the respondents replied that it would not really make a difference, and a mere 7 percent considered that we would have much better government. Very few respondents (3 percent), however, would say that we would end up with worse or much worse government.

As shown in table 4.5, gender continues to be an important factor in respondents' opinions on the issue of the representation of women: women are more likely than men to believe that equal representation of women in the House of Commons would make for better government. Interestingly, the gender of the interviewer ceases to have a significant impact on responses to this question (see table 1.D11). While education continues to be a factor, it is only a higher level of education that significantly increases the likelihood of a favourable response (and level of information no longer has an effect; see table 1.D11). Those whose mother tongue is neither English nor French are more sceptical, perhaps because they are not particularly likely to consider gender imbalance to be a problem to begin with.

Where laissez-faire individualism shapes perceptions of whether or not the underrepresentation of women is a problem, populism seems to be the operative value when it comes to views on the consequences of improving descriptive representation (table 4.6). The one exception seems to lie with the views of majoritarian individualists. Their almost unanimous conviction that the country would be better off if we worried less about equality, and the lower priority that they accord to the needs and rights of minorities, combine to restrain their populist impulse. Where these conflicting impulses are weaker, however, a populist strain significantly enhances the likelihood of linking gender balance to better government. This is particularly true of the populist liberals and the radical collectivists; indeed, Pitkin (1967) links a preoccupation with descriptive representation to a predilection for direct democracy. If representative government must substitute for direct democracy, there must at least be a correspondence between the legislature and the nation to ensure that the legislature does what the people themselves would have done if they could act directly. In short, "if the legislature is a substitute for the assemblage of the whole people, it should approximate the original as closely as possible" (ibid., 86).

Opinions on this question are also shaped by an empirical belief in discrimination. Those who perceive discrimination in the workplace are more likely (44 percent) to believe that correcting the gender imbalance would enhance the quality of government. On the other hand, those who cleave to a traditional conception of women's place are less likely (27 percent) to think that any improvement would result.

Interestingly, those who have been party members themselves are more likely to see better government resulting from equal representation of women in the House (see table 1.D11). As we shall see, however, this belief does not translate into enhanced support for requiring the parties to choose as many female as male candidates – it is one thing to acknowledge the existence of a problem, but quite another to be ready to endorse remedial action.

Overall, the balance of opinion (59 percent) is against actually requiring the parties to offer balanced slates of candidates. As detailed in table 4.5, only 41 percent of respondents favoured such a requirement. Opposition increases slightly (four percentage points) when the word "quotas" is included in the question (which was done with a random half of this subsample); the effect, however, is fairly modest. There is an interesting exception to this pattern: among the least informed, explicit use of the word "quotas" actually increases support by a full 18 percentage points (data not shown). Apparently, providing a clearer sense of what such a requirement might entail actually works to enhance support among this group. The least informed comprise only a small proportion of our respondents. It is striking, however, that the very same effect is observed – with a different subsample – when we look at attitudes regarding the representation of visible minorities.

The gender of the interviewer has little, if any, impact on responses to this gender issue (see table 1.D12). Responding to a woman, men may tend to feel constrained to pay what amounts to lip service to the notion that the underrepresentation of women in the House of Commons is a problem; they draw the line, however, when it comes to endorsing affirmative action to correct the imbalance.

As we can see (table 4.5), women, union members, blue-collar workers and those with non-English and non-French mother tongues are all more likely to favour a requirement that parties have equal numbers of male and female candidates. Support is particularly high among Quebeckers and those with less education and/or lower incomes. Catholicism, however, ceases to have a significant effect on opinions, once residence in Quebec is taken into account (see table 1.D12).

Higher levels of political information significantly diminish support for any such requirement (see table 1.D12), despite the fact that the more informed are more likely to recognize gender imbalance as a problem. Only 24 percent of the best informed favour requiring parties to act on this issue.

As shown in table 4.6, opinions on this question are clearly rooted in basic political values. Not surprisingly, it is the combination of minoritarianism, egalitarianism and collectivism that produces the strongest support for a requirement that parties offer more balanced slates. Fully half of the radical and party collectivists favour such a requirement. The strong strain of individualism that characterizes the minoritarian individualists does not preclude support, however, when it appears in combination with a pervasive concern for the needs and rights of minorities. This lends considerable force to Cairns' analysis of the challenge that the minoritarian impulse poses to majoritarianism and, by extension, to traditional patterns of representation. Cairns points in particular to a growing suspicion of "theories and practices of representation that imply or assert that representatives can be trusted to speak for citizens/constituents when they lack the defining characteristics of the latter" (1991, 84).

The impact of populist values is also apparent (see table 4.6), confirming the connection between populist impulses and enhanced concern for descriptive representation. The technocratic liberals – the one grouping that lacks a populist strain – stand out for their lack of support for the imposition of any requirement on the parties to improve the descriptive accuracy of representation in the House of Commons.

Support for requiring political parties to offer balanced slates of candidates is enhanced by an empirical belief in discrimination against women. Those who believe that discrimination makes it extremely difficult for women to obtain jobs equal to their abilities are significantly more likely (48 percent) to endorse affirmative action to require equal numbers of women candidates than are those who do not perceive discrimination in the workplace (28 percent).

Discrimination has also been cited as one of the factors that works to exclude members of visible minorities from elected office. The attainment of direct representation in the House of Commons has become a priority for members of some visible minorities, and in the months preceding the last federal election there was a good deal of media coverage of their pursuit of candidacies, especially in the metropolitan Toronto area. Visible minority candidates are said to have been kept out of competitive constituencies in the past by a combination of prejudice on the part of established party hierarchies, fears of racist reactions on the part of voters, or simply doubts about the commitment of prospective candidates to their chosen party (see Stasiulis and Abu-Laban 1990).

When we asked our subsample of respondents about the under-representation of members of visible minorities in the House of Commons, we found some similarities to the pattern of responses that we observed regarding women, but also some interesting differences. First, respondents were generally less likely (23 percent) to deny that the lack of members from visible minorities is a problem; however, they were no more likely to characterize it as a very serious problem. Second, we can see (table 4.7) that gender continues to be a significant determinant of opinion on the issue of descriptive representation. Women are more likely than men to see the underrepresentation of visible

Table 4.7

Distribution of opinions about the representation of visible minorities in the House of Commons
(percentages)

	Serious or very serious problem	Better or much better government	Favouring requirement
Atlantic	43	44	54
Quebec	47	38	58
Ontario	39	34	41
Manitoba/Saskatchewan	34	35	42
Alberta	28	32	31
British Columbia	41	36	32
Men	34	33	39
Women	48	40	53
Under 45	41	36	46
45 and over	40	38	44
Low education	44	38	57
Medium education	39	36	44
High education	37	33	29
Low income	49	41	54
Medium income	40	37	45
High income	30	31	35
Blue collar	41	37	50
White collar	40	36	43
Unionized	44	38	47
Nonunionized	39	36	44
English	37	36	38
French	45	36	59
Non-charter language	49	45	48
Catholic	44	39	54
Protestant	30	27	35
Canada	40	36	45

The wording of the questions was the following:

d8 As you may know, there are very few members of visible minorities in the House of Commons. In your view is this a VERY SERIOUS problem, a SERIOUS problem, NOT A VERY SERIOUS problem or NOT A PROBLEM at all?

d9 If there were more members of visible minorities in the House of Commons do you think we would have MUCH BETTER government, BETTER, WORSE or MUCH WORSE government or do you think it WOULDN'T REALLY MAKE A DIFFERENCE?

d10 Would you FAVOUR or OPPOSE [quotas] requiring the parties to choose more members of visible minorities as candidates?

Note: There were two versions of questions d8, d9 and d10, one referring to women, one to visible minorities. The respondents were randomly selected to answer one or the other set of questions.

minorities as a problem. This is interesting, because it cannot simply be attributed to a desire for consistency in responses. The female respondents in this subsample were not asked for their views on the question of women in the House of Commons and thus could have felt no constraint to appear even-handed.

What is different about the determinants of views regarding the underrepresentation of women versus members of visible minorities is that region comes into play much more in the case of visible minorities. Residents of all three Prairie provinces are less likely to consider the lack of members of visible minorities in the House of Commons to be a problem, while residents of the Atlantic provinces and especially Quebec are more likely to feel that there is indeed a problem. Those who have neither official language as their mother tongue are also more likely to describe the underrepresentation of members of visible minorities as a problem. Protestants and those with higher incomes, however, are less likely to see a problem. Although the more informed are more likely to consider the lack of gender balance as a problem, level of political information has little impact when the underrepresentation of visible minorities is the issue (see table 1.D13), perhaps reflecting its lesser prominence on the public agenda. If anything, those with a university education are less likely to see a problem with a lack of minority representation.

Like opinions about the underrepresentation of women, opinions about the lack of visible minorities in the House of Commons are rooted in basic political values. The operative values, however, are not the same. Populist liberals, minoritarian individualists, radical collectivists and party collectivists alike are all significantly more likely to perceive a problem with respect to the representation of minorities. What seems to be the driving force is the combination of egalitarianism and minoritarianism – egalitarianism alone is not sufficient. The technocratic liberals have an egalitarian strain but it appears in the company of majoritarianism. Like the majoritarian individualists, they are significantly less likely to perceive a problem with the lack of visible minorities in the House. Minoritarianism may also be insufficient if the egalitarian strain is weak; once the effects of empirical beliefs about discrimination are taken into account, the minoritarian individualists cease to be significantly different from the majoritarian individualists and the technocratic liberals on this question of minority representation (see table 1.D13).

Awareness of discrimination against members of visible minorities is indeed a key factor shaping views on this question. Those who agree that discrimination makes it extremely difficult for members of visible minorities to find jobs equal to their abilities are significantly more likely (52 percent) to characterize their underrepresentation in the House as a problem.

When asked whether increasing minority representation in the House would result in better government, the distribution of responses was very similar to that obtained with respect to correcting the gender imbalance. Fifty-seven percent felt that it would not really make a difference and only 5 percent thought that it would result in much better government. Seven percent, however, actually considered that it would result in worse or much worse government.

Looking first at those who were more likely to see the lack of minority representation as a problem, we can see (table 4.7) that women, residents of the Atlantic provinces and those with neither official language as their mother tongue are also more likely to believe that increasing minority representation would make for better government. Conversely, turning to those who were less likely to perceive a problem, we see that Protestants and those with higher incomes are also significantly less likely to feel that better government would be the result.

Empirical beliefs about the existence of discrimination continue to drive opinion: those who believe that discrimination makes it extremely difficult for members of visible minorities to find jobs commensurate with their abilities are also more likely (45 percent) to think that increasing minority representation in the House would result in better government.

When we look at the role of underlying political values (see table 4.8), we can see that both the radical and party collectivists are sanguine about the effects of improving the representation of visible minorities in the House of Commons. What seems to be key here is the rejection of individualism: both collectivist groups are distinguished by their refusal to accept the notion that most people who fail to get ahead have only themselves to blame; these groups are more likely to blame the system. The views of the populist liberals and the minoritarian individualists are more equivocal; only when it is accompanied by a belief in the fact of discrimination does their minoritarian impulse translate into the view that better government will result from increased minority representation. Once the effects of beliefs about discrimination are taken into account, their views on this question are not significantly different from those of the technocratic liberals and the majoritarian individualists (see table 1.D14).

When respondents were asked whether or not parties should be required to choose more members of visible minorities as candidates, the explicit use of the word "quotas" had the effect of making a

Table 4.8
Political values and opinions about the representation of visible minorities in the House of Commons
(percentages)

	Serious or very serious problem	Better or much better government	Favouring requirement
Technocratic liberals	26	29	30
Populist liberals	43	39	40
Minoritarian individualists	43	38	60
Majoritarian individualists	30	29	35
Radical collectivists	46	38	46
Party collectivists	52	48	64

For the wording of the questions, see table 4.7.

favourable response somewhat less likely (except among the least informed where, again, it had the opposite effect). Opposition to such a requirement increased by nine percentage points when the word "quotas" was used. Overall, 55 percent were opposed to having such a requirement, which is very close to the figure of 59 percent obtained when increasing the number of women candidates was the issue.

As shown in table 4.7, women, the less educated, those with lower incomes, residents of the Atlantic provinces and Quebeckers are all more likely to favour a requirement that parties increase the number of visible minority candidates, with francophones supporting such a requirement despite apparent scepticism about the effects of increasing the number of members of visible minorities in the House. It is worth noting that fully 60 percent of francophone Quebeckers favour affirmative action to ensure more candidates from visible minorities. On the other hand, Albertans, British Columbians, Protestants and those with a higher level of education are significantly less likely to favour requiring action from parties on this issue. Albertans and Protestants were two of the groups who were less likely to consider the under-representation of members of visible minorities to be a serious problem to begin with. The better informed are also significantly less likely to favour a requirement that parties have more visible minority candidates (see table 1.D14); as well, like the better educated, the more informed were significantly less likely to support imposing any requirement on parties with respect to women candidates.

It is also worth noting two factors that do not have a significant impact on opinion on this question. Union members were more likely than average to see a problem with the underrepresentation of members of visible minorities and they were somewhat more likely to favour affirmative action in the case of female candidacies, but they were not significantly more likely to support similar action with respect to visible minorities. Similarly, despite being more likely to perceive a problem with the underrepresentation of visible minorities and to favour affirmative action in the case of female candidacies, members of minority language groups failed to emerge as particularly strong supporters of affirmative action on behalf of visible minorities. Awareness of their own numerical underrepresentation in the House of Commons may temper their support for affirmative action that addresses the problem of visible minorities alone.

Turning to the fundamental political values underlying opinion on this issue, we can see that minoritarianism appears to be the basic operative value. This is especially evident in the case of the party collectivists and the minoritarian individualists, but all four of the groupings that give priority to the needs and rights of minorities are more likely to favour imposing a requirement on the parties to ensure minority candidacies. In the case of the minoritarian individualists, this minoritarianism is once again enough to override their individualistic beliefs (see table 4.6). A significant part of the effect of populist liberalism, however, is mediated through the empirical belief in the existence of discrimination against visible minorities in the workplace (see table 1.D15). Again, this belief that discrimination makes it extremely difficult for members of visible minorities to find jobs equal to their abilities acts as a powerful independent determinant of opinion.

Finally, we should note one factor that does not have a significant effect on opinions about this issue of requiring more minority candidates: party membership (see table 1.D15). Those who are (or have been) members of a political party are not significantly less likely to favour such a requirement (though party members were somewhat more likely to balk when it came to requiring equal numbers of male and female candidates).

PARTY DEMOCRACY

Party membership is also not a significant determinant of opinion when it comes to questions dealing with the way that the federal parties choose their leaders. No matter is more central to questions of internal party democracy than the way that the parties choose their leaders; the quality of internal party democracy, in turn, has important implications for the quality of representative democracy in general in Canada. Our system of representative democracy operates through political parties. Political parties stand between citizens and their government, mediating the processes of authorization and accountability alike. It is the political parties that organize competition for elected office and it is through them that governments are formed and held accountable for their actions. In choosing their leader, parties are choosing a potential prime minister, making the leadership convention "the most important extra-governmental political institution in Canada" (Courtney 1986, 102).

Leadership conventions have been criticized from a number of angles (see Perlin 1988): their cost, which may risk making some candidates beholden to large private contributors and may deter other qualified candidates from running at all; a style of campaigning that devalues genuine policy debate, aided and abetted by the "horse-race" focus of media coverage (see Fletcher 1988; Brady and Johnston 1988); and balloting rules that can work to deny the election of compromise candidates (see Levesque 1983). Particularly relevant to our concerns is the representativeness of leadership selection processes. Despite affirmative action requirements that ensure minimum proportions of female and youth delegates, the federal parties remain vulnerable on this score. Women remain underrepresented (see Brodie 1988) and the cost of participation results in a status bias in delegate representation (see Stewart 1988).

In order to measure opinions on the process of leadership selection, we first asked our respondents how satisfied they are with the way that the federal parties choose their leaders. Despite the fact that two of the three major parties had recently held leadership conventions, a substantial proportion of our respondents (29 percent) had no opinion. Of those who did have an opinion on this question, half (50 percent) were somewhat satisfied and a further 7 percent were very satisfied. Fourteen percent, however, declared themselves to be not satisfied at all. That so many were at least somewhat satisfied is surprising in view of the negative publicity surrounding the last Liberal leadership convention.

As we can see (table 4.9), no group stands out as being particularly satisfied – or dissatisfied – with the way that parties choose their leaders. While Protestants and residents of the Atlantic provinces are the most likely to express satisfaction, socio-demographic differences on this question are generally muted. There is one notable exception, however. Quebeckers are considerably less likely to declare themselves satisfied with the process of leadership selection. This is telling, because Quebec has had longer exposure to the democratization of the leadership selection process. It was the PQ that first initiated a ballot for all party members to choose their party leader. We also found that those with more information are significantly less likely to express satisfaction (see table 1.D16). Those who actually knew the names of all three party leaders were the least likely to be satisfied with the way that the leaders are chosen.

Table 4.9
Distribution of opinions about the way federal parties choose their leaders
(percentages)

	Somewhat or very satisfied	Favouring a law
Atlantic	66	33
Quebec	42	39
Ontario	64	26
Manitoba/Saskatchewan	61	20
Alberta	56	31
British Columbia	61	20
Men	56	26
Women	58	33
Under 45	57	32
45 and over	56	26
Low education	60	35
Medium education	56	30
High education	55	22
Low income	56	32
Medium income	58	28
High income	51	32
Blue collar	60	28
White collar	55	32
Unionized	56	30
Nonunionized	57	29
English	62	26
French	43	37
Non-charter language	62	31
Catholic	52	35
Protestant	63	22
Canada	57	29

The wording of the questions was the following:

The next questions are about the way FEDERAL parties choose their leaders.

p1 Are you VERY satisfied, SOMEWHAT satisfied, NOT VERY satisfied, NOT AT ALL SATISFIED with the way the parties choose their leaders, or DON'T YOU HAVE AN OPINION?

p2 Should there be a law controlling the way parties choose their leaders or should it be up to the parties to decide?

On all of the questions we have examined so far, we have found a significant gender gap. Women have tended to be more critical than men of existing arrangements. Women differ little from men, however, when it comes to satisfaction with the way that parties choose their leaders. This may reflect the impact of the affirmative action taken by the federal parties, as well as the fact that one federal party – the NDP – had recently chosen a woman as its leader. In general, however, NDP supporters are less likely (53 percent) to be at least somewhat satisfied with the way leaders are chosen than are prospective Conservative (60 percent) or Liberal (65 percent) voters (data not shown).

Broadening public participation is, of course, a priority for those who favour a less-mediated form of democracy, and debate about processes of leadership selection has revolved around the question of the appropriate weight of "the brass versus the grass" (Stewart 1988). Turning to the role of basic political values, we can see (table 4.10) that dissatisfaction is most evident among the radical collectivists. This is the grouping that combines a populist desire to bring decisions closer to the grass roots with an ability to conceive of democracy without political parties. For the other populist groupings, however, a common belief in the necessity of parties seems to mute their criticism of the parties' internal processes of leadership selection.

Is leadership selection a private, internal party matter or is it to be seen as "a matter in the public domain" (see Ontario, Commission on Election Contributions and Expenses 1986, 78)? The view that leadership selection *is* in the public domain serves as a justification for legislating controls. There have been calls, in particular, for applying the

Table 4.10
Values and opinions about the way federal parties choose their leaders
(percentages)

	Somewhat or very satisfied	Favouring a law
Technocratic liberals	62	23
Populist liberals	56	31
Minoritarian individualists	57	27
Majoritarian individualists	60	28
Radical collectivists	46	33
Party collectivists	57	34

For the wording of the questions, see table 4.9.

model of election expense legislation to party leadership campaigns and many of the same arguments made in support of controls on the financing of election campaigns have been extended to the financing of leadership campaigns. Regulation is seen as a way of guarding against undue influence on the part of wealthy contributors and of opening up the process to candidates of modest means. Those who oppose such regulation do so on various grounds. Some fear, for example, that disclosure would deter contributions, while others argue that subsidies (with their threshold requirements) would only reinforce the advantages that the established candidates enjoy over less well known ones (for a discussion of the arguments on both sides, as well as some caveats, see Wearing 1988). Regulation could, of course, apply as well to non-financial aspects of the leadership selection process, such as eligibility and balloting procedures.

Are Canadians ready to support the legislation of controls? We asked those who had an opinion about the way parties choose their leaders whether there should be a law controlling the leadership selection process or whether it should be up to the parties to decide. Fully 71 percent believed that the decision should be left to the parties. This seems to confirm Wearing's observation that Canadians tend to view political parties as essentially private, self-governing institutions (Wearing 1988). Not surprisingly, the less satisfied respondents are with the way the federal parties choose their leaders – and the more cynical they are about politics and politicians in general – the more likely they are to favour legislation. Yet even among those who declare themselves not at all satisfied with current practices, only a slight majority (56 percent) are ready to endorse legislation controlling the way that the federal parties choose their leaders.

Table 4.9 demonstrates that Quebeckers, residents of the Atlantic provinces, women and those with less education are all more likely to favour a law on leader selection. While Catholics also appear more likely to favour legislation, this is largely because Quebec respondents are mainly Catholics. Once language and province of residence are taken into account, Catholics no longer appear to be significantly different in their views (see table 1.D17). British Columbians, residents of Manitoba and Saskatchewan, Protestants and those with a higher level of education, however, are less likely to favour legislation. Interestingly, women are more likely to favour a law, even when they are satisfied with the existing process of leadership selection, and surprisingly, those who are (or have been) party members are not significantly more likely than non-members to think that this is a matter for the parties themselves to decide (see table 1.D17).

Looking at political values, we can see (table 4.10) that populist views have only a modest effect on these opinions. This is especially true of the minoritarian individualists and the majoritarian individualists, both of whom share an antipathy to state intervention. Despite their populist views, they differ relatively little in their opinions from the technocratic liberals. Populist views need to be supplemented by statist beliefs about the desirability of government intervention in order to translate into appreciably greater support for a law to govern the way that federal parties choose their leaders.

RECAPITULATION

We can characterize Canadians' beliefs about the workings of representative democracy in the following ways:

1. There is dissatisfaction with the way that our electoral system translates votes into seats. There is a strong regional dimension to this dissatisfaction, with residents of Alberta and Quebec being least likely to find the current process acceptable. It should be emphasized, however, that in no region of the country does more than a bare majority find the workings of the present system acceptable.

2. There is a readiness to entertain the notion of separating the choice of local representative from the choice of the party to form the government. Those likely to have more experience of the existing system and more knowledge of its workings, however, were less ready to endorse the idea of a two-vote system.

3. There is much less readiness to impose limits on the number of years that MPs can serve and only a minority would allow MPs to change their parties between elections without obtaining a new mandate in a by-election.

4. While many respondents saw some problem with the under-representation of women and members of visible minorities in the House of Commons, relatively few considered it to be a very serious problem. Canadians are divided over whether there should be a law requiring parties to nominate more candidates from both these categories. Even though a slight majority is opposed to the idea, 40 percent are willing to force political parties to increase the number of female and visible minority candidacies.

5. There was little evidence of widespread dissatisfaction with the way that federal parties choose their leaders, nor of a desire to legislate controls on the leadership selection process. Many believe that this matter should be left to the parties themselves to decide.

6. Women are consistently less likely to find the current arrangements

acceptable and more likely to endorse changes. While concerned about the underrepresentation of women as MPs, their reformist preferences do not appear to be simply self-regarding. Women are also more likely than men to view the lack of representation of members of visible minorities in the House of Commons as a serious problem.

7. Those with a higher level of education are more likely to be concerned about gender balance in the House of Commons, but less likely to endorse affirmative action. In general, those with a higher level of education were more reluctant to endorse changes in the existing arrangements, whether that meant a two-vote system, limited terms for MPs or controls on the process of party leader selection.

8. Quebeckers are more likely to be critical of current arrangements and to favour changes. While Albertans also hold distinctive views on a number of these issues, their criticism is focused on the electoral system, and any greater readiness on their part to endorse the reforms discussed in this chapter is restricted to limiting MPs' terms. Where Albertans stand out is in their opinions about the underrepresentation of visible minorities. They are less likely both to see a problem and to support affirmative action to require more visible minority candidates.

9. Populist values are associated with enhanced support for changes – a two-vote system and a limit on MPs' terms – that could make for greater grassroots control of elected representatives. While populist values do not affect views about the way that the electoral system translates votes into seats, they do tend to make for somewhat greater dissatisfaction with the way that the parties choose their leaders. With the exception of the radical collectivists, however, this dissatisfaction is muted and individualism acts as a brake when it comes to endorsing regulation of the leadership selection process.

10. When the issue is requiring parties to offer more balanced slates with respect to women and members of visible minorities, minoritarianism is the operative value and individualism no longer acts as such a restraint.

5

ATTITUDES ABOUT ELECTORAL FINANCE

W<small>E NOW TURN</small> our attention to Canadians' views about electoral finance. This is a central consideration in the mandate of the Commission but also in the design of any kind of electoral procedure. As the proverb says, "money is the sinew of war," and elections are often seen as a (civilized) war in which contestants fight for the right to govern. From the voters' perspective, the issue is this: in order to be able to choose freely and intelligently among various parties and candidates, voters must be sufficiently informed about what parties and candidates stand for, what they promise to do, what they have done in the past and their background in general. Bringing that information to voters is costly. Should we let parties and candidates spend as much as they wish to inform voters or should we impose limits? Should the government help defray some or all of the expenses incurred? Should the government regulate parties' and candidates' sources of revenue? These are the difficult and crucial issues that are explored in this chapter.

We look first at spending, and more specifically at party spending. The party spending issue is essentially whether or not there should be limits on the amount of money parties and candidates are allowed to spend. The *Canada Elections Act* fixes a per-voter ceiling on party spending, with a sliding scale for candidates at the local level. The basic rationale for imposing such limits is to prevent any party or candidate from spending in an exorbitant manner and enjoying an unfair advantage over its opponents. We explore the issue of whether Canadians approve of the general principle of imposing limits on party expenses.

Although elections are about the choice of members of Parliament and of the party that will form the government, many groups may have a direct stake in the outcome. The question is whether such groups should be allowed to spend money to promote their positions during an election campaign. This question is particularly sensitive, given the fact that groups may overwhelmingly support a given party or candidate. The *Canada Elections Act* prohibits election expenditures by anyone other than parties, candidates or their representatives. The clause has been successfully challenged by the National Citizens' Coalition on the ground that it infringes upon the rights to freedom of thought, belief, opinion and expression guaranteed by the *Canadian Charter of Rights and Freedoms* (see Paltiel 1989). As a consequence, interest groups were able to spend freely during the last federal election campaign. We examine where Canadians stand on this issue.

The second major set of questions pertains to the other side of the balance sheet, that is, the revenues necessary to finance election expenses. There are three potential external sources of revenue for parties and candidates: individuals, groups (including corporations and unions) and the government. We determine to what extent each of these sources is deemed to be legitimate in the eyes of Canadians. There is widespread consensus on the appropriateness of contributions by individuals. There is debate, however, with respect to the two other sources. In the province of Quebec, contributions by "legal persons" (that is, groups) are banned, on the basis that only those who have the right to vote should have the right to give money and possibly affect the outcome of the election. Such a ban does not exist in the other provinces or at the federal level, perhaps because it is felt that groups are affected by government decisions and should thus be allowed to participate in this way in election campaigns.

We also assess the legitimacy of public funding in Canada. The *Canada Elections Act* stipulates that candidates and parties that satisfy certain conditions can receive a partial refund. There is also a tax credit for donations to parties and candidates. Similar provisions are made for provincial elections. The rationale for public funding is that it facilitates access for those who have little financial backing and it prevents political parties and candidates from becoming beholden to wealthy backers. The major objection is that public funding makes parties less dependent on their members and less responsive to grassroots demands (Koole 1989, 210). We examine how sensitive Canadians are to such considerations.

Even if contributions from these various sources are allowed, there remains the question as to whether they should be regulated in some fashion. Three types of regulation have been put in place in various jurisdictions. First, there are regulations on the amount of contributions. The standard justification for these limits is that they prevent individuals or groups from giving very large sums of money and exercising undue influence over a party or candidate. The federal law places no limit on the size of contributions but limits do exist in a number of provinces. Second, the law may force parties and candidates to disclose the identity of contributors and the amounts given; this is the case for federal and most provincial elections. The usual reason advanced for such regulation is that, when contributions are made public, any undue influence on politicians can be monitored and, hence, potentially deterred. Third, in the specific case of public funding, it must be decided which parties and candidates should be eligible. At the federal level, only candidates who receive at least 15 percent of the votes and parties that spend at least 10 percent of the maximum allowed are eligible for public reimbursement. We examine public opinion on these various questions.

We wish not only to describe the views of Canadians on these matters but also to see how these views vary across subgroups and how they relate to the basic values and beliefs examined in chapters 2 and 3. We pay particular attention to two socio-economic characteristics: region and income. Region particularly concerns us because of important variations in provincial legislation. Specifically, the province of Quebec has adopted the most stringent set of regulations for electoral finances (see Paltiel 1989), and we are interested in determining to what extent public opinion in Quebec differs from that in the rest of Canada. As for income, its relevance to the study of attitudes about electoral finances seems obvious. We would expect personal finances to affect how one would like to regulate the use of money in elections; specifically, those with low incomes may feel somewhat disadvantaged by their lack of financial resources and be more concerned with imposing limits on party expenditures and revenues. We should remember, however, that attitudes about the role of money in politics do not vary substantially among income groups (see Chapter 3) and that Meisel and Van Loon's 1966 study for the Committee on Election Expenses (Barbeau Committee) did not find a clear relationship between income and opinions about electoral finance. It remains to be seen whether any relationship emerges between income and regulations deemed desirable.

The basic justification for the regulation of electoral finances is to ensure that all voters, parties and candidates compete on an equal footing; the basic objection is that it is an inappropriate reduction of voters', parties' or candidates' freedom of expression. Regulating electoral finances runs counter, then, to the individualistic goal of minimizing restrictions on individual autonomy. The debate about electoral finances is also very much a debate about the proper role of the state. We may thus expect the two collectivist groupings identified in

Chapter 2 to be more supportive of state regulation, and the two individualist groupings to be less supportive.

Finally, respondents' views about electoral finances should hinge on their beliefs about politicians and money. The more one distrusts politicians and is cynical about the role of money in politics, the more likely one is to conclude that it is necessary to impose strict limits on electoral finances.

LIMITS ON PARTY SPENDING

The principle of limits on party spending is almost unanimously accepted in Canada. Only 7 percent of respondents in our survey indicated that parties should be allowed to spend as much as they want (question f1). We tested the firmness of their position by asking those who were in favour of the disclosure of contributions (later in the questionnaire) whether limits are necessary even if the source of the money is known. Only 8 percent reconsidered their position and concluded that limits may not be required.

Support for the idea of limiting party spending has always been very strong in Canada. Gallup reports that as early as 1949, 86 percent of those with an opinion thought that "there should be a limit on the amount each party can spend in an election campaign"; the percentages were 91 percent in 1961 and 89 percent in 1972 (Gallup Report 27 May 1972).

The idea also enjoys wide acceptance in the United States. When Americans are asked what changes they would like to see in the way political campaigns are conducted, the most frequently mentioned suggestion is to cut spending (Gallup 1982). Similarly, a Roper poll revealed that, among six suggestions for electoral reform, the most favoured among Americans in 1983 was limits on spending: it was selected by 60 percent of the sample, compared to 41 percent for the second most popular idea, ceilings on contributions (*Public Opinion* 1984, 31).

For the purpose of the analysis, we have collapsed responses to questions f1 and f9; an individual who first told us that he or she was in favour of a limit, but who later said that limits are not necessary if donations are disclosed, is considered to be against spending limits. On that score, 88 percent of our sample still wanted limits. The issue of spending limits is so consensual in Canada that there can hardly be substantial variations among groups. As expected, support for limits is greatest in Quebec. Women, those with a university degree and those with a low income are also more favourable to limits. The relationship with income, however, is tenuous, and differences among groups are small (table 5.1).

Table 5.1

Distribution of opinions about party spending

(percentages)

	Supporting limits in party spending
Atlantic	88
Quebec	92
Ontario	87
Manitoba/Saskatchewan	90
Alberta	85
British Columbia	84
Men	86
Women	90
Under 45	87
45 and over	89
Low education	88
Medium education	87
High education	91
Low income	90
Medium income	87
High income	86
Blue collar	87
White collar	88
Unionized	88
Nonunionized	88
English	86
French	91
Non-charter language	90
Catholic	90
Protestant	86
Canada	88

Opinions were tapped through two questions (f1 and f9). Those who think there should be limits to party spending (f1) but that limits are not needed if we know where the money is coming from (f9) are considered to oppose limits.

The wording of the questions was the following:

One of the issues we would like to talk to you about is campaign spending.

f1 Do you think that political parties should be allowed to SPEND AS MUCH AS THEY WANT in an election campaign OR should there BE A LIMIT on what they can spend?

f9 Is there STILL a need for limits on political party spending if we know where the money is coming from?

We also tested whether opinions on spending limits were related to basic political values and beliefs. On the whole, the relationship is quite weak, perhaps because there is so little variation to begin with. The main exception is the greater support found for limits among the radical collectivists: only 6 percent of them opposed limits, compared to between 11 and 14 percent in the other groups. It is not surprising that this group, with its strong collectivist and anti-party leanings, is particularly willing to favour state regulation of parties' behaviour.

In sum, nine Canadians out of ten approve of the principle of placing limits on party spending. Opinions on this question are firm and unrelated to beliefs about politicians, parties and money. Those most supportive of limits are the radical collectivists.

SPENDING BY GROUPS

Elections provide citizens with the opportunity to choose among parties and candidates. It is understandable that the rules that first come to mind with respect to campaign spending concern parties and candidates; however, other actors may well intervene in a campaign. Many corporations, unions and other organized groups have a direct stake in an election and may find it in their interest to support or attack candidates or parties that are either favourable or opposed to policies they care about. On the one hand, it can be argued that it is important that voters be exposed to as many viewpoints as possible, not only those put forward by parties, and that organized interests be allowed to advertise and promote their positions. On the other hand, prohibition of spending by organized interests can be justified on the ground that there is the risk that groups with a great deal of money will have undue influence and may jeopardize fair competition among parties.

How do Canadians feel about this issue? We have a series of five questions on this issue in our questionnaire (questions f12 to f17). We first deal with interest groups. A random half of our sample were given the standard argument for allowing group advertising (that it is a right in a democracy), and were asked if they agreed that spending should be allowed. The other half were given the usual argument for not allowing group advertising (that groups with money will have too much influence), and were asked if they agreed with banning such advertising. None of our respondents was given the two arguments (our pre-test showed that the question was becoming too complex). We find that each of the two arguments makes sense to a clear majority of Canadians. Seventy-six percent of those who were presented with the positive side agreed that groups should be allowed to advertise, and 68 percent of those who were presented with the negative side agreed that they should not be allowed (table 5.2).

Table 5.2
Canadians' opinions about group advertising
(percentages)

	In favour of controls
1. Interest groups: with argument against controls (f12)	24
2. Interest groups: with argument for controls (f13)	68
3. Corporations (f14)	55
4. Unions (f15)	58
5. Parties and groups (f17)	90
6. Private corporations	63
7. Interest groups like...	61
8. Unions	64

Sources: Items 1 to 5: Blais and Gidengil 1990; items 6 to 8: Environics, *The Focus Canada Report* 1990, chap. 3.

The wording for items 1 to 5 was the following:

f12 Now what about election advertising by interest groups? Some say interest groups SHOULD be allowed to advertise to promote their positions on the election issues because that is *their right in a democracy.* BASICALLY do you AGREE or DISAGREE with this view?

f13 Now what about election advertising by interest groups? Some say interest groups SHOULD NOT be allowed to advertise to promote their positions during campaigns, otherwise groups with lots of money will have *too much influence on the election.* BASICALLY do you AGREE or DISAGREE with this view?

f14 What about CORPORATIONS: should they be allowed to advertise to promote their positions during election campaigns?

f15 And UNIONS? (Should UNIONS be allowed to advertise to promote their positions during election campaigns?)

f17 If you had to choose between the following two options, which would you choose:
having spending controls on political parties and [interest groups] [corporations and unions]
　　OR
having no spending controls at all?

The wording for items 6 to 8 was the following:

6. Do you approve or disapprove of government regulations controlling the amount of money private corporations can spend promoting their points-of-view during elections?

7. Do you approve or disapprove of government regulations controlling the amount of money interest groups like the National Citizens' Coalition, the Canadian Alliance for Free Trade or the Pro-Life and Pro-Choice movements can spend promoting their points-of-view during elections?

8. Do you approve or disapprove of government regulations controlling the amount of money that unions can spend promoting their points-of-view during elections?

Three conclusions can be reached from these results. First, the standard arguments do have appeal to Canadians. The issue raises a real dilemma: Canadians are concerned with freedom of speech as well as with undue influence, and it is sometimes not possible to reconcile these two objectives. Second, the distribution of responses suggests that Canadians are somewhat more sensitive to the rights of groups than to the risk of undue influence. The balance of opinion tilts (slightly) toward allowing groups to advertise. This is particularly interesting, given the overwhelming support for limits on party spending. It could be that, because they do not mistrust interest groups as much as parties, Canadians do not perceive regulations on interest group spending to be as necessary. Alternatively, limits on spending may be more acceptable than outright prohibition of advertising.

Third, it appears that many Canadians have not thought about this issue and that their opinions are, therefore, rather soft. When they are presented with only one side of the issue, they agree with it. An individual with a firm view on the question would react the same way (that is, in favour of or against advertising), whatever the argument put to him or her. This is not what we observed; however, it is not surprising that many Canadians do not have firm views on this issue. After all, the issue is complex and has not been extensively discussed in the public arena. Furthermore, the propensity to agree with a statement, be it positive or negative, is not greater among the least politically informed, which suggests that the opinions of a wide spectrum of Canadians are pliable.

The next two questions in our survey asked whether corporations and unions should be allowed to advertise during election campaigns. Canadians are almost evenly divided, a slight majority favouring the banning of such advertising. In fact, 52 percent would like to see such a ban on both corporations and unions, 39 percent no ban on either, 5 percent a ban only on unions and 3 percent a ban on corporations only. Canadians are more concerned with the potential intervention of corporations and unions in a campaign than with that of interest groups. For instance, one-third of those who agreed, when given a positive argument, that interest groups should be allowed to advertise ("it is their right"; see question f12) would not extend that right to corporations. Interest groups are perceived to be more benign than corporations and unions, probably because the groups that many people spontaneously think of are those involved in a cause, such as the environment or abortion, and thus defending values rather than interests, and not the far more numerous business groups, to which, presumably, Canadians would react in the same way as they do with respect to corporations. This is what a focus group discussion, which took place prior to our survey, seemed to indicate (see Massie 1990).

Finally, we asked our respondents the most difficult question of all, that is, what they would do if they had to treat parties and groups the same way: would they prefer having spending controls on both or no controls at all (question f17)? The response was unequivocal: 90 percent opted for controls. Eighty-nine percent of those who agreed that interest groups have the right to advertise (question f12) would accept controls if the option of dealing differently with parties was ruled out. This clearly indicates that Canadians are resolved to control party spending. If this implies that groups also have to be controlled (an idea about which there is no consensus), then so be it.

These results are similar to those obtained by Environics in its fall 1990 omnibus survey. Some 60 percent (excluding those with no opinion) said that they approve of government regulations controlling the amount of money corporations, unions and "interest groups like the National Citizens' Coalition, the Canadian Alliance for Free Trade or the Pro-Life and Pro-Choice movements" can spend "promoting their points of view during elections." For corporations and unions, approval of regulations is a little higher (six percentage points) in the Environics survey, which refers to controls on spending rather than an outright ban. The most interesting point, perhaps, is that complete prohibition received almost as much support as the setting of limits. Support for controls on interest groups, however, was as strong in the Environics survey as it was with respect to corporations and unions, most likely because the question led people to focus their attention on the role of business groups that were actively involved in the last federal election. Spontaneously, many Canadians react differently to the involvement of interest groups and of corporations (or unions), as our survey shows. When they are reminded that the distinction may be very hazy, they treat groups as they do corporations, not the other way around.

We do not have any data that would allow us to track the evolution of opinions on these matters. There is also very little data on public attitudes in other countries. The scant evidence we do have indicates that the large Political Action Committees (PACs) in the United States have a very poor public image. A Louis Harris poll in 1982 found that only 20 percent of Americans approved of "big company" PACs and 27 percent of labour ones (Sorauf 1988, 232). Although support was higher for environmental and women's PACs (around 50 percent), there is no doubt that PACs are looked upon with great suspicion. Canadians appear to be somewhat sanguine about group involvement, for the very good reason that they have not had first-hand experience with it, with the exception of the 1988 federal election. Even then, group spending was minuscule compared to that in the United States.

We have constructed a scale made up of responses to the questions about interest groups, corporations and unions. (The correlation between views on the latter two is 0.83, and between these two and views on interest groups – questions f12 and f13 – in the order of 0.4 and 0.3, respectively.) Respondents were given a score ranging from 0 (if they systematically opposed advertising by interest groups, corporations and unions) to 1 (if they would allow advertising by each of these three sources). The mean score is 0.46, a reflection of the lack of consensus on the issue.

The most powerful predictor of opinions on the acceptability of group advertising is political cynicism. As shown in table 5.3, the more one distrusts politicians, the less willing one is to let groups advertise during a campaign. It is interesting to note that distrust of politicians leads one to support controls on groups. What really happens, of course, is that those who do not trust politicians simply want to have every aspect of electoral finances tightly controlled. It is not only cynicism about politicians, but also cynicism about parties and the role of money that induces a willingness to ban direct group intervention in election campaigns (see table 1.D19). There is no evidence, however, that opinions stem from basic political values, a fact consistent with the observation, made earlier, that opinions on this issue are particularly pliable. It would seem that Canadians react to this question on the basis of their feelings about groups and politicians, rather than on the basis of principles.

Among the socio-economic variables, education is most strongly related to views about the appropriateness of group advertising (table 5.4). The better educated are particularly open to group involvement in campaigns: their average score on our scale is 0.54, compared to 0.44

Table 5.3
Political cynicism and opinions about group advertising

Political cynicism	Mean score on group advertising
Low	.41
Medium	.46
High	.51

Note: The score on group advertising is made up of responses to questions f12 to f15. The higher the score, the more favourable one is to allowing group advertising. Respondents are divided into three groups according to their score on the political cynicism scale. The more one distrusts politicians, the higher his/her score on the political cynicism scale (see table 3.4).

Table 5.4
Distribution of opinions about group advertising

	Mean score on group advertising
Atlantic	.45
Quebec	.43
Ontario	.49
Manitoba/Saskatchewan	.41
Alberta	.49
British Columbia	.46
Men	.47
Women	.45
Under 45	.48
45 and over	.42
Low education	.44
Medium education	.44
High education	.54
Low income	.47
Medium income	.42
High income	.50
Blue collar	.42
White collar	.48
Unionized	.46
Nonunionized	.46
English	.47
French	.42
Non-charter language	.48
Catholic	.44
Protestant	.47
Canada	.46

Note: The score on group advertising is made up of responses to questions f12 to f15. The higher the score the more favourable one is toward allowing group advertising.

for those with low and medium levels of education. It may be that the better educated, who tend to be heavily involved in associations of all sorts (Milbrath 1965), feel great sympathy toward groups in general and are more reluctant to support regulations targeted at groups rather than at parties or individuals.

On the whole, regional variations on this issue are rather muted. We should note an exception: respondents from Manitoba and Saskatchewan are least favourable to group involvement. We also find that support for group advertising is particularly weak among middle-income people; perhaps they perceive themselves as being less well organized than both the rich and the poor, and are therefore more wary of group interventions in election campaigns.

Canadians are ambivalent about the desirability of prohibiting group advertising. They seem not to distrust groups as much as they do parties, and are thus more reluctant to control them. At the same time, they are concerned with the possibility that groups with a great deal of money will have too much influence on the election. Furthermore, they do not have firm views on the matter and their responses vary according to the wording of questions. They are also less preoccupied with the issue than Americans, perhaps because they have no first-hand experience with the implications of a laissez-faire approach (the infamous PACs). Thus, the balance of opinion is slightly in favour of a ban on group advertising; and there is no doubt in the minds of Canadians that they are willing to accept limits on group spending if that is what is required to maintain limits on party spending, which they find absolutely essential.

REVENUE

Individual Contributions

Even those who call for strict regulation of campaign spending recognize that some spending is necessary in order for parties and candidates to convey their messages to voters. Once this is acknowledged, the question must be raised as to where parties and candidates will find the money to pay for their campaign spending. There are three external sources of funds: individuals, groups and the government. We have taken for granted that individual contributions are perceived to be legitimate in our society (but see section E of appendix B for a reconsideration of this assumption). As Sorauf (1988, 70) notes, the common view is that individual contributions do not threaten the integrity of the system. Debate has focused instead on the conditions that must be met for contributions to be acceptable.

The first question concerns the size of contributions. Federal legislation places no ceilings on them, but some provincial legislation does. In Quebec, the limit has been set at $3 000, but in Alberta and Ontario, limits are quite generous, at $30 000 and $14 000, respectively, in an election year. Canadian legislation is rather permissive on this score. In the United States, the *Federal Election Campaign Act* sets limits of $1 000 on individual contributions to candidates and of $5 000 on PAC contributions.

A second issue to be considered is whether the identity of contributors and the amount given should be disclosed. Canadian federal law requires that all donations of $100 or more must be fully reported and disclosed. Similar provisions exist in most provinces. Disclosure is usually justified on the grounds that it allows citizens to find out whether any special favour has been exchanged for donations, and builds confidence in the electoral process by making the whole process public. It is sometimes objected to because it may infringe on private life and/or hurt those who contribute to losing parties and candidates.

Let us examine Canadians' views on these matters by looking first at the size of contributions. Fifty-nine percent of our respondents believed that there should be a ceiling on contributions (question f2). When they were asked what that ceiling should be, the variations were substantial: 23 percent of those favourable to a ceiling would like it to be $100 or less, but 9 percent opted for a ceiling of $10 000 or more. The modal and median response was $1 000. At the same time, we should not forget that 41 percent were opposed to any limits whatsoever. We are thus faced with two very different positions – strict limits of $1 000 or less versus no controls at all – supported by over 40 percent each. The "compromise" position – ceilings somewhere between $1 000 and $10 000 – was chosen by a small minority. This suggests that any legislation that sets limits of more than $10 000, or even of $3 000, as in Quebec, is likely to be found unsatisfactory by the bulk of the population. In fact, it seems to be very difficult to come up with any acceptable option, since Canadians are strongly divided on this issue.

We cannot tell whether public opinion on limits to contributions has evolved over time; there is no way, either, to compare attitudes in Canada with those in other countries. The only piece of information we have comes from a 1983 Roper poll indicating that, in the United States, among six suggestions for electoral reform, ceilings on contributions (amount unspecified) were the second most popular option after limits on spending, chosen by 41 percent of respondents. In the United States, as in Canada, citizens are more concerned with cutting spending than with limiting revenues. Not surprisingly, those who favour controls on spending are also more likely to favour ceilings on contributions. The relationship, however, is not as strong as we might have thought. Among those in favour of spending limits, 39 percent still believe that people should be allowed to give as much as they want to a party.

The standard substitute for ceilings on donations has been disclosure. The argument is that the best defence against corruption is information. From that point of view, it is imperative that parties reveal the identity of contributors and of the amounts given. Canadians over-whelmingly agree with the desirability of disclosure (table 5.5). Gallup has obtained similar responses at various points in time. The results of the 1965 Canadian National Election Study were, however, quite different (see Meisel and Van Loon 1966): at the time, only 47 percent agreed with the idea of requiring parties to disclose the names of contrib-utors. (There was an additional question on the disclosure of amounts, with similar results.) The difference cannot be imputed to any change in public opinion, since Gallup reports similar figures over a 23-year period; rather, we would suggest that the wording used in the Canadian National Election Study may have inadvertently scared some people away from disclosure. The reference to the disclosing of names may have led some to think that names would have to be published in the media. Notwithstanding this, the evidence indicates that Canadians' support for the principle of disclosure is long-standing.

Disclosure is not, however, perceived to be a panacea. Ninety-two percent of those in favour of disclosure still saw a need for limits on party spending (question f9). It is important to keep in mind that many more Canadians approve of limits on spending (93 percent) than of disclosure (79 percent). Making revenue sources public is seen as a positive step but not as the most crucial one.

Table 5.5
Canadians' opinions about disclosure of contributions
(percentages)

	In favour of disclosure
RCERPF survey (1990)	79
Gallup (1949)	83
Gallup (1964)	85
Gallup (1972)	86
Canadian National Election Study (1965)	47

Sources: Blais and Gidengil (1990); *Gallup Report* (24 May 1972); CNES (1965).

In our survey, the question (f8) was:
"Do you think political parties should be required or not be required to reveal who gives them money?"

The Gallup question was:
"Do you think that political parties should or should not publish details of their political funds, that is, make public the sources from which they get their money?"

The Canadian National Election Study question was:
"Should parties be required to disclose the names of their contributors?"

We can now consider how opinions on these various issues vary among groups. We first examined opinions about ceilings on contributions (table 5.6). Respondents from the West are more likely to say that people should be allowed to give as much as they desire. Opposition to a ceiling is also particularly high among Protestants, women and younger respondents. The relationship with age is particularly interesting. Among those born after 1965, there is a majority (58 percent) opposed to ceilings; the percentage decreases to 46 percent among those born between 1956 and 1965 and to 40 percent in the other age groups (data not shown).

Support for ceilings increases with the level of information (table 1.D20): 67 percent of the best-informed group said that there should be a limit to the amount of money people can give to parties. It would seem that being more informed leads one to favour limits to contributions. The better informed are also more consistent in their views on finances. They are more likely to want limits on contributions if they believe in limits on spending; questions f1 and f2 are correlated at 0.12 among those of low information level, 0.17 for those of average level and 0.26 for the top level (note, however, that we do not observe the same pattern with respect to the ban on group contributions). The tendency to focus on spending and not to be overly preoccupied with revenues prevails to a greater extent among the least informed.

In table 5.6, we see how opinions about the proper level of ceilings varied across regions and groups. (The question was, of course, asked only of those in favour of a fixed amount.) Westerners again stand out as the most permissive. Perhaps the most interesting finding, however, is the lack of any significant relationship between income and opinions on ceilings. The rich do tend to select somewhat higher ceilings than the poor, but the differences are relatively small and are not statistically significant when other socio-economic characteristics are controlled (table 1.D21). People's personal financial situations affect responses to a much smaller extent than might be anticipated.

Variations in the desirability of disclosure tend to be small, as the great majority of Canadians are in favour of disclosure (table 5.7). Support reaches its peak among those with a university education.

Opinions on these issues reflect beliefs about political life. With respect to ceilings, perceptions of the impact of money in elections play a crucial role. Support for ceilings reached 70 percent among those who believe that the party that spends the most wins the election, compared to 52 percent among those who reject such a view (data not shown). The fact that most Canadians are sanguine about the impact of money on electoral outcomes accounts, in great part, for the rather timid support for ceilings.

Table 5.6
Distribution of opinions about contribution ceilings

	Opposed to ceilings on donations (%)	Mean amount deemed appropriate ($)
Atlantic	45	2 296
Quebec	36	2 188
Ontario	40	2 038
Manitoba/Saskatchewan	46	3 038
Alberta	46	3 147
British Columbia	48	3 001
Men	38	2 542
Women	45	2 131
Under 45	45	2 673
45 and over	35	1 932
Low education	43	1 788
Medium education	42	2 344
High education	36	3 140
Low income	43	1 849
Medium income	43	2 492
High income	36	2 726
Blue collar	44	1 927
White collar	40	2 551
Unionized	42	2 400
Nonunionized	41	2 324
English	42	2 520
French	38	2 049
Non-charter language	43	2 356
Catholic	39	2 188
Protestant	44	2 384
Canada	41	2 375

The questions were the following:

f2 What about people who give money to political parties? Do you think people should be allowed to GIVE AS MUCH MONEY AS THEY WANT to a political party, OR do you think the AMOUNT SHOULD BE LIMITED?

f2b What do you think the limit should be on how much a person can give to a party? Should it be one hundred dollars, five hundred, one thousand, five thousand, ten thousand dollars or more than ten thousand dollars?

Those choosing a "more than $10 000" target were put at $20 000 and "other" responses were left out.

Table 5.7
Distribution of opinions about disclosure
(percentages)

	In favour of disclosure of contributions
Atlantic	78
Quebec	75
Ontario	81
Manitoba/Saskatchewan	78
Alberta	80
British Columbia	85
Men	82
Women	76
Under 45	78
45 and over	81
Low education	74
Medium education	79
High education	89
Low income	74
Medium income	81
High income	84
Blue collar	75
White collar	81
Unionized	81
Nonunionized	79
English	81
French	75
Non-charter language	79
Catholic	77
Protestant	79
Canada	79

For the wording of question f8 in our survey, see table 5.5.

Canadians overwhelmingly approve of the principle that campaign finances should be made public and that, consequently, parties should fully disclose their revenue sources. Respondents were divided on the desirability of ceilings on contributions, a slight majority being in favour of them. The preferred ceiling was set at $1 000, which is much below the amounts established by provincial laws. Finally, cynicism about the role of money in politics enhances support for regulation of contributions.

Group Contributions

While individual contributions are generally perceived to be legitimate in our society, the appropriateness of group contributions and public funding is a more contentious issue. Let us first deal with groups. Two basic positions clash on this issue. On the one hand, it can be argued that it is only individuals who have the right to vote and that, therefore, only individuals should be allowed to give money to parties and candidates. Otherwise, individuals who are members of organizations with money will have a greater say in the election. On the other hand, it can be pointed out that government policies have an impact on groups as well as on individuals and that it is therefore entirely appropriate for groups to be able to give financial support to parties or candidates whose positions they find most congenial. It has also been suggested, more pragmatically, that there is no use prohibiting contributions from groups since groups can easily circumvent the rules by channelling the money through individual donations.

In Canada, the dominant position on this issue has been the laissez-faire approach. At the federal level, as well as in nine provinces, there is no prohibition on non-individual contributions. The exception is the province of Quebec, where contributions from "legal persons" are banned. Furthermore, in the 1988 election, Conservative candidates from the province of Quebec declared that they would voluntarily abide by the Quebec provincial rule, a gesture that could not fail to put the whole issue higher on the agenda.

What, then, is the view of Canadians on non-individual contributions? As shown in table 5.8, a slight majority agrees with the existing federal laissez-faire approach, at least with respect to corporations and interest groups; opinion is evenly divided with regard to unions, which seem to elicit greater distrust. Of course, a substantial minority feels that group contributions should be prohibited, but it would seem that Canadians are more concerned with controlling spending than with regulating revenues. Not surprisingly, opinions on contributions are correlated with those on spending. For instance, the correlation between responses on union contributions and advertising is 0.40, yet there is also some disjunction. Among those who would ban political advertising by corporations, 48 percent are willing to allow them to contribute. Perhaps the impact that groups may exercise through direct intervention in a campaign is more clearly unacceptable than the more indirect one that flows through contributions.

In the 1965 Canadian National Election Study, a sample of Canadians was asked whether it was a good thing for parties to receive contributions from business corporations or trade unions (see Meisel and Van Loon 1966). Only 31 percent and 28 percent of those expressing an opinion said it was a good thing in the case of corporations or unions, respectively. Unfortunately, however, it is impossible to tell whether

Table 5.8
Canadians' opinions about group contributions
(percentages)

	In favour of allowing contributions
1. Corporations (f4)	61
2. Unions (f5)	49
3. Interest groups (f6)	62
4. Corporations	53
5. Unions	48

Sources: Items 1 to 3: our survey; items 4 and 5: *The Gallup Report* (11 September 1986).

The wording for items 1 to 3 was the following:

Should the following organizations have the right or NOT have the right to give money to political parties?

f4 First, what about corporations? (Should corporations have the right or NOT have the right to give money to political parties?)

f5 Unions? (Should unions have the right or NOT have the right to give money to political parties?)

f6 And interest groups? (Should interest groups have the right or NOT have the right to give money to political parties?)

The wording for items 4 and 5 was the following:

"In Canada political parties can receive donations from unions and corporations. In your opinion should both unions and corporations be allowed to donate to political parties, unions and corporations only, or should neither of these organizations be allowed to donate funds?"

all those who thought it was a bad idea would have been ready to impose an outright ban. We thus do not know whether opinions on this issue have shifted over the long haul. More recently, in 1986, a Gallup poll indicated that Canadians were almost equally split on the appropriateness of donations by corporations and unions (table 5.8). The wording of the question was somewhat different from ours but the pattern is much the same. Canadians are divided on this issue, with a slight edge to the laissez-faire approach in the case of corporations.

Opinions on the appropriateness of group contributions vary among regions and groups (see table 5.9). We have collapsed answers to the three questions on interest groups, corporations and unions into a scale ranging from 0 to 1. High scores on the scale indicate permissive attitudes toward non-individual contributions. The average score is 0.58, a reflection of the overall reluctance to prohibit such donations.

Perhaps the most interesting finding is the absence of a difference between Quebec and the rest of Canada on this question. Quebec is the

Table 5.9
Distribution of opinions about group contributions

	Mean score on the group contribution scale
Atlantic	.63
Quebec	.58
Ontario	.58
Manitoba/Saskatchewan	.53
Alberta	.58
British Columbia	.55
Men	.56
Women	.60
Under 45	.61
45 and over	.53
Low education	.55
Medium education	.57
High education	.61
Low income	.56
Medium income	.57
High income	.61
Blue collar	.58
White collar	.58
Unionized	.57
Nonunionized	.58
English	.57
French	.58
Non-charter language	.64
Catholic	.58
Protestant	.57
Canada	.58

Note: The scale is made up of responses to questions f4 to f6. The higher the score, the more favourable one is toward allowing group contributions.

only province where non-individual donations are prohibited, and thus one might have expected Quebeckers to be more opposed to group contributions. This is not the case, however. They are more favourable to limits on party spending (and, we shall see in section E of appendix B, to public funding), and more likely to want a ban on group advertising, yet they do not particularly endorse a ban on group donations. (In fact, only 34 percent of Quebeckers said that corporations should not have the right to give money.) There is more support for regulation in Quebec, which is in line with stricter provincial legislation, but the correspondence is confined to general orientations; it does not necessarily apply to specific aspects of the electoral law.

In general, opinions are weakly related to socio-economic variables. Variations across income groups, especially, are not substantial. There is, however, some indication of a generational difference. Those born before 1946 are less favourable to allowing group contributions. On two crucial issues related to contributions – whether groups should be allowed to give money and whether there should be ceilings – the younger generation appears to be more permissive.

Opinions about the appropriateness of group contributions are strongly affected by political beliefs. Those who are cynical about politicians and the role of money in politics are less likely to find group contributions acceptable (table 5.10). Citizens' views on the matter, however, seem to be largely unrelated to basic political values (see table 1.D23); thus we observe the same pattern as for group spending. People do not appear to respond to issues having to do with the role of groups on the basis of their fundamental political values. This suggests that on this set of issues, opinions are not firmly formed, as indeed the sharply different response in our two subsamples to the questions on group advertising indicates.

There is an important exception to this pattern, however. The technocratic liberals are more willing than others to allow group

Table 5.10
Political cynicism, beliefs about money and opinions about group contributions

	Mean score on the acceptability of group contributions
A. Political cynicism	
Low	.63
Medium	.60
High	.49
B. Motivation of contributors	
Expect something	.52
Do not expect something	.62
C. Impact of money in elections	
Money buys election	.50
Money does not buy election	.63

Note: The group contribution scale is made up of responses to questions f4 to f6. The higher the score the more favourable one is toward allowing group contributions. Respondents are divided into subgroups according to their score on the political cynicism scale (see table 3.4), and to their responses to questions f18 (motivation) and f20 (impact).

contributions; their mean score on the group contributions scale is 0.63, compared to between 0.52 and 0.58 among the other groups. As we pointed out in Chapter 2, the other five groupings are all characterized by a populist strain, which entails a concern with grassroots politics and a distrust of all kinds of intermediaries, including groups. It appears that Canadians do not distrust groups as much as they do parties and politicians. Still, their populist leanings induce them to be at least somewhat ambivalent.

In short, Canadians are ambivalent and divided on the desirability of group contributions. They do not have firm views on the matter, but their spontaneous reaction is laissez-faire, consistent with the absence of federal legislation in this area. Interestingly, respondents from Quebec do not favour banning such contributions, contrary to the provincial legislation that prohibits contributions from "legal persons." Quebeckers do tend to support stricter regulation of campaign finances, but that support does not show up in the specific case of group contributions. Questions involving groups seem to elicit different types of responses, perhaps because the implications are not as clear to many citizens.

On one aspect of group contributions, however, opinion *is* clear. Ninety-one percent of those who believe that corporations and unions should have the right to contribute also support the idea of requiring these groups to obtain approval from their shareholders or members.

Public Funding

Another source of revenue is public funding. Public funding can be direct – that is, the government defrays some or all of the expenditures incurred by parties and candidates during a campaign – or indirect – that is, the government induces individuals and groups to contribute through a system of tax deductions or credits. Both types of public funding exist in Canada. Parties and candidates that satisfy certain conditions can receive a partial refund for their campaign expenditures. Individuals receive a tax credit for their donations. The standard argument in favour of direct public funding is that it offsets the disadvantage facing parties and candidates that have little financial support. The usual objection is that it makes parties dependent on the state and less sensitive to the views of their members. Indirect public funding solves this problem, since the state limits itself to inducing private contributions. However, it does not necessarily make the competition any fairer. (This depends on how tax credits or deductions actually work: in Canada, the NDP seems to have been the main beneficiary. See Seidle 1985.)

How do Canadians react to public funding? The idea of direct public funding is not very popular with the Canadian public. Sixty-four percent of our respondents believed that the government should not reimburse any of the money spent by parties and candidates during an election campaign (question f10). Indirect public funding, through a tax credit, is a little more acceptable: 47 percent of our sample agreed with it (question f3). Note that a random half was reminded that such a tax credit was similar to the one existing for charitable donations; providing that information did not affect responses. Canadians are evenly split on the question, however it is posed.

The 1965 Canadian National Election Study included some questions about public funding on behalf of the Advisory Committee on Election Expenses (Meisel and Van Loon 1966). Canadians were first asked whether "the government should pay all, some or none of the costs of political campaigns." Only 26 percent of those with an opinion said that the government should not pay anything. This is very far from the 64 percent observed in our survey. It is important to note, however, that the 1965 question, contrary to the one in our survey, did not explicitly refer to parties' and candidates' spending. It is, of course, easier to agree with the abstract idea of the government paying some unspecified campaign costs when the direct link to party and candidate spending is not presented.

In the same 1965 survey, only 32 percent of respondents indicated that they were in favour of "allowing people to deduct from their income tax the money they give to parties and candidates, in the same way that they deduct money they give to charity" (Meisel and Van Loon 1966). This is much lower than the 47 percent we found in 1990. Again, the two questions are not identical, one referring to deductions and the other to credits, but the fact that in 1990 variations in the wording of the question did not affect responses suggests that support for indirect public funding may have grown slightly. This may reflect experience with tax credits, which have become a reality since the 1965 study. Perhaps, also, as Canadians have become more wary of government intervention, they have come to the view that if there is to be some form of public funding, it should be as indirect as possible. In our survey, fewer than half of those in favour of a tax credit for contributions supported partial reimbursement of campaign expenditures.

In the same vein, Gallup has asked the following question at various times: "It has been suggested that the federal government provide a fixed amount of money for the election campaigns of candidates for federal seats in the House of Commons, and that all private contributions from other sources be prohibited. Do you think this is a good idea or a poor idea?" The question puts forward a radical option –

the banning of all private contributions combined with public funding; that radical idea is, however, well received by the public. In 1984, 62 percent of Canadians thought it was a good idea (table 5.11).

These are startling results. At first glance, they seem difficult to square with the findings reported above about the state of public opinion on contributions by groups and public funding. If 62 percent agree with the banning of all private contributions combined with public funding, how is it that only 39 percent seem to be in favour of prohibiting contributions by corporations and that only 38 percent would like the government to reimburse some of the expenses incurred by parties and candidates? It is possible that people are willing to ban private contributions only if there is public funding, and vice versa. We find this highly implausible, however, and believe that the results reflect strong support for stringent limits on spending, which is implied in the question (there would be a fixed amount of money), and about which there is near unanimous agreement, as was pointed out previously.

Whatever the exact interpretation, table 5.11 suggests that support for direct public funding has decreased in Canada, which is in line with our assertion that the large gap between the findings of the 1965 Canadian National Election Study and our own survey with respect to direct public funding is probably not entirely due to different wordings and may well reflect real changes in the public mood. The Gallup data also suggest (again, it is important to keep in mind that the question is extremely

Table 5.11
Support for a combination of limited spending, public spending and a prohibition on private contributions in Canada and the United States
(percentage supportive)

	Canada	United States
1974	83	—
1977	—	64
1978	75	—
1979	—	66
1982	—	64
1984	62	59
1987	—	51

Sources: Canada: *The Gallup Report* (29 March 1984); United States: *The Gallup Report* (March 1987).

The question was:

"It has been suggested the federal government provide a fixed amount of money for the election campaigns of candidates for federal seats in the House of Commons, and that all private contributions from other sources be prohibited. Do you think this is a good idea or a poor idea?"

complex and that it is not clear what is being measured) that Canadians used to be more supportive of public funding than Americans but that the difference has considerably diminished in recent times.

We conclude this overall review of the evidence with data from Norway. In the 1965 National Election Study, Norwegians were asked the following question: "It has been suggested that the government should give contributions to the parties' activities before the elections. Do you think that it would be a good idea or a bad idea for the government to help pay the costs of political campaigns?" The question was posed before the introduction of public funding in Norway. Only 30 percent of those with an opinion liked the idea, an indication that public funding is not necessarily more popular in Europe than in North America. Canadians' reluctance about direct public funding does not appear to be exceptional.

Opinions on the appropriateness of the two different types of public funding vary among regions and respondent groups (see table 5.12). The most important regional variation is the greater support for public funding, both direct and indirect, in Quebec and the greater opposition in Alberta and British Columbia. Support for public funding in Quebec seems to reflect a greater willingness to accept government regulation in that province.

In general, opinions are weakly related to socio-economic variables. Variations across income groups, especially, are not substantial. The greatest difference occurs with respect to direct public funding, and even there it is rather modest: direct public funding is approved by 40 percent of the low-income group but only 29 percent of the high-income one.

Opinions about direct public funding and tax credits do reflect basic political values. As expected, the two collectivist groupings are more favourable to both forms of public funding (table 5.13). The majoritarian individualists, for their part, support tax credits but oppose public reimbursement of campaign expenditures. We can see here how the two forms of public funding elicit different reactions. The idea of direct public funding puts collectivists and individualists in opposition. People like (or dislike) public reimbursement because they are favourable (or unfavourable) to state intervention in general. Since the public mood is presently one of resistance to government intervention, direct public funding does not receive much support. With respect to tax credits, they are an indirect form of government intervention which the collectivists approve, and which individualists also like because they reward individual initiative on the part of contributors.

Finally, the modalities of public funding have to be defined. The

Table 5.12
Distribution of opinions about direct and indirect public funding for parties and candidates
(percentages)

	Supporting direct public funding	In favour of tax credits
Atlantic	39	50
Quebec	49	59
Ontario	32	43
Manitoba/Saskatchewan	35	46
Alberta	26	36
British Columbia	26	37
Men	33	47
Women	40	47
Under 45	38	46
45 and over	34	48
Low education	42	53
Medium education	34	44
High education	33	45
Low income	40	47
Medium income	36	45
High income	29	47
Blue collar	34	45
White collar	41	51
Unionized	35	47
Nonunionized	37	47
English	30	41
French	49	58
Non-charter language	41	54
Catholic	44	54
Protestant	26	41
Canada	36	47

The questions were the following:
f10 Do you think the government should reimburse ALL, SOME or NONE of the money spent by parties and candidates during an election campaign?
f3 Should people who give money to political parties [get a tax credit in the same way they are given a credit for donations to charity?] [get a tax credit to reduce the income tax they pay?]

most critical question is that of eligibility. In federal elections, only candidates who receive at least 15 percent of the votes are eligible for partial reimbursement of their campaign expenditures. Similar thresholds exist in the provinces, and range from 10 to 20 percent. From a comparative perspective, these thresholds are rather high. For instance,

Table 5.13
Values and opinions about direct and indirect public funding for parties and candidates
(percentages)

	Agreeing with direct public funding	Agreeing with tax credits for contributions
Technocratic liberals	34	39
Populist liberals	31	36
Minoritarian individualists	39	45
Majoritarian individualists	28	52
Radical collectivists	43	51
Party collectivists	44	52

For the wording of the questions, see table 5.12.

the equivalent threshold in Australia is 4 percent. It has been argued that such a high threshold jeopardizes the capacity of new or minor parties to compete with established parties (Paltiel 1989). A low threshold (or no threshold at all) is more likely to facilitate access for new parties and candidates. The standard argument for stringent conditions is that only candidates and parties with substantial support should receive public funding.

How do Canadians react to the idea of a vote threshold for public funding? The response may depend on the level of that threshold. We therefore devised an experiment. One (random) third of our sample was asked about a threshold of 20 percent, another about one of 10 percent and the third group about one of 5 percent (question f11). On the whole, Canadians are divided on this issue but their responses are affected very little by the exact threshold. Fifty-one percent even agreed with a 20 percent threshold (it should be kept in mind that the question was put only to those who supported some direct public funding); support for thresholds of 5 percent and 10 percent increased to only 59 percent. These results suggest that Canadians do not have clear views on the exact conditions that candidates should fulfil in order to receive public funding. They remain reluctant to endorse public funding and are therefore prone to impose some threshold. At the same time, they do not like the idea of giving any special advantage to the traditional parties, which they tend to distrust; that consideration militates against any threshold. As a consequence, much ambivalence prevails.

Two socio-economic variables – region and gender – are related to opinions on eligibility for public funding (see tables 5.14 and 1.D26). The

Table 5.14
**Distribution of opinions about eligibility for public
funding**
(percentages)

	Believing that all parties and candidates should get reimbursed
Atlantic	47
Quebec	33
Ontario	53
Manitoba/Saskatchewan	40
Alberta	50
British Columbia	47
Men	37
Women	50
Under 45	45
45 and over	42
Low education	48
Medium education	42
High education	40
Low income	41
Medium income	47
High income	43
Blue collar	44
White collar	43
Unionized	42
Nonunionized	44
English	50
French	33
Non-charter language	49
Catholic	38
Protestant	52
Canada	43

The question was the following:
f11 Do you think that ALL political parties and candidates should
get some reimbursement or ONLY THOSE who get at least
[5] [10] [20 percent] of the vote?

regional pattern is somewhat complex: while respondents from Atlantic
Canada, Ontario, Alberta and British Columbia were evenly divided on
whether public funding should be available for every party, only
40 percent of respondents in Manitoba and Saskatchewan and 33 percent
of Quebeckers agreed with the idea. Women are more opposed to restrictions: 50 percent of them would like all parties and candidates to receive
public funding, compared to just 37 percent of men. Women are more

favourable to public funding to begin with (see table 5.12) and would like it to be as widely available as possible.

Political values also help to shape opinions about eligibility for public funding (table 1.D26). Only 36 percent of majoritarian individualists agreed with the idea that all parties and candidates should be eligible for public funding. The majoritarian individualists have two good reasons to oppose the idea: their laissez-faire orientation induces them to resist public funding in general, and their concern with the rights of the majority makes them less sensitive to the problems faced by minor parties.

To sum up, Canadians express strong resistance toward the most direct form of public funding, that is, reimbursement of campaign expenditures. There is some indication that this resistance has grown over time, possibly as a result of the rise of anti-state sentiment. Indirect public funding, through tax credits, is somewhat more acceptable: close to one-half of our respondents were in favour of it.

THE FEASIBILITY OF CONTROLS

A majority of Canadians would like to see controls placed on spending by parties, corporations and unions, and on the size of contributions, sources of which should be made public. There is no structured predisposition, however, to limit (or not limit) party revenues across the board. Opinions on the desirability of ceilings on individual contributions are weakly related to opinions on the appropriateness of contributions by corporations, unions and interest groups (the correlation coefficients range from 0.08 to 0.11).

The question of the perceived effectiveness of such controls remains. Canadians may support controls on campaign finances in the abstract, yet not believe that these controls are actually feasible. Perhaps they would be ideal in a perfect world, but simply cannot be achieved in the real world of politics, as parties, candidates and groups can easily find ways to circumvent the law. Sorauf (1988, 325) argues that there is great scepticism in the United States about the actual implementation of controls. According to him, there is a widespread assumption that "the clever and the powerful, armed with clever advice, can escape the restrictions of the law and, more than that, turn them to their advantage."

We tapped Canadians' views on the matter through two questions. We first inquired whether they thought it was impossible to really control party finances (question f21). To those who said yes, we asked whether they would go so far as saying that attempting to control is a futile exercise (question f22). The combination of these two questions gives us three groups:

1. the optimists, who believe that controls are quite possible;
2. the ambivalent, who believe that real controls may not be feasible but that regulations may still achieve something and are thus helpful; and
3. the pessimists, who conclude that controls are simply a waste of time and energy.

In our survey, 49 percent were ambivalent, 42 percent optimists and 8 percent pessimists. Many Canadians have doubts about the implementation of controls, but very few conclude that they are useless.

It is in central Canada that optimism about the feasibility of controls is the greatest (see table 5.15). Regional differences do not vanish when political cynicism is taken into account (table 1.D27), which suggests that perhaps distance from the centre also fosters a greater sense of powerlessness, a feeling that one does not have much control over one's environment. It is also interesting to note that optimism is particularly high in Quebec, the province where the strictest regulations have been put in place. Education is also a good predictor of perceptions. Fifty-four percent of those with a university degree can be characterized as optimists, compared to 37 percent among less-educated respondents. Again, the relationship is not explained by the lesser cynicism of the better educated and may instead reflect deeper feelings about the possibility of controlling one's environment. Low-income people also express greater pessimism, but that link vanishes when other socio-economic variables are factored in (table 1.D27).

There is also a rather strong link between political cynicism and scepticism about the feasibility of controls. We find that 51 percent among those who scored low on the political cynicism scale were optimists, but only 34 percent among the highly cynical. This, of course, raises a dilemma: the more you distrust politicians, the more you want to control them but the less confidence you have in society's capacity to actually control them. The dilemma should not be overstated. Very few Canadians believe that controls are entirely useless.

On the whole, Canadians are moderately optimistic about the possibility of genuine controls on campaign finances. They do not expect these controls to be fully effective but still believe that they are worthwhile. Scepticism is more pervasive among the lesser educated and outside central Canada; this is a reflection, perhaps, of a larger sense of powerlessness. It is weaker in the one province that has adopted the most rigorous set of restrictions; at the very least, experience with tougher rules has not made Quebeckers more prone to believe that attempts at regulating campaign finances are futile. Finally, scepticism is enhanced by the strong sense of political cynicism that prevails in Canada.

Table 5.15
Distribution of opinions about the feasibility of controls for party electoral spending
(percentages)

	Optimists about the feasibility of controls
Atlantic	38
Quebec	44
Ontario	45
Manitoba/Saskatchewan	38
Alberta	42
British Columbia	36
Men	44
Women	40
Under 45	43
45 and over	40
Low education	37
Medium education	41
High education	54
Low income	37
Medium income	42
High income	49
Blue collar	38
White collar	44
Unionized	43
Nonunionized	41
English	42
French	42
Non-charter language	41
Catholic	42
Protestant	41
Canada	42

The question was the following:

f21 It is impossible to really control what political parties receive and spend in an election. (BASICALLY, do you AGREE or DISAGREE?)

RECAPITULATION

We may conclude that:

1. There is a strong consensus on the desirability of limits on party spending and of the disclosure of contributions.
2. Canadians are more concerned with controlling expenditures than with controlling revenues. Only a slight majority favours ceilings on individual contributions.

3. Views about what groups should have the right to do in a campaign tend to be pliable.
4. Most Canadians oppose public funding of campaign expenses.
5. Most Canadians find controls on election finances helpful even though they have some doubts about their feasibility.
6. On the whole, public opinion tends to be consistent with present legislation, which consists of strict controls on spending and little regulation of revenues. The major departure concerns public funding, which is opposed by most Canadians.
7. It is in Quebec that support for the regulation of election finances is strongest and in the West that it is weakest. The findings with respect to Quebec are particularly interesting, since that province has adopted the strictest legislation in that domain. On the whole, the regulatory approach in Quebec is well accepted.
8. Low-income people do not systematically request stronger control of election finances.
9. Cynicism about politicians and the role of money in politics enhances support for controls on electoral finances.
10. Opinions about the appropriateness of public funding stem in part from attitudes about the role of the state. Collectivists tend to support public funding and individualists are likely to oppose it.

6

ATTITUDES ABOUT ELECTORAL COMMUNICATION

Without money, parties and candidates would not be able to run campaigns. Rules about who can spend money, and how much, and where and how parties can get the necessary revenues, are crucial. Money is, however, merely a means for parties and candidates to inform citizens about their positions and to try to convince them to vote in a certain way, which is what an election campaign is really about. As Elster (1986) has argued (see also Fishkin 1992), the forum is to politics what the market is to the economy. Therefore, rules about how that forum should be structured, and how communication between parties and candidates, on the one hand, and voters, on the other hand, should take place, are fundamental.

We consider Canadians' views about how communications should proceed in an election campaign. There are four basic means by which party leaders and candidates can communicate their messages to the voters:

1. they can talk directly to them, in private or public meetings;
2. they can reach them through the media, mainly via advertising;
3. they can rely on the media to report their positions; and
4. they can participate in televised debates.

The last three options involve the media. In option 2, politicians control the messages that are sent to voters, while option 3 leaves them no control, as it is the media that decide which messages will make the news. Option 4 is intermediary; politicians do the talking in response to journalists' questions, and neither side is allowed to screen out messages. We examine how the public assesses these various sources of information and, in one case, whether they would like to establish new rules to improve the process.

We would expect people of different levels of information and education to have different perspectives on how communication should take place in election campaigns. A person who rarely follows politics is likely to be looking for different kinds and sources of information than the person who follows politics closely. It is thus important to distinguish the views of the better informed and of the least informed, as well as those of the better educated and the least educated, as education can be seen to facilitate the processing of information.

We also want to assess how much of the cynicism expressed toward politicians and parties extends to the media. How much do Canadians distrust the media? Are those who are more cynical about politicians also more cynical about the media? And does that cynicism induce voters to request less-mediated types of electoral communication, such as debates?

Finally, we consider the link between political values and attitudes about electoral communication. We especially determine whether there is, as in the case of finances, a cleavage between individualists and collectivists as to the proper role of the state in regulating electoral communication. We examine the impact of populist leanings on Canadians' attitudes; specifically, we explore whether populism enhances support for less-mediated forms of communication, especially debates.

PARTY ADVERTISING

We first look at the least-mediated form of political communication (short of meetings): party advertising. From the voters' perspective, party advertising presents one major advantage and one major liability. Its great virtue flows from its unmediated character. Parties are able to communicate directly with voters, without journalistic interference regarding which messages deserve or do not deserve to reach voters. Its main limitation is its partiality, in the two senses of the word. The message comes from one specific source and, most of the time, provides information about only one party or candidate, thus making comparisons difficult. The source of the information also has clear interests at stake and there is, therefore, the presumption that the message may be biased in some way.

In our survey, we sought our respondents' perceptions of the utility of party advertising and their attitudes about imposing limits on its use. With respect to perceptions, we gave them the two standard arguments for and against advertising: that we need it because it is direct, or that it is not of much use because it is not really informative, and asked them to choose the position closest to their own point of view. We also experimented with the order in which positions were presented, which allowed us to test the firmness of opinions (questions m13a and m13b).

The extreme position – that we could do away with advertising altogether – is rejected by two-thirds of Canadians. This does not mean that people are convinced of the great value of campaign ads; rather, most of us reach the conclusion that ads are not entirely useless. Indeed, the mere fact that as many as one-third believed that we would be better off without these ads is indicative of the strong scepticism they elicit. In all likelihood, many Canadians are ambivalent: they distrust party ads but concede that they may sometimes play a useful role. It should be noted that we found an order effect. The option presented last was selected slightly more often; the difference, however, was not very large (14 percentage points), indicating that opinions were moderately firm.

We also inquired whether there should be limits on party advertising. We asked our respondents to choose between two positions, one arguing for limits to ensure fair competition and the other arguing against them on the basis of freedom of speech (questions m12a and m12b), and we again experimented with the order of presentation. Fully three-fourths of the sample came down on the side of limits. Again, responses revealed an order effect (15 percentage points); the effect decreased with information level (data not shown). The order effect was most substantial in the case of the minoritarian and majoritarian individualists: support for limits dropped 20 percentage points and 25 percentage points, respectively, when the libertarian argument regarding freedom of speech was presented last rather than first.

Once more we discover a strong willingness to control party spending, but specifically with respect to advertising. Opinions on the appropriateness of limits on party advertising are, of course, related to opinions on limits on party spending in general. The relationship, however, is far from perfect. Nineteen percent of those in favour of overall limits on spending would not have specific limits on advertising. Somewhat more problematic is the fact that 50 of the 188 respondents opposed to limits on party spending would like to see limits placed on advertising. It seems that being presented with an argument for limits moved them to reconsider their position.

Opinions on this question are related to socio-economic variables (see table 6.1). Quebeckers, once again, are more favourable to controls: 81 percent believed that we should limit party advertising, compared

Table 6.1
Distribution of opinions about party advertising
(percentages)

	In favour of limits on party advertising
Atlantic	75
Quebec	81
Ontario	76
Manitoba/Saskatchewan	78
Alberta	73
British Columbia	74
Men	76
Women	78
Under 45	78
45 and over	75
Low education	73
Medium education	78
High education	82
Low income	75
Medium income	79
High income	80
Blue collar	76
White collar	77
Unionized	79
Nonunionized	76
English	75
French	80
Non-charter language	81
Catholic	78
Protestant	76
Canada	77

The questions were the following:

m12a Which of the following two statements comes closer to your own opinion?
We should limit spending on party advertising, otherwise parties with more money will have an unfair advantage.

    OR

Freedom of speech is such a fundamental right that parties should be allowed to advertise as much as they wish.

m12b Which of the following two statements comes closer to your own opinion?
Freedom of speech is such a fundamental right that parties should be allowed to advertise as much as they wish.

    OR

We should limit spending on party advertising, otherwise parties with more money will have an unfair advantage.

Note: Each respondent was (randomly) assigned one of the two questions. The results of the two questions are collapsed.

to 75 percent in the rest of Canada. The better educated and better informed (see table 1.D28) are also more supportive of controls. The difference, however, is confined to question m12a. In that question, the argument that freedom of speech is fundamental and that parties should be allowed to advertise as much as they wish, which was presented last, was found convincing by 40 percent of the least-informed respondents but by only 23 percent of the best-informed group. When the arguments were presented in the reverse order (question m12b), there was hardly any difference.

We would expect respondents' positions on whether there should be limits placed on party advertising to be related to perceptions of the utility of that type of electoral communication. There is indeed a relationship, but a modest one. Eighty-three percent of those who thought we could do without party ads supported limits, compared to 74 percent among those who said that we need ads. When other factors are controlled, however, the difference is reduced to only five percentage points. Furthermore, these perceptions do not account for the greater support for controls in Quebec and among the better informed and university educated (table 1.D28).

Attitudes about controls on party advertising are shaped as much by feelings about politicians as by reactions to advertising as such (table 1.D28). Support for controls reached 80 percent among the most cynical group, compared to 74 percent and 76 percent among the medium- and least-cynical groups, respectively.

MEDIA COVERAGE

For most people the main source of information about election campaigns is the news (Fletcher 1981; Robinson and Levy 1986). The quality of media coverage of election campaigns is therefore of paramount importance. In order to be able to make sound judgements about the merits and drawbacks of the various candidates, voters must be able to rely on sources of information that are accurate (party positions on various issues, for instance, must be reported faithfully), diverse (that is, presenting a range of different perspectives) and balanced (the different parties and candidates must be treated fairly).

To what extent are Canadians satisfied with the quality of information provided by media coverage of election campaigns? In our survey, we asked our respondents to assess the media on two general criteria: accuracy and fairness (questions m1 and m2). On these two scores, the overall evaluation was quite positive: 76 percent felt the media do a good or a very good job in accurately reporting on federal election campaigns, and 63 percent believed that they treat all parties fairly.

Such positive evaluations have been documented in previous surveys. A June 1986 Environics poll indicated that three in four Canadians thought that journalists were very or somewhat honest. The same survey showed Canadians more likely to believe journalists (64 percent) than pollsters (33 percent) or politicians (2 percent) when it came to understanding how the public felt about various issues; these figures changed little from an earlier poll in 1980. Nor are these reactions peculiar to Canada. A *Los Angeles Times* survey conducted in 1985 showed that only 5 percent of Americans felt that the news media were doing a bad job (Schneider and Lewis 1985).

We also wanted to know whether people think the news media pay enough attention to smaller parties (question m3). On that more specific point, the media are perceived less favourably: 57 percent said that too little attention is given to smaller parties. That sentiment is, of course, more widespread among supporters of smaller parties, but half of Conservative and Liberal supporters also agreed with the assessment. It would seem that this coverage imbalance is not considered to be a major problem, as it does not affect overall media evaluations too strongly: 57 percent of those who said too little attention is paid to smaller parties still concluded that the media do a good job in treating parties fairly. Canadians would like to know more about smaller parties, especially since they are dissatisfied with the traditional major ones, but they do not blame the media too harshly for lack of coverage.

In order to better understand the sources of evaluations of the quality of media coverage, we constructed a scale based on responses to the two general questions dealing with the media (m1 and m2). The correlation between the two questions is 0.58. We gave a score of 3 for those who said that the media do a very good job, and 0 for those who answered that the media do a very poor job. We added the scores for the two questions and divided by 6, which allows total scores on the scale to vary between 0 and 1. The average score is 0.68, a reflection of the overall positive assessment.

As shown in table 6.2, evaluations of the media's role in election campaigns are somewhat more positive in the East and more negative in the West, mostly because supporters of the Reform Party tend to be more critical of the media (53 percent said that the media do a poor job of treating the parties fairly, compared to 37 percent among supporters of the three major parties). Men and the better educated also tend to be more critical. Political information plays a role as well: those with a low level of information give a mean score of 0.74, compared to 0.67 and 0.60, respectively, for the medium- and high-level groups. These differences are maintained after controls (table 1.D29). It seems that the better

Table 6.2
Distribution of opinions about media coverage of election campaigns

	Average scale on evaluation of media coverage
Atlantic	.70
Quebec	.72
Ontario	.68
Manitoba/Saskatchewan	.65
Alberta	.62
British Columbia	.62
Men	.63
Women	.73
Under 45	.65
45 and over	.71
Low education	.74
Medium education	.67
High education	.59
Low income	.70
Medium income	.67
High income	.59
Blue collar	.69
White collar	.67
Unionized	.68
Nonunionized	.67
English	.65
French	.71
Non-charter language	.72
Catholic	.70
Protestant	.66
Canada	.68

The questions were the following:

Now some questions about campaigns and the media.

m1 How good a job do you feel the media do in accurately reporting on federal election campaigns? Do they do a VERY GOOD job, a GOOD job, a POOR job or a VERY POOR job?

m2 How good a job do you feel the media do in treating all the federal political parties fairly? Do they do a VERY GOOD job, a GOOD job, a POOR job or a VERY POOR job?

Note: The scale is made up of responses to questions m1 and m2. The higher the scale, the more positive the evaluation of media coverage.

informed use more stringent criteria in their assessments. Even in those groups, however, the overall balance of opinion is slightly positive.

Finally, evaluations of the quality of media coverage are not related to basic political values and beliefs. This is particularly true in the case of cynicism. There is simply no difference in the average scores given by those with high, medium and low levels of political cynicism (data not shown). Canadians perceive the world of the media as being quite distinct from that of politics. Distrust of politicians does not lead to distrust of journalists.

TELEVISED LEADERS DEBATES

Televised leaders debates now exist in a number of countries: Sweden, the Netherlands, France, Germany, Israel, the United States and Canada. They represent an additional source of information for voters, with some peculiar characteristics with respect to the roles played by politicians and the media. In Canada, at least, both politicians and the media play a central role in deciding whether there will be debates and how these debates will be structured. Representatives from the parties and the media must agree on every detail of their format, and, failing such an agreement, no debate occurs, as was the case in the federal elections of 1972, 1974 and 1980. In televised debates, at least the way they have been organized in Canada, both the media and politicians find themselves moderately constrained. Politicians do not control the agenda, as they do in their advertisements, since they must respond to questions and arguments from journalists and other politicians, but at least their messages can reach the voters without direct interference from journalists. Journalists are not able to highlight those messages they deem to be the most important or relevant and screen out others, as they do in news coverage, but they can force politicians to address some issues that are systematically avoided in party ads.

In Canada, as well as in the United States, about two-thirds of the electorate usually watches some part of the debates in those elections where they occur (LeDuc and Price 1990; the proportion tends to be somewhat lower in Europe: see Bernier and Monière 1991). Similarly, in our survey, 64 percent of the respondents said that they had watched leaders debates in 1984 and/or 1988.

Do debates enhance the quality and quantity of information available to voters? On the one hand, it can be argued that debates are at the very heart of what politics is about, that it is only through the confrontation of ideas and personalities that citizens can sort out the merits and limits of various candidates and parties. From that perspective, voters need forums, like the leaders debates, which "serve the majority of the electorate better than any other single campaign communication device that attempts to present both the candidates' personality and their positions on issues" (Kraus 1988, 5) by enabling them to compare directly the options they will have to choose from. On the other hand, the standard objection to debates is that they "emphasize image over substance and add little to the public's knowledge either of the issues or of the candidates" (Swerdlow 1984, 12). From that perspective, the medium of television is such that debates are won or lost not on the basis of the ideas that are discussed, but on mere images; the leader with the most appealing smile or face, who appears to be calm and self-confident and who knows when and how to look at the camera, will come out looking like the best leader, however shallow his or her ideas may be.

We presented our respondents with these two standard arguments for and against debates (questions m8 and m9). Sixty-seven percent of the sample agreed with the statement that debates provide the best opportunity to compare leaders' positions on election issues. As to the outcome of debates, Canadians are evenly divided on whether it is ideas or images that count the most. When responses to these two questions are combined, we find that 40 percent of the sample were systematically positive about debates (they believed that debates give the best opportunity to compare and that ideas count more than images), and 23 percent were systematically negative.

Many Canadians are concerned with the biases inherent in television and are aware that style is important in debates. On the whole, however, they perceive content to count as much as images and think that, at the very least, debates allow them to compare leaders. They are thus moderately positive about the merits of debates.

This modestly positive assessment emerged as well when respondents were asked to rate the relative utility of debates when it comes to deciding how to vote (question m5). Sixty percent found them at least somewhat useful and only 18 percent said that they were entirely useless. Similar findings came out of an Environics poll conducted in December 1988: half of Canadians stated that the 1988 debate had been at least somewhat important in helping them decide for which party to vote.

It is fair to conclude, therefore, that Canadians like televised leaders debates. They have some concerns about the important role that images play in the process, but they still watch them, and find them to be useful because they feel that debates enable them to obtain a better grasp of the differences among leaders and parties. The scant evidence we have suggests that their reaction is not different from that of people in other countries. In the United States, Gallup reports that "for more than

25 years the public has indicated strong support for the idea of having the candidates present their views in a series of nationally televised programs"; in 1976, 77 percent (of those with an opinion) favoured having debates in the next presidential campaign. Similarly, in the 1976 German election, 75 percent of voters watched at least part of the leaders debate, which was held three days before the election, and 75 percent liked the program very much or much. The same positive evaluation is found in France and the Netherlands (Bernier and Monière 1991).

There is, of course, no guarantee that each election will have leaders debates. We have had them in Canada for two elections in a row but only in four cases out of seven since the first debate took place in 1968. The question is, therefore, whether Canadians feel that debates are important enough to warrant being imposed by law. We asked our respondents whether they would want a law requiring party leaders to participate in a televised debate (question m6a). People were divided on the issue, but a slight majority (58 percent) would approve of such a law. It is not altogether clear whether those who approve of legally imposing debates are fully aware of all the related implications; the law would have to specify the modalities of the debates. Perhaps some might reconsider the question if those implications were pointed out. What the survey does indicate, however, is that debates are perceived to be an important source of information, and that many Canadians are willing to consider the option of ensuring, through a law, that debates do take place.

Finally, we inquired about who should participate in the debates. The issue, of course, is whether debates should be restricted to "serious" candidates in order to facilitate exchanges and discussion, or widened to as many participants as possible in order that voters can be exposed to a great variety of viewpoints. We offered our respondents three options:

1. the leaders of the three major parties;
2. the leaders of all parties with members in Parliament; or
3. the leaders of all registered parties (there were 10 in the 1988 election).

The last option was the most popular, with 54 percent choosing it (excluding no opinions and combinations). Again, we find Canadians willing to hear more from and about smaller parties and wanting them to participate fully in the political forum; indeed, those who think the media do not pay enough attention to smaller parties, as well as those who would vote for smaller parties, are also more likely to want to have leaders of all registered parties participate in the debates. Even among those who would vote Liberal or Conservative, however, close to half are willing to have all leaders involved (data not shown). There is widespread sentiment that the system should be more open to smaller parties, a sentiment fuelled in part by strong negative feelings about the established parties. This sentiment also reflects populist leanings: the technocratic liberals were less likely (44 percent) than those with a populist strain to favour including all of the registered political parties in debates.

People with a low level of income and education whose mother tongue is neither French nor English, and younger respondents, especially those born after 1965, are more favourable to mandatory debates (table 6.3). It is the least informed who see the greatest advantages in leaders debates: their support for mandatory debates reached 69 percent, compared to 47 percent among the better informed. For the former, debates constitute a great opportunity to assemble as much information as possible in a very short period of time; indeed, it is for the least informed that debates provide the greatest marginal gain in information. Those who follow campaigns very closely are likely to learn much less than those who hardly keep up with the news (Sears and Chaffee 1978). It is perhaps telling that the group that is the most supportive of mandatory debates is the one whose mother tongue is neither French nor English: 72 percent of them would want a law imposing leaders debates. This is perhaps the group for whom political information is the most difficult to acquire and for whom debates count the most.

For the same reasons, the better educated and better informed tend to find debates less useful in helping them decide how to vote; they are generally less positive in their judgements about the value of debates, and as a consequence are less inclined to support a law requiring leaders to participate in debates. Even controlling for a whole set of perceptions, beliefs and political values, the better informed remain less supportive of mandatory debates (table 1.D30). It is possible that the better informed are also concerned with the complexities involved in state-organized debates, and are therefore reluctant to adopt such an innovation. The point should not be overstated, however: almost half of the most informed still support mandatory debates.

Opinions about the desirability of debates are closely linked to evaluations of their utility. The most crucial consideration is whether debates provide the best opportunity to compare leaders (see table 1.D30). Seventy percent of those who believed that debates do indeed provide the best opportunity to compare leaders were favourable to mandatory debates. It is also interesting to note that the evaluations of those

Table 6.3
Distribution of opinions about mandatory leaders debates
(percentages)

	In favour of mandatory debates
Atlantic	65
Quebec	63
Ontario	57
Manitoba/Saskatchewan	51
Alberta	54
British Columbia	54
Men	56
Women	61
Under 45	60
45 and over	55
Low education	67
Medium education	59
High education	44
Low income	66
Medium income	57
High income	49
Blue collar	64
White collar	56
Unionized	60
Nonunionized	58
English	54
French	63
Non-charter language	72
Catholic	63
Protestant	52
Canada	58

The question was the following:
m6a Do you think the law should require party leaders to participate in a televised debate at each election?

who did not watch the debates in 1984 or 1988 were almost as supportive of mandatory debates as the evaluations of those who did watch and found them useful (see, again, table 1.D30). In fact, 64 percent of those who did not watch the debates believed there should be a law requiring them. This is a clear indication that non-exposure to debates should not be construed as a negative assessment of their utility.

As we argued at the outset, debates represent an additional source of information for the electorate, on top of party ads and media coverage. An important feature of debates is that party leaders can communicate their messages to voters without the interference of journalists. We would thus expect those who are dissatisfied with media coverage to express greater faith in the utility of debates, in which the media play a minor role. It seems, however, that the more one trusts the media, the more positive one tends to be about debates (data not shown), and that attitudes about the media do not have an independent impact on opinions about mandatory debates (table 1.D30). The better educated and better informed tend to be more critical about any source of information, be it party ads, media coverage or debates (a similar pattern has been observed in the United States; see Schneider and Lewis 1985). It seems that the more one knows about politics, the more critical one becomes about all information sources. This pattern could be attributed to the diminishing marginal return of information, because, beyond a certain level, one gains less and less from exposure to additional information, and every source of information is assessed more negatively.

Finally, attitudes about debates are strongly affected by political cynicism and basic political values: 64 percent of the most cynical group supported mandatory debates, compared to 50 percent among the least cynical. To put it bluntly, the less you trust politicians, the more you want to force them to participate in a debate where they will have to defend their positions. Likewise, the technocratic liberals were alone among our six types in having a majority who opposed mandatory debates (52 percent). It does indeed make sense that the sole group that rejects populist values is most strongly opposed to mandatory debates. Debates can be characterized as a populist device that allows a direct relationship between people and politicians (and all five of the groupings with a populist strain are more likely to agree that debates give voters the best opportunity to compare the leaders' positions). This does not fit the standard technocratic approach to politics, with its heavy emphasis on the role of experts, but is in line with widespread feelings within large segments of the population. We should also note that support for mandatory debates reached its peak (70 percent) among the party collectivists. As expected, those who are more favourably disposed to state intervention in general are less wary of regulating electoral communication. Many Canadians are, nonetheless, willing to impose debates, despite their general laissez-faire orientation.

RECAPITULATION

The findings reported in this chapter lead to the following conclusions:

1. The majority of Canadians support limits on party advertising.
2. On the whole, evaluations of media coverage of election campaigns tend to be positive.
3. Most Canadians watch leaders debates and believe that they provide the best opportunity to compare leaders, even though they express some concern about the important role images play in those debates.
4. Canadians are divided on the desirability of mandatory debates, but a small majority approves of them.
5. The better educated and better informed are more critical about each source of electoral communication, probably because, beyond a certain point, the marginal gain in information provided by each of these sources rapidly diminishes.
6. Those who are more cynical about politicians are more likely to support limits on party advertising and mandatory debates. Political cynicism, however, does not lead to criticism of how the media cover election campaigns.
7. The most compelling consideration that induces many Canadians, especially those less socialized to Canadian politics, to approve of mandatory debates is the belief that debates enable them to compare leaders.
8. Support for mandatory debates is enhanced by pervasive populist values in large segments of the population.

7

OVERALL
EVALUATION OF
ELECTORAL
PROCEDURES

Wᴇ ʜᴀᴠᴇ ᴇxᴀᴍɪɴᴇᴅ how Canadians react to various aspects of the electoral law, including the translation of votes into seats, the role of MPs, party democracy, finances and communication. It is now time to adopt a broader perspective and look at how the entire system is perceived. In our survey, we tapped this global evaluation through three questions: one that inquired about the overall level of satisfaction with the way federal elections work in Canada (question e1), and two in which respondents were asked first to compare electoral arrangements in Canada with those in the United States (question e3), and then those existing for federal elections with those for provincial elections (question e5). Each of these questions was followed by an open-ended question, in which respondents could explain and elaborate on their positions. For a random half of the respondents, this set of questions came at the very beginning of the questionnaire; for the other half, the questions came after the sections on the specifics of electoral law (but before the sections on political values and beliefs). This experiment allowed us to check the firmness of global evaluations.

Our first objective was, of course, to characterize as accurately as possible the overall legitimacy of federal elections. One of the basic functions of elections is to "help to preserve government's stability by containing and channelling away potentially more disruptive or dangerous forms of mass political activity" (Ginsberg 1982, 7). That function can be fulfilled only if citizens believe that elections work properly; otherwise, elections fail to enhance support for political leaders and the regime.

The evidence presented in previous chapters suggests reasons for both satisfaction and dissatisfaction with present rules. On the one hand, we saw in Chapter 5 that federal legislation, with rather strict controls on spending but little regulation of revenues, tends to be consistent with public opinion. On the other hand, chapters 4 and 6 have pointed out some aspects of the electoral process that a majority of Canadians would like to change: most Canadians don't like the way the electoral system translates votes into seats, would like to be able to separate the choice of local representative from the choice of the party to form the government, and would approve of a law requiring party leaders to participate in televised debates.

The question is, of course, whether the reasons for satisfaction outweigh those for dissatisfaction. We determine what kinds of considerations, about which aspects of the electoral process, have the greatest impact on overall evaluations. We pay particular attention to two questions. First, how crucial are attitudes about the electoral system? Is it possible to enhance satisfaction with electoral arrangements without changing the electoral system? Second, to what extent do attitudes about electoral finances shape one's overall evaluation? Our own study has been predicated on the assumption that finances are central to the whole electoral process, and it will be interesting to see whether this is indeed the case when we look at the legitimacy of the system.

Overall evaluations not only summarize specific judgements on specific aspects of electoral arrangements – they are also likely to reflect basic political values and beliefs. We wish, particularly, to examine how political cynicism affects evaluations. Are the most cynical respondents, whatever their views on specific arrangements, more critical of the whole system? The same question applies, indeed, to populism. Do the strong populist leanings of many Canadians express themselves in scepticism and dissatisfaction with the way representative democracy works in Canada?

Finally, we ascertain variations in satisfaction across regions and groups. Even if there is widespread satisfaction, the existence of deep dissatisfaction among subgroups would indicate that the legitimacy of elections is in jeopardy. As in previous chapters, regional variations are of paramount concern. Previous chapters have shown that residents of Alberta and Quebec hold quite specific views on a number of issues. Does it follow that residents of these two provinces feel less satisfied, overall, with the way elections work in Canada?

LEVEL OF SATISFACTION

Canadians are moderately satisfied with the way federal elections work (table 7.1). Of course, many may not have thought about this a great deal, and we therefore explicitly mentioned in our question that it was quite possible not to have an opinion. Sixteen percent of our respondents said that, indeed, they had no opinion. Among those who did have an opinion, the dominant position was one of modest satisfaction. Canadians do not exhibit any great enthusiasm about how elections work in Canada, but neither do they express a deep sense of discontent. As well, responses did not vary according to their placement in the questionnaire.

We asked everyone (except those who were very satisfied with the existing rules) what they thought should be changed in order to have a better system for federal elections (question e2). Forty-six percent of the sample could not mention any specific change. Among those who did have some idea, responses covered a wide range of options, without any one option receiving top priority. The following suggestions each received between 40 and 80 mentions: equal representation by

Table 7.1
Overall evaluation of electoral procedures
(percentages)

	Group 1	Group 2	Total sample
A. Satisfaction			
Very satisfied	11	5	8
Somewhat satisfied	48	44	46
Not very satisfied	18	23	21
Not at all satisfied	9	9	9
No opinion	14	19	16
B. Evaluation Canada/USA			
USA better	15	17	16
Canada better	27	23	25
Neither better	38	41	39
No opinion	20	19	20
C. Evaluation federal/provincial			
Federal better	8	7	8
Provincial better	21	19	20
Neither better	64	66	65
No opinion	7	7	7

The questions were the following:

e1 On the whole, are you VERY satisfied, SOMEWHAT satisfied, NOT VERY satisfied or NOT AT ALL satisfied with the way federal elections work in Canada, or DON'T YOU HAVE AN OPINION on this?

e3 In general, would you say elections work better in the UNITED STATES, work better in CANADA, or NEITHER works better than the other?

e5 How about federal and provincial elections? Which would you say work better: FEDERAL elections, PROVINCIAL elections, or NEITHER works better?

Note: Group 1 was asked the questions at the very beginning of the questionnaire and group 2 only after section D.

province/region; proportional representation; having two votes; and reducing/controlling spending. The necessity of having candidates of great intellectual and moral standing and of giving greater responsibility to voters was also stressed by a good number of respondents. The latter responses did not point to any specific institutional change, but reflected strong cynicism about politicians.

Table 7.2 lists the major institutional options that Canadians have in mind when they think about improving the existing system. The most striking fact is that half of respondents could not point to any specific change that they would like to see. This is partly a reflection of relative satisfaction with existing rules. Indeed, the percentage unable to mention anything was highest among the somewhat satisfied (56 percent; the question was not put to the very satisfied nor to those with no opinion) and lowest (25 percent) among the very dissatisfied. The paucity of suggestions, however, also stems from the fact that most people have not thought about these issues a great deal. Not surprisingly, the probability of a suggestion substantially increased with the level of political information: the percentage of "no response" increased from 30 percent among the best informed to 68 percent among the least informed.

It is noteworthy that none of the various options for electoral reform identified by our respondents had any wide appeal. The domain most frequently referred to was electoral finance. This is not an

Table 7.2
Changes to electoral procedures suggested by respondents
(percentages)

	Group 1	Group 2	Total sample
Territorial representation	7	5	6
Ballot	4	7	5
Proportional representation	2	3	3
Voting procedures	4	1	3
Electoral finances	6	7	7
Other	32	31	32
None/Don't know	46	46	46

The question was the following:

e2 What do you think should be changed to have a better system for federal elections?

Note: Group 1 was asked the question at the very beginning of the questionnaire and group 2 only after section D. Only first mentions are considered here.

artificial effect of our questionnaire's focus on this issue, since those who were asked the question at the very beginning of the questionnaire mentioned electoral finances with the same frequency. The other four issues – territorial representation, the ballot, proportional representation and voting procedures – all seemed to be of somewhat lesser importance. Those who were asked the question at the beginning of the interview were more likely to mention right-to-vote rules, possibly because this was the first item indicated in the introduction to question e1; those who had the question at the end of the interview were more likely to mention changes in the ballot (having two votes), probably because question d5 had focused their attention on that particular item. It is also interesting to note that among the five issue areas distinguished here, the one most often mentioned by those who were not at all satisfied with the existing system was territorial representation (it was referred to by 23 respondents, that is, 9 percent of the strongly dissatisfied), which suggests that the issue of regional representation is of great concern to some Canadians.

Those groups that were the most and the least satisfied with existing rules are identified in table 7.3. Those who were not at all satisfied were given a score of 0, and those who were very satisfied a score of 3, with scores of 1 and 2, respectively, for the not very and somewhat satisfied. The average score was 1.64, a reflection of a modest degree of satisfaction.

The most striking cleavage is the regional one. The level of satisfaction decreases as one moves from east to west: 42 percent of respondents (all percentages, here and below, exclude those with no opinion) in western Canada were not satisfied with the way elections work, compared with 33 percent in central Canada (Quebec and Ontario) and 28 percent in Atlantic Canada. These regional variations should not be overstated: in each region a majority expressed some degree of satisfaction; however, these differences are significant. Moreover, they are much starker among those who were asked the question toward the middle of the questionnaire, that is, after the sections on electoral finance, the media and various representation issues. Specifically, the percentage of dissatisfied respondents in the West jumped from 34 percent at the beginning of the questionnaire to 50 percent when the question was posed later. It seems that the more Westerners think about the way elections work in Canada, the more dissatisfied they become. This should not be imputed to the particular set of issues our questionnaire focused upon; we did not have questions dealing with territorial representation or Senate reform, issues that are particularly salient in the West. It should be pointed out that in both variants of the experiment, the

Table 7.3
Determinants of satisfaction with existing electoral procedures

	Mean score on satisfaction
Atlantic	1.80
Quebec	1.65
Ontario	1.69
Manitoba/Saskatchewan	1.49
Alberta	1.50
British Columbia	1.53
Men	1.67
Women	1.60
Under 45	1.67
45 and over	1.58
Low education	1.56
Medium education	1.66
High education	1.69
Low income	1.56
Medium income	1.67
High income	1.71
Blue collar	1.62
White collar	1.65
Unionized	1.67
Nonunionized	1.62
English	1.61
French	1.70
Non-charter language	1.65
Catholic	1.66
Protestant	1.64
Canada	1.64

For the wording of question e1, see table 7.1.

Note: Those who said they were not at all satisfied were given a score of 0, those not very satisfied a score of 1, those somewhat satisfied a score of 2 and those very satisfied a score of 3.

evaluation section came before the sections on political values and beliefs, and that evaluations, therefore, could not have been contaminated by responses to questions about political cynicism.

Are these general evaluations rooted in assessments of specific components of the electoral law or do they merely reflect citizens' visceral reactions to politics? Although basic political values and beliefs play an important role, as we will see later, there is no doubt that opinions about at least some of these issues do affect evaluations (see tables 7.4 and 1.D31). The link, moreover, is entirely consistent. With a caveat to be discussed below, those whose views coincide with the existing state of affairs tend to be more satisfied with the status quo; those whose views depart from existing arrangements are, naturally, more dissatisfied. This indicates that we are justified in conceptualizing evaluations as a sort of overall judgement on existing institutions. It should be pointed out that the link between opinions and evaluations is closer among those who were asked the evaluation question later in the interview (data not shown); these respondents had more time to think about the issues and to offer a reasoned judgement. The difference, however, should not be overstated. Basically, the same relationships emerge, though in a somewhat weaker fashion, in the "early" group.

Judgements about the electoral system are the most powerful consideration. Those who do not accept the "first-past-the-post" system are much more likely to express dissatisfaction with existing institutions (see table 7.4). This makes perfect sense. The way in which votes are translated into seats is probably the most crucial rule of all: not only does it affect the actual number of seats parties receive, but by anticipation

Table 7.4
**Overall degree of satisfaction and opinions about
specific electoral arrangements**

	Mean score on satisfaction
A. Judgement on first-past-the-post system	
Completely unacceptable	1.52
Somewhat unacceptable	1.60
Somewhat acceptable	1.80
Completely acceptable	1.91
B. Opinion on spending limits	
Support	1.62
Oppose	1.75
C. Score on the acceptability of group contributions	
0.00 *(strongly opposed)*	1.47
0.33	1.64
0.67	1.67
1.00 *(strongly favourable)*	1.73

See tables 4.1, 5.1 and 5.9 for question wording.

Note: Those who said they were not at all satisfied were given a score of 0, those not very satisfied a score of 1, those somewhat satisfied a score of 2 and those very satisfied a score of 3.

voters are induced not to support parties that they like because they are perceived to have no chance of winning the election (Blais and Carty 1991). This is probably the reason that the electoral system is the institution that has been the most systematically researched (Lijphart 1985) and debated (Blais 1991).

The two other important issues, in terms of their effects on evaluations, are spending limits and group contributions. We have underlined, in Chapter 5, Canadians' great concern with spending limits, and it is quite normal that the concern be reflected in overall assessments of electoral procedures. It may seem to be somewhat odd, however, that those few who oppose spending limits and who thus oppose the existing rules (since there are clear limits to what parties and candidates can spend in a campaign) end up being more satisfied with the way that federal elections work. This apparent paradox can be explained rather simply: many Canadians dramatically overestimate the amounts spent by parties and candidates. Both the focus group discussions that preceded the survey and our own pre-tests showed that Canadians believe that "hundreds of millions of dollars" (Massie 1990, 12) are being spent on campaigning. Those in favour of spending limits thus do not favour the status quo as they perceive it. They want stricter limits, and it is for that reason that they are dissatisfied. This highlights the difficulty of having spending limits that Canadians will find satisfactory. To the extent that people systematically overestimate actual spending, they are bound to find existing rules wanting.

The other important issue is group contributions. Those who oppose group contributions are less likely to feel content with the way elections work in Canada. The issue is fundamental. It pertains to the very definition of who is allowed to intervene in election campaigns. The question was deemed to be sufficiently serious by the Quebec caucus of the Conservative party to justify experimenting with a complete ban on group contributions in the 1988 federal election. Our study confirms that it does have some resonance at the mass level. At the same time, as we observed in Chapter 5, views about which groups should be allowed to contribute tend to be pliable. The American experience suggests that if groups were to become much more visible in election campaigns, the existing permissive mood could easily give way to strong demands for strict regulations.

Evaluations of existing electoral procedures are also related to basic beliefs and political values, the most crucial of which is cynicism. The more cynical one is about politicians, the less likely one is to be satisfied with the way elections work (see tables 7.5 and 1.D31). Evaluations reflect not only reactions to specific provisions of the electoral law but

Table 7.5
Beliefs, values and the overall degree of satisfaction with the electoral process

	Mean score on satisfaction
A. Political cynicism*	
Low	1.88
Medium	1.55
High	1.44
B. Values**	
Technocratic liberals	1.72
Populist liberals	1.61
Minoritarian individualists	1.68
Majoritarian individualists	1.64
Radical collectivists	1.55
Party collectivists	1.58

Note: Those who said they were not at all satisfied were given a score of 0, those not very satisfied a score of 1, those somewhat satisfied a score of 2 and those very satisfied a score of 3.

*For question wordings and scale, see tables 3.1 and 3.4.

**On this typology, see tables 2.1, 2.2 and 1.D1.

also feelings about politicians in general. We noted in Chapter 5 that political cynicism has been on the increase recently in Canada. Our findings suggest that this trend must have depressed somewhat the level of satisfaction with the electoral process. The fact that Canadians complain relatively little about the way elections work, despite their cynical views of politicians, is remarkable.

Lastly, the collectivists tend to be more critical of existing procedures, while technocratic liberals express a greater degree of satisfaction. To the extent that Canadian federal legislation is, on the whole, rather permissive and refrains from stringent regulations, the collectivists, who believe in the merits of government intervention, are bound to be disappointed. It is also interesting to observe that satisfaction reaches its peak among the sole group without a populist strain. This confirms that populist feelings, as well as cynicism, contribute to depressing the level of satisfaction with existing electoral procedures.

All in all, Canadians seem relatively satisfied with the way federal elections work. Those whose views on various aspects of the electoral law coincide with the existing state of affairs express greater satisfaction, which indicates that general evaluations are rooted in judgements about the appropriateness of various particular measures. We also find, however, that assessments depend to a great extent on level of political trust: the more one trusts politicians, the more positive one is about the electoral process. Finally, evaluations reflect basic views about the role of the state, with the collectivists being the most critical of the dominant laissez-faire approach in the electoral process.

COMPARING CANADIAN AND AMERICAN ELECTIONS

We asked our respondents to compare the way elections work in Canada and in the United States (question e3). It would, of course, have been interesting to have them compare Canada with many other countries but the United States is clearly the country about which Canadians know the most and with which comparisons can be most easily established. Twenty percent of respondents did not have an opinion about this issue. If one adds to these respondents all those who could not evaluate how elections work in Canada, to whom the comparative question was not put, we can conclude that one Canadian in three has no opinion on the issue. Among those with an opinion, about half believed that neither system works better, approximately 30 percent preferred the Canadian approach and 20 percent opted for the American type of elections. This reflects a modest level of satisfaction with existing arrangements. Perceptions of the comparative value of the two systems are, of course, related to overall evaluations. Only 15 percent of those who were satisfied with the existing rules preferred the U.S. system, compared with 29 percent of those who were dissatisfied. It should be noted, however, that even in that latter case the American arrangements did not have wide appeal.

We attempted to examine the reasons why some respondents believed that elections work better in Canada and others preferred the American system. Twenty-five percent of our respondents could not mention any reason. The major advantage of the U.S. system, in the eyes of those who liked it, was the fact that it is a presidential system; this was mentioned by 93 respondents, that is, 31 percent of those mentioning a reason why they thought U.S. elections work better.

Those who preferred the Canadian system were able to point to more reasons for their preference. The most frequent reason, with 77 mentions, was the parliamentary system. On both sides, then, the system of government is the dimension that comes most often to mind as distinguishing Canadian and American elections. These spontaneous responses suggest that the presidential system may be slightly favoured over the parliamentary one. But those who believed that Canadian elections work better offered three other reasons with some frequency. Forty-eight respondents indicated that, in their view, Canadian elections are better because they are fairer and more democratic, while only 12 respondents said the reverse. We do not know precisely which rules made them believe this but it is probably reasonable to assume that at least some of them must have thought about campaign finances (34 respondents explicitly referred to campaign finances as being better in Canada, with no one saying that they were better in the United States), the domain where American and Canadian practices differ the most substantially. Fifty respondents also pointed out that elections are less complicated in Canada, and 39 others said that they like the fact that campaigns in Canada are shorter. In short, elections are perceived to work a little better in Canada than in the United States because they appear to be fairer and simpler, advantages that more than make up for the main attraction of American elections, which is the fact that voters are allowed to vote directly for the president.

Table 7.6 indicates which groups preferred the Canadian or American system. Those who believe that Canadian elections work better were given a score of 1, those who prefer American elections a score of 0, and those who believe that neither works better a score of 0.5. The average score was 0.56, indicating a modest preference for the Canadian system.

Albertans are distinctive in their positive evaluation of the American system. While in the rest of Canada those choosing the Canadian system greatly outnumber those opting for the American one (leaving aside those seeing no difference), in Alberta a slight majority prefer the American system. The appeal, however, does not extend to the other western provinces. The reactions of Quebeckers are somewhat more surprising: almost as many (95) preferred the American system as the Canadian one (116). The reason lies in the strong appeal of the presidential system in Quebec. Among those who preferred the American system, half spontaneously referred to the presidential system as the reason for their preference.

Those with a university degree stood out as much more likely to prefer the Canadian electoral system. Among the lesser educated, those choosing the Canadian system also slightly outnumbered those favouring the American one (27 percent versus 19 percent), but the majority view (55 percent) was that there is no difference. The university educated, by contrast, selected the Canadian approach in a proportion of 46 percent, against 18 percent for the American one, while only 36 percent saw no difference.

In short, when Canadians are asked to compare Canadian and American elections, they indicate a slight preference for the Canadian approach. Canadian elections are perceived to be simpler, shorter and

Table 7.6
Comparative evaluations of Canadian and U.S. electoral procedures

	Mean score
Atlantic	.60
Quebec	.53
Ontario	.59
Manitoba/Saskatchewan	.58
Alberta	.49
British Columbia	.54
Men	.55
Women	.57
Under 45	.55
45 and over	.57
Low education	.54
Medium education	.53
High education	.64
Low income	.57
Medium income	.55
High income	.56
Blue collar	.54
White collar	.56
Unionized	.55
Nonunionized	.57
English	.56
French	.53
Non-charter language	.60
Catholic	.55
Protestant	.56
Canada	.56

For the wording of the question, see table 7.1.

fairer. The main attraction of the American system is that it allows citizens to vote directly for the president. Preference for the Canadian system reaches its peak among the better educated, and its low point in Alberta.

COMPARING FEDERAL AND PROVINCIAL ELECTIONS

Finally, we asked Canadians to compare how federal and provincial elections work in Canada. Two-thirds of respondents did not see any basic difference between the two (see table 7.1). Among those who did see a difference, the great majority believed that provincial elections work better than federal elections. The reasons given refer, in various ways, to the fact that the province is a smaller unit, which makes for closer contacts between voters and politicians. The factor mentioned most often, for instance, was the fact that candidates are more accessible and better known at the provincial level. The better evaluation given to provincial elections, therefore, stems from a general sense of proximity, rather than from the perception that provincial laws are more adequate than federal legislation.

As was the case with Canada–United States comparisons, we constructed a scale with a value of 1 for those who believed provincial

Table 7.7
Comparative evaluation of federal and provincial electoral procedures

	Mean score on satisfaction
Atlantic	.53
Quebec	.52
Ontario	.56
Manitoba/Saskatchewan	.65
Alberta	.63
British Columbia	.59
Men	.57
Women	.56
Under 45	.57
45 and over	.57
Low education	.56
Medium education	.57
High education	.57
Low income	.56
Medium income	.59
High income	.56
Blue collar	.57
White collar	.57
Unionized	.57
Nonunionized	.56
English	.57
French	.56
Non-charter language	.60
Catholic	.56
Protestant	.58
Canada	.57

For the wording of the question, see table 7.1.

elections work better, 0 for those who thought federal elections are better, and 0.5 for those who saw no basic difference between the two. The average score was 0.57, indicating a preference for provincial elections.

In table 7.7, we see that respondents from the Prairies were more likely to choose provincial elections. Quebeckers, on the other hand, were less likely to believe that provincial elections work better than federal ones. However, they were simply more likely to see no difference between federal and provincial elections. This was the case for 84 percent of Quebec respondents, compared to 66 percent of respondents in the rest of Canada. It is a particularly puzzling result, since the province of Quebec has the most distinct set of campaign regulations. Paradoxically, it is in the province where federal and provincial legislation deviates the most substantially that federal and provincial elections are perceived to be the most similar. This suggests that people in Quebec use different criteria when comparing federal and provincial elections. The reason mentioned most often for preferring provincial elections in Quebec was that they are better organized and fairly run, while in the rest of the country, as we have indicated above, the greater accessibility of provincial MPs was most frequently cited.

RECAPITULATION

1. All in all, Canadians are relatively satisfied with the way federal elections presently work.
2. When asked to compare Canadian and American elections, Canadians express a slight preference for the former, which are perceived to be simpler and fairer.
3. Most Canadians see little difference in the way in which federal and provincial elections work.
4. Dissatisfaction with existing electoral procedures is greater in the western provinces.
5. Satisfaction with the electoral process increases with level of education.
6. Those whose views on specific aspects of the electoral law are consistent with the existing arrangements tend to be more satisfied, which indicates that rules do affect evaluations.
7. The issue with the greatest impact on evaluations is the electoral system itself. Those who find it unacceptable that a party can win a majority of seats without having a majority of votes are much less likely to be satisfied with the way elections work. Evaluations, however, also hinge on attitudes about electoral finances; those concerned with controls on party spending and favourable to banning group contributions tend to be less satisfied. Thus, judgements about

the electoral system play a paramount but not overwhelming role in overall evaluations.

8. Political cynicism strongly affects evaluations. The more cynical one is, the less content one is with existing arrangements. It is indeed remarkable that Canadians complain so little about electoral procedures, given their high degree of political cynicism.

9. The liberal technocrats are more satisfied with the way elections work, an indication that populist leanings serve to depress satisfaction. The collectivists, for their part, express less satisfaction, most likely because they would prefer stricter government regulation of the various aspects of the electoral process.

8

CONCLUSION

Wₑ HAVE SURVEYED Canadians' attitudes about several aspects of electoral democracy. In this concluding chapter, we want to highlight what we take to be the basic orientations of Canadian public opinion about electoral institutional arrangements. Before doing so, however, we must tackle the important issue of whether or not there is genuine public opinion on these matters.

We can test the firmness of opinions through experimentation. To the extent that people have firm views on a given topic, their responses should not be affected by the order in which the different options are presented, by the placement of the question in the questionnaire, or by slight variations in the actual wording of the question. Because we were concerned with the potential softness of opinions on some issues, we resorted to a number of experiments of this type in our survey. The results of these experiments have been presented and discussed in various parts of the text.

In table 8.1, the findings with respect to the 10 experiments used in this study are summarized. The impact of these experiments usually tends to be small. The median impact is five percentage points; it is less than 10 points in seven cases out of ten. The most important exception is, of course, the experiment concerning advertising by interest groups. We have already stressed the softness of opinions about the role of groups in election campaigns. At the same time, it should be kept in mind that this is an exception: the typical experiment moves responses by only a few percentage points. The experiments do not indicate a generalized pliability of attitudes on the issues covered in this study.

We also need to consider whether the patterns that we have observed would still hold if we sorted out those with no opinion/knowledge of electoral arrangements. The responses given to the whole set of issues examined in this study by those with and without an opinion on the acceptability of the first-past-the-post system are compared in table 8.2 (question d1). Question d1 explicitly reminded interviewees that it was quite possible (and, by implication, legitimate) not to have

Table 8.1
Impact of experiments: an overview

Topic	Description of the experiment	Impact (%)
Representation of women (d10)	The question asks whether the respondent favours or opposes requiring parties to choose as many women as men candidates. One version of the question refers to quotas, the other version does not.	4
Representation of visible minorities (d10)	The question asks whether the respondent favours or opposes requiring parties to choose more members of visible minorities candidates. One version of the question refers to quotas, the other version does not.	9
Tax credits (f3)	The question asks whether the respondent believes people who give money to parties should get a tax credit. One version mentions "to reduce the income tax they pay," the other "in the same way they are given a credit for donations to charity."	1
Advertising by interest groups (f12, f13)	The question asks whether the respondent believes interest groups should be allowed to advertise. One version presents only one argument in favour of allowing advertising, the other only one argument against allowing advertising.	43
Spending controls (f17)	The question asks the respondent to choose between two options: spending controls on parties and groups or no spending controls at all. One version refers to interest groups, the other to corporations and unions.	2
The usefulness of party ads (m13a, m13b)	The question asks the respondent to choose between two statements: one arguing that we could do without advertising, and one arguing that we need party advertising. The order in which the two statements are presented is reversed in the two versions of the question.	15
Limits on party advertising (m12a, m12b)	The question asks the respondent to choose between two statements: one arguing that we should limit spending on advertising, and one arguing that parties should be free to advertise as much as they wish. The order in which the two statements are presented is reversed in the two versions of the question.	15
Overall evaluation	The question asks how satisfied the respondent is with the way federal elections work in Canada. Half the respondents are asked the question at the beginning of the questionnaire, and half are asked near the end.	6
Comparison of U.S. and Canadian elections	The question asks whether the respondent believes elections work better in the United States or Canada. Half the respondents are asked the question at the beginning of the questionnaire, and half are asked near the end.	4

Table 8.1 (cont'd)
Impact of experiments: an overview

Topic	Description of the experiment	Impact (%)
Comparison of federal and provincial elections	The question asks whether the respondent believes federal or provincial elections work better. Half the respondents are asked the question at the beginning of the questionnaire, and half are asked near the end.	2

Note: The impact refers to the difference, in percentage points, in the distribution of responses between the two versions of the question. We use the response category that elicits the greatest difference.

an opinion on the issue. Indeed, 34 percent of those interviewed did say that they had no opinion. Should the responses of that third of the sample to questions dealing with other issues, such as electoral finances, be taken seriously? Would we get different results if we took these respondents out of the analysis?

Clearly, the differences between those with and those without an opinion on the electoral system are quite small with respect to the many other issues that we have examined here (see table 8.2). The average difference is a mere five percentage points and the difference is less than 10 percentage points in 31 instances out of 39. Taken together, tables 8.1 and 8.2 strongly suggest that most Canadians have relatively firm views about how representative democracy should work, at least in its broad outlines. There is no evidence for the possibility that respondents might be answering questions on these issues more or less randomly (which would have indicated a lack of firm opinions).

On many issues, Canadians are split on what they consider to be the most appropriate way to run elections. There are, however, a few instances where a clear majority emerges in support of a given option. It is, we believe, interesting to highlight those options that do get wide approval. The analyses presented in chapters 4 through 6 indicate that a strong majority of Canadians believe that:

1. there should be strict limits on campaign spending;
2. parties should be required to reveal their sources of financing;
3. the government should not reimburse any of the money spent by parties and candidates during an election campaign;
4. MPs who want to change party affiliation between elections should be required to resign their seat in Parliament; and
5. it should be up to parties to decide how to choose their leaders.

Table 8.2

Comparing the responses of those with and without an opinion on the electoral system

(percentages)

Question		With an opinion	Without an opinion	Difference
E1	Very or somewhat satisfied	64	66	2
E3	Where elections work better	34	25	9
E5	Provincial elections work better	21	23	2
F1	Support spending limits	93	94	1
F2	Support ceilings	62	54	8
F2b	Support ceilings of $1 000 or less	70	71	1
F3	Support tax credits	44	52	8
F4	Support contributions by corporations	60	65	5
F5	Support contributions by unions	48	52	4
F6	Support contributions by groups	61	63	2
F7	Groups need approval	89	94	5
F8	Support disclosure	82	73	9
F10	Support reimbursement	33	44	11
F11	Reimbursement for all	40	48	8
F12	Support group advertising	76	75	1
F13	Support ban on group advertising	68	70	2
F14	Support advertising by corporations	44	48	4
F15	Support advertising by unions	42	43	1
F17	Support controls	91	88	3
F21	Believe in the feasibility of controls	45	36	9
M1	Media = accurate	73	83	10
M2	Media = fair	60	70	10
M3	Too little attention to smaller parties	56	57	1
M5	Debates very or somewhat useful	59	59	0
M6	Support compulsory debates	55	65	10
M7	All leaders in debates	51	57	6
M8	Debates allow to compare	64	75	11
M9	Debates = image	54	43	11
M12a	Support limit on advertising	72	64	8
M12b	Support limit on advertising	85	83	2
M13a	Need advertising	75	76	1
M13b	Need advertising	60	62	2
D5	Support two votes	74	80	6
D6	Support term limits	37	42	5
D7a	Allow MPs to change parties	30	28	2
D7	MPs follow public interest	33	43	10
D8	Representation = serious problem	36	35	1
D9	Representation = better government	37	36	1
D10	Support quotas	38	53	15

We should note that there is another option that does get wide approval and that does not appear on our short list: this is the idea that there should be two votes – one to choose the local MP and another to choose a party. This idea strikes a responsive chord among those who favour a more populist style of politics. We wonder, however, about the firmness of views on this question. This issue has not been publicly debated and Canadians are unlikely to be aware of some of its ramifications. Ideally, we would have tested the firmness of opinion by presenting the opposing sides of the argument to random halves of our sample. The constraints of questionnaire length, however, prevented us from probing more deeply. What we have uncovered here is simply the face appeal of the idea.

On other issues, opinions are more or less evenly split. There is, therefore, no clear signal as to what the Canadian public might desire, for the very simple reason that the public is divided. Among these issues, a particularly important and sensitive one concerns the role of groups in election campaigns. We have seen that no clear majority emerges for allowing or not allowing interest groups, corporations and unions to give money and/or advertise. We have also stressed the extent to which opinions on these matters are pliable. There are two points, however, on which Canadians overwhelmingly agree. First, groups should be required to receive formal approval from their members (shareholders, in the case of corporations) before contributing to a party. Second, if they had to choose between having spending controls on parties and groups or no controls at all, Canadians are unequivocal: they want controls. The first finding, in particular, reveals strong support for some regulation of group involvement in election campaigns.

We indicated in the introduction that one of our objectives was to ascertain the degree of correspondence between public opinion and the current electoral law. Table 8.3 indicates the issues where we find the majority to be in agreement with existing rules and those where there is some discrepancy. The table shows that the correspondence is not close, cases of disagreement being as numerous as cases of agreement. The picture is only a little more encouraging if we restrict our attention to those issues where there is a clear majority. Among the five propositions listed above, three are instances in which public opinion is consistent with the electoral law and two are cases where it is not. All in all, then, the evidence suggests that public opinion has had little impact on electoral law.

The fact that most Canadians, nonetheless, feel relatively satisfied with the way elections work in Canada may seem paradoxical. If there is little correspondence between existing rules and majority preferences, how is it that dissatisfaction is not greater?

Table 8.3
Correspondence between public opinion and public policy

Majority agrees with existing policy	Majority disagrees with existing policy
Spending controls	Ceilings on contributions
Group contributions	Tax credits
Disclosure of contributions	Public funding
No term limits	Mandatory debates
No quotas	Electoral system
No regulation of party leadership selection	MPs' party switching

Note: We have excluded issues with respect to which opinions seem particularly pliable; that is, those on group advertising and the idea of having two votes.

One possible explanation is that even though there is little congruence, overall, between public opinion and the electoral law, there is correspondence on those issues that matter the most, and that is why most Canadians express relative satisfaction. We cannot provide a full test of that hypothesis since we do not know what importance respondents attached to the various issues. We do know, however, which issues have the greatest impact on overall evaluations. These are first and foremost the electoral process, spending limits and group contributions. The first constitutes an instance of discrepancy between public opinion and the law, and the latter two are cases of correspondence. That correspondence has to be qualified, however. As we showed in Chapter 7, those who support spending controls are *less* satisfied, an indication that they would want stricter controls. Likewise, even the majority that is favourable to group contributions believes that groups should get formal approval from their members, a point about which the existing law is silent. All in all, then, there is no evidence of greater congruence between public opinion and public policy on the most important issues.

In this respect, it may be useful to dwell on how reactions to the existing electoral system relate to overall evaluations. As we have indicated, opinions as to whether it is acceptable for a party to win a majority of seats without having a majority of votes tend to depress satisfaction, since more Canadians find it unacceptable than acceptable. Yet, it should be kept in mind that fully 34 percent of our respondents did not have an opinion on the issue. Furthermore, among those who found the system unacceptable, only a minority said it is completely unacceptable. This group, which felt strongly and negatively about the plurality rule, represented only 8 percent of the total sample.

We believe that the relative satisfaction with the present electoral process may be a reflection of the absence of any appealing alternative option. On the one hand, Canadians value the fact that they can choose their government. Seventy-six percent believed that things would be worse if we stopped having elections; only 3 percent said they would be better (question tst7). On the other hand, elections do not seem to work any better elsewhere, or at least in the United States. There does not seem to be any compelling reason for complaint.

There is thus presently no serious problem with respect to the legitimacy of electoral procedures. If that were to be the determining factor in deciding what kind of electoral reform to embark upon, then we would have to conclude that substantial reform does not appear to be imperative. There is simply no issue where a strong majority disagrees with the existing law and that exerts a significant impact on overall evaluations. There is no specific reform that, on the basis of the survey evidence analysed in this study, appears likely to enhance substantially the degree of satisfaction with the electoral process.

Of course, there are some options that our survey indicates could possibly buttress the perceived legitimacy of the process. The first and most obvious possibility is some type of proportional representation. The survey indicates potential sympathy for proportional representation, but it is a very complex issue that deserves a much more thorough analysis than can be accomplished within the confines of this study. A second option would be to impose stricter spending controls, although the problem with this option is one of feasibility, given the spiralling costs of campaigns.

In terms of the perceived legitimacy of the process, then, the overall message is that things are basically satisfactory and there is no imperative need for reform. On a broader level, however, things are not so satisfactory. Although Canadians are generally satisfied with the process, they do not like the outcome: they simply do not have a great deal of confidence in those whom they elect.

This raises another important question: would it be possible to improve public confidence in politicians through electoral reform? We should stress at the outset that we can only offer tentative answers. Political cynicism stems from many factors and it is extremely difficult to isolate the specific impact of electoral procedures. We saw in Chapter 3 that political cynicism has increased over time in Canada. It seems very unlikely that the increase can be imputed to electoral arrangements, which have remained basically unchanged in the 1980s. There are clearly other factors at work – the economy, constitutional conflicts and strong discontent with the Conservative government – that must be kept in mind.

Only a comparative study across systems with different institutions could address the question of the impact of electoral arrangements in a satisfactory way. As we noted in Chapter 3, the degree of political cynicism in Canada seems similar to that found in the United States, but is generally greater than that in Europe. The question is whether electoral arrangements may be responsible for these variations. Unfortunately, the evidence on this is scarce. A study by Miller and Listhaug (1990), however, is suggestive. They examine trends in political cynicism in Norway, Sweden and the United States over the period 1964–86 and show that confidence declined in the three countries; it later recovered in Norway, while it continued to plummet in Sweden and the United States. They argue that political cynicism receded in Norway because the creation of new parties in the early 1970s provided the disaffected with a means of representation, while in the more rigid Swedish and American party systems dissatisfaction with the existing parties was progressively transformed into general cynicism. The analysis rests on a very limited comparison and is only indicative. It does suggest, however, that cynicism is likely to rise when voters who are deeply dissatisfied with a given party perceive no viable alternative.

Some findings in our survey are consistent with the view that Canadians are cynical about politicians in part because they feel their choices are too limited. A majority believes that the media should pay more attention to smaller parties and that leaders of all parties should be allowed to participate in the televised debates. It should be noted, however, that such positive predispositions toward smaller parties do not extend to a willingness to make public funding available to all parties. Nevertheless, the more positively one feels about smaller parties, the more cynical one tends to be (data not shown), a pattern that is consistent with Miller and Listhaug's (1990) interpretation.

This suggests that one way to fight political cynicism would be to facilitate the entry of new parties. On this criterion, the Canadian system is found wanting: 81 percent said it is difficult for new parties to have candidates elected (question p3). Two types of institutional arrangements would make it easier for new parties to form and grow. The first consists of switching from the simple plurality system to either proportional representation or a majority system. (For an estimation of the effect of electoral systems on the number of parties, see Blais and Carty 1991.) The second is to make all parties and candidates eligible for public funding, a proposition that most Canadians oppose but that comparative experience suggests could enhance confidence in the political system.

The comparative perspective can also be applied within Canada. The province of Quebec has adopted the strictest set of regulations with respect to electoral finances; it is only in that province, for instance, that group contributions are banned. We may, therefore, ask what the Quebec experience suggests to be some of the consequences of greater regulation of campaign finances. The findings of our survey indicate that the regulatory approach is well received in Quebec. Quebeckers are more favourable to public funding as well as to controls on party and group spending. We also showed in Chapter 4 that they are more willing to support changes to current arrangements – to regulate the way parties choose their leaders, for instance. It is particularly interesting, in this respect, that Quebeckers (together with Ontarians) are among the most optimistic about the feasibility of controlling campaign finances.

Greater support for regulation in Quebec could reflect the fact that Quebeckers are simply more favourable to state intervention in general, or it could stem from their positive evaluation of the Quebec legislation. The first interpretation is not borne out by the finding in Chapter 2, that Quebeckers are not more likely to be members of our two collectivist groups. While there is no way that this can be demonstrated with the existing data, it is at least possible, then, that direct experience with a regulatory approach has convinced Quebeckers that the whole electoral process ought to be closely regulated. At the very least, the Quebec experience is not considered to be a failure. In fact, there are indications that it may be viewed as a major success.

We also found that political cynicism is lower in Quebec than in the rest of the country. Could it be that a stricter set of regulations contributes to building some confidence in the political system? Again, there is no way to tell with any degree of certainty. As we noted, the lesser cynicism in Quebec may be attributed, at least in part, to the fact that the prime minister comes from that province. Indeed, support for the Conservative party is higher in Quebec. Even when we control for vote intention, however, cynicism remains lower in Quebec (data not shown). Again, we cannot rule out the possibility that stricter electoral laws are a contributing factor.

The Quebec experience, therefore, suggests that perhaps the adoption of tighter controls on campaign finances could contribute to a reduction in the level of political cynicism in Canada. As in the case of cross-national comparisons, we are on shaky ground, and the most that can be claimed is that the evidence is not inconsistent with such a hypothesis.

In short, our study finds no evidence of strong discontent with existing electoral arrangements. From that perspective, there does not seem to be an urgent need for a major overhaul of the electoral law. There is, however, pervasive frustration with the outcome of the electoral process; many Canadians have lost confidence in their elected representatives. The comparative perspective, within and outside Canada, suggests that stricter regulation of electoral finances, and a party system that posed fewer barriers to new parties, might help to restore some degree of public confidence.

APPENDIX A

SAMPLE DESIGN AND DATA COLLECTION PROCEDURES

This appendix is an edited excerpt from the technical documentation prepared by the Institute for Social Research (ISR). It provides details on the sampling design and data collection procedures used in the survey, as well as a listing of the variables used in the analysis, the categories developed in coding the open-ended questions and a copy of the survey instrument, including the exact wording in French and English of all questions and the order in which they were asked. The complete technical ISR report can be obtained from the Institute for Social Research, York University, 4700 Keele Street, North York, Ontario M3J 1P3. Other inquiries about the data set should also be addressed to the ISR. The report should be cited as follows:

Northrup, David, and Anne Oram. 1991. *A Survey of Attitudes About Electoral Reform: A Study for the Royal Commission on Electoral Reform and Party Financing – Technical Documentation.* Toronto: York University, Institute for Social Research.

STUDY DESCRIPTION

The Survey of Attitudes About Electoral Reform was conducted for the Royal Commission on Electoral Reform and Party Financing under the direction of Professors André Blais and Elisabeth Gidengil at the Institute for Social Research, York University, between August and December 1990. Almost 2 950 thirty-minute interviews were completed with a random sample of Canadians between 13 September and 4 November.

Random digit dialling (RDD) procedures were utilized to select the telephone numbers for the survey. All interviewing was completed (in English and French) from ISR's centralized telephone facilities using Computer Assisted Telephone Interviewing (CATI) techniques. The Institute uses software from the Computer-Assisted Survey Methods Program (CSM) at the University of California, Berkeley.

The questionnaire included about 130 items on election interest, evaluation of the way elections and campaigns work, election spending, third-party advertising during elections, the role of the media and televised debates, the way the system of government and political parties work, knowledge questions about party leaders, values and a battery of socio-demographic items.

CATI was utilized for several experiments in question wording and order in the Survey of Attitudes About Electoral Reform. There were different versions of questions dealing with the implications of tax credits for money given to political parties, election advertising by interest groups, election spending controls and representation in the House of Commons. Question order experiments included the placement of questions designed to determine an overall evaluation of the way elections work in Canada either at the beginning of or midway in the survey, the order in which arguments about third-party spending were advanced and the order of questions dealing with satisfaction and contact with elected representatives.

SAMPLE DESIGN

The sample for the Survey of Attitudes About Electoral Reform was designed to represent the adult population (18 years of age or older) that resides in one of the 10 Canadian provinces and that are Canadian citizens, speak one of the official languages (English or French) and reside in private homes (residents of old age homes, group homes, educational and penal institutions were excluded). Because the mode of data collection for the survey was telephone, the 1.8 percent of Canadian households without a telephone were eliminated from the sample population (Canada, Statistics Canada 1985).

Selection of Households

A two-stage probability selection process was utilized to select respondents for the survey. The first stage was the contact of households by the random selection of residential telephone numbers. A complete listing of all residential telephone numbers in Canada would have been the appropriate sampling frame for the survey; unfortunately, such a listing does not exist.

Telephone books are not an acceptable surrogate. Unlisted numbers and numbers for people who have recently moved are not included. People who do not have their name in the telephone book are not a random subset of the population (Tremblay and Hofmann 1983). Sampling from telephone books would systematically exclude these people.

Use of random digit dialling for selecting telephone numbers gives all households, not just those listed in telephone directories, an equal and known probability of selection. All telephone numbers in Canada consist of a three-digit area code, a three-digit central office code (the first three digits of the seven-digit telephone number) and a suffix (the last four digits of a telephone number). It is possible to determine area codes, central office codes and suffixes in use by referring to telephone and city directories. With this knowledge, it is possible to construct a listing of all possible numbers in Canada. A computer is then used to generate a random sample of telephone numbers from this listing.

Because such a sample will include numbers that are nonresidential or are not in service, and because an interview will not be completed in every household that is selected for a study (some households will refuse to be interviewed and some households will not contain an eligible respondent), the sample selected must be in excess of the desired number of completions. Based on information from Statistics Canada and previous work completed at ISR, a projection of the required sample size could be calculated.

Selection of Respondent

The second stage of sample selection was random selection of an adult household member as the respondent. This stage of sample selection was completed by selecting the household member, 18 years of age or older, who had the most recent birthday and was a Canadian citizen. (A discussion of the use of the most recent birthday as the method of selecting respondents can be found in O'Rourke and Blair 1983.)

Sample Size, Sample Release and Data Collection

Given the target number of 2 800 completed interviews, it was necessary to draw a sample of approximately 9 330 telephone numbers. This number was calculated as follows: 9 330 x .50 [proportion of numbers predicted to be eligible households] x .60 [proportion of households willing to participate] = 2 800.

Because of the proportion of numbers that are eligible households and, more importantly, because the response rate may vary for each survey, it is appropriate to release less than the total sample at the beginning of data collection. Once data collection is about half to three-quarters completed, the proportion of sample numbers that are eligible households and the response rate can be predicted and the total sample release can be adjusted. Once it became apparent that the response rate was going to exceed the prediction of 60 percent, a proportion of the sample was not released. The total number of telephone numbers released for interviewing was 8 638.

It should be noted that the sample comprised 43 replicates of 200 telephone numbers. Because each replicate is an independent sample of all telephone numbers with the appropriate distribution of numbers for each province, it is possible to adjust the size of the sample without negatively affecting the representativeness of the sample.

Regional Sample Distribution

Minimal sample sizes were established for each region: 400 in the Atlantic provinces (distributed proportional to the population of the four provinces); 600 in Quebec; 600 in Ontario; 400 in Manitoba and Saskatchewan (distributed proportional to the population of the two provinces); 400 in Alberta; and 400 in British Columbia. With the exception of Nova Scotia and New Brunswick, the number of completions obtained approximates the number of completions required. In making comparisons between the Atlantic provinces and the rest of Canada, appropriate weights were utilized.

Weighting Description

Weights, designed to adjust for unequal probabilities of selection within households and the disproportionate sample allocation among the provinces, were attached to the data set.

The probability of an adult member of the household being selected for an interview varied inversely with the number of people living in that household (in a single-adult household there is a 100 percent chance of selection and in a three-adult household there is only a 33 percent chance of selection). As a result, it is possible that the data are biased, because one-person households are over-represented in the sample. Some practitioners of survey research weight in order to compensate for the unequal probabilities of selection – one-adult house-holds are given a weight of one, two-adult households a weight of two, three-adult households a weight of three, etc.

DATA COLLECTION PROCEDURES AND RESPONSE RATES

The telephone interviewing was conducted from ISR's centralized CATI facility. Each supervisory station is equipped with a video display terminal that repro-duces an image of the interviewer's screen and a ROLM CBX telephone commu-nications system. This allows supervisors to monitor an interviewer's calls and visually verify that the interviewer has recorded the respondent's answer correctly.

Data Collection Procedures

In Quebec the initial call was always made by a French-speaking interviewer. The first call attempt for the rest of the country was made in English. Whenever a household or respondent indicated that he or she wished to be interviewed in the other language, an interviewer with the appropriate language skills called back.

In the most extreme case, 37 calls were made to complete the interview. However, typically only a small number of calls were required to complete each interview. About three-quarters of the completions required five or fewer call attempts. All telephone numbers received a minimum of 12 call attempts before the fieldwork was completed, and to maximize the likelihood of finding respondents at home, calls were scheduled during the day, evening and weekend.

All households that refused to participate in the survey were contacted a second time; approximately 30 percent of the first refusals (467 respondents or 16 percent of all interviews) completed the interview on the second or subse-quent contact after the initial refusal.

Whether the respondent refused during the initial contact, the number of call attempts, the number of times the telephone was answered and other variables that describe the data collection process are included as part of the data set.

Response Rate

There are numerous ways to calculate response rates in survey research (Groves 1989; Groves and Lyberg 1988; Frey 1983; Dillman 1978). The method used in this project was conservative; most other ways of calculating response rate would produce inflated values. The response rate was defined as the number of completed interviews divided by the estimated number of eligible households times 100 percent.

A response rate of 65 percent was obtained, which compares favourably to that obtained in other national telephone surveys conducted at ISR. The National Election Survey had a final response rate of 57 percent and the National Survey of Civil Liberties had a rate of 64 percent (Northrup 1989). The relatively high response rate for this survey probably results from three factors: (1) the sponsorship of the survey by a Royal Commission; (2) the desire of Canadians to make their views known on electoral reform (interviewers told respondents that this was their chance to have a say in the way elections work in Canada and this apparently struck a chord with many people who were feeling a lack of confidence in government in the aftermath of the Meech Lake debate); (3) an unusually high level of refusal conversions.

Details on the calculation of the response rate are as follows. Of the 8 638 telephone numbers included in the sample, 4 361 were eligible households. Ineligible households (respondent was unable to speak either English or French, or was not healthy enough to complete the interview; nonresidential and not in service numbers, etc.) accounted for 3 961 of the telephone numbers. It was not possible to determine the eligibility status for 316 of the sample telephone numbers. For response rate calculations, it was assumed that the proportion of these 316 numbers that were household numbers was the same as it was in the rest of the sample. This proportion is called the "household eligibility rate."

Variation in response rates between provinces was pronounced but not unexpected. Geographical variation in response rates is typical of studies conducted at ISR. Considerable variation in response rates has been found for provincial telephone surveys (Bates 1984), national telephone surveys (Northrup 1989; Bryant et al. 1990) and national mail surveys (Northrup 1985). Geographical variation in response rates has also been noted by American survey researchers (Dunkleberg and Day 1973; Fitzgerald and Fuller 1982; Steech 1981). Most authors have noted that response rates are lower in larger urban areas. Not surprisingly, the response rate was higher than average in three of the four Atlantic provinces and Alberta and Saskatchewan, the provinces with smaller proportions of their population residing in major urban centres; and lowest in Ontario, Quebec and British Columbia, the provinces with the larger proportion of their population residing in major urban centres.

CATI Experiments Utilizing Random Numbers

CATI facilities were used to vary item wording and order in the Survey of Attitudes About Electoral Reform. An example of a wording experiment is instructive. There were two versions of the tax implications of giving money to political parties (f3). Each version of the item is presented below.

First version:
> Should people who give money to political parties get a tax credit in the same way they are given a credit for donations to charity?

Second version:
> Should people who give money to political parties get a tax credit to reduce the income tax they pay?

The responses for the item – yes; no; don't know; and refused – were the same in both versions of the item.

Which version of the item the respondent was given depended on the value of random number 2 (identified in the data set as *rn*2). In the example above, *rn*2 had a value of "0" or "1." During the conduct of the interview CATI would, on the basis of the value of *rn*2, present the interviewer with the appropriate version of the question for the respondent (for example, if *rn*2 was "0" then the interviewer read the first version of the item to the respondent). The values for each random number, associated with each of the CATI experiments, were assigned to each telephone number in the sample before the interviewing commenced. (Because not all telephone numbers in the sample resulted in a completed interview, the proportions of the sample receiving each version of the item may not be identical.)

The following items made use of random numbers for wording experiments: f3, f12, f13, f17, d8, d9, d10, v9. The following items incorporated order experiments: the block of questions e1 to e6, m12 and m13, and the block of items d12 to d17.

Examination of the frequency distribution for items containing experiments should be informed by the distribution for each version of the item. The variable label for each item containing wording experiments includes the random number. Tabulation of the item by the random number (a cross-tabulation) will detail the marginal distribution to each version of the experimental item.

APPENDIX B

ATTITUDES ABOUT ELECTORAL REFORM

Note: For questions with two versions, each version was asked of half the sample. See the section "CATI Experiments Utilizing Random Numbers" in appendix A for details.

Introductory Questions

Record respondent's gender.

- ❏ male
- ❏ female
- ❏ not sure yet

Section E: Evaluation

We would like to know how you feel about the way federal elections work in Canada, who has the right to vote, what is allowed in election campaigns, how to vote and how candidates get elected.

e1.   On the whole, are you *very* satisfied, *somewhat* satisfied, *not very* satisfied or *not at all* satisfied with the way federal elections work in Canada, or *don't you have an opinion on this?*

- ❏ very satisfied
- ❏ somewhat satisfied
- ❏ not very satisfied
- ❏ not at all satisfied
- ❏ don't have an opinion on this
- ❏ refused

e2.   What do you think should be changed to have a better system for federal elections?

- ❏ mentions information

    specify_____

- ❏ no mention
- ❏ don't know
- ❏ refused

e3.   In general, would you say elections work better in the *United States*, work better in *Canada*, or *neither* works better than the other?

❏ work better in the United States

❏ work better in Canada

❏ neither works better

❏ don't know

❏ refused

e4.   In what way do they work better in [either United States or Canada, depending on previous answer]?

❏ mentions information

specify_____

❏ no mention

❏ don't know

❏ refused

e5.   How about federal and provincial elections in [respondent's province]?

Which would you say work better: *federal* elections, *provincial* elections, or *neither* works better?

❏ federal elections

❏ provincial elections

❏ neither works better

❏ don't know

❏ refused

e6.   In what way do [either federal or provincial elections, depending on previous answer] work better?

❏ mentions information

specify _____

❏ no mention

❏ don't know

❏ refused

Section F: Finances

f1.   One of the issues we would like to talk to you about is campaign spending. Do you think that political parties should be allowed to *spend as much as they want* in an election campaign *or* should there *be a limit* on what they can spend?

❏ as much as they want

❏ there should be a limit

❏ don't know

❏ refused

f2. What about people who give money to political parties? Do you think people should be allowed to *give as much money as they want* to a political party *or* do you think the *amount should be limited?*

❏ as much as they want

❏ should be limited

❏ don't know

❏ refused

f2b. What do you think the limit should be on how much a person can give to a party? Should it be one hundred dollars, five hundred, one thousand, five thousand, ten thousand dollars, or more than ten thousand dollars?

❏ one hundred dollars

❏ five hundred dollars

❏ one thousand dollars

❏ five thousand dollars

❏ ten thousand dollars

❏ more than ten thousand dollars

❏ other

specify_____

❏ don't know

❏ refused

f3. (version 1)

Should people who give money to political parties get a tax credit in the same way they are given a credit for donations to charity?

❏ yes

❏ no

❏ don't know

❏ refused

f3. (version 2)

Should people who give money to political parties get a tax credit to reduce the income tax they pay?

❏ yes

❏ no

❐ don't know

❐ refused

f4.   Should the following organizations have the right or *not* have the right to give money to political parties?

First, what about corporations? (Should *corporations* have the right or *not* have the right to give money to political parties?)

❐ yes, have the right

❐ no, not have the right

❐ don't know

❐ refused

f5.   Unions? (Should *unions* have the right or *not* have the right to give money to political parties?)

❐ yes, have the right

❐ no, not have the right

❐ don't know

❐ refused

f6.   And interest groups? (Should *interest groups* have the right or *not* have the right to give money to political parties?)

❐ yes, have the right

❐ no, not have the right

❐ don't know

❐ refused

f7. (version 1)

Should corporations be required to get approval from their shareholders before giving money to a political party?

❐ yes

❐ no

❐ don't know

❐ refused

f7. (version 2)

Should unions be required to get approval from their members before giving money to a political party?

❐ yes

❐ no

❏ don't know

❏ refused

f8.   Do you think political parties *should* be required or *not* be required to reveal who gives them money?

❏ yes, should be required

❏ no, should *not* be required

❏ don't know

❏ refused

f9.   Is there *still* a need for limits on political party spending if we know where the money is coming from?

❏ yes

❏ no

❏ don't know

❏ refused

f10.   Do you think the government should reimburse *all*, *some*, or *none* of the money spent by parties and candidates during an election campaign?

❏ all

❏ some

❏ none

❏ don't know

❏ refused

f11. (version 1)

Do you think that *all* political parties and candidates should get reimbursed or *only those* who get at least [5, 10 or 20 percent – respondents were asked about one of the three percentages] of the vote?

❏ all

❏ only those who get [5, 10 or 20 percent]

❏ don't know

❏ refused

f11. (version 2)

Do you think that *all* political parties and candidates should get some reimbursement or *only those* who get at least [5, 10 or 20 percent] of the vote?

❐ all

❐ only those who get [5, 10 or 20 percent]

❐ don't know

❐ refused

f12. Now what about election advertising by interest groups? Some say interest groups *should* be allowed to advertise to promote their positions on the election issues because that is their right in a democracy. *Basically*, do you *agree* or *disagree* with this view?

❐ basically agree

❐ basically disagree

❐ don't know

❐ refused

f13. Now what about election advertising by interest groups? Some say interest groups *should not* be allowed to advertise to promote their positions during campaigns, otherwise groups with lots of money will have too much influence on the election. *Basically*, do you *agree* or *disagree* with this view?

❐ basically agree

❐ basically disagree

❐ don't know

❐ refused

f14. What about *corporations*: should they be allowed to advertise to promote their positions during election campaigns?

❐ yes

❐ no

❐ don't know

❐ refused

f15. And unions? (Should *unions* be allowed to advertise to promote their positions during election campaigns?)

❐ yes

❐ no

❐ don't know

❐ refused

f17. (version 1)

If you had to choose between the following two options, which would you choose: having spending controls on political parties *and* interest groups, *or* having no spending controls at all?

❐ controls

❐ no controls

❐ don't know

❐ refused

f17. (version 2)

If you had to choose between the following two options, which would you choose: having spending controls on political parties *and* corporations and unions, *or* having no spending controls at all?

❐ controls

❐ no controls

❐ don't know

❐ refused

f18. Now we would like to have your views about money and elections. *Basically*, do you *agree* or *disagree* with each of the following statements.

Anybody who gives money to a political party expects something in return, like a job or a contract.

(*Basically*, do you *agree* or *disagree?*)

❐ basically agree

❐ basically disagree

❐ don't know

❐ refused

f19. People with money have a lot of influence over the government.

(*Basically*, do you *agree* or *disagree?*)

❐ basically agree

❐ basically disagree

❐ don't know

❐ refused

f20.   The party that spends the most during a campaign is almost sure to win the election.

(*Basically*, do you *agree* or *disagree?*)

☐ basically agree

☐ basically disagree

☐ don't know

☐ refused

f21.   It is impossible to really control what political parties receive and spend in an election.

(*Basically*, do you *agree* or *disagree?*)

☐ basically agree

☐ basically disagree

☐ don't know

☐ refused

f22.   [If basically agree (f21):] Then would you say trying to control contributions and spending is just a waste of time and energy *or* is it still worth trying?

☐ waste of time and energy

☐ still worth trying

☐ don't know

☐ refused

Section M: Media and Campaign

m1.   Now some questions about campaigns and the media.

How good a job do you feel the media do in accurately reporting on federal election campaigns? Do they do a *very good* job, a *good* job, a *poor* job, or a *very poor* job?

☐ very good

☐ good

☐ poor

☐ very poor

☐ don't know

☐ refused

m2.   How good a job do you feel the media do in treating all the federal political parties fairly? Do they do a *very good* job, a *good* job, a *poor* job, or a *very poor* job?

☐ very good

☐ good

❐ poor

❐ very poor

❐ don't know

❐ refused

m3. **What about small parties that don't win many votes? Do the media pay them *too much*, *too little*, or *about the right amount* of attention?**

❐ too much

❐ too little

❐ about the right amount

❐ don't know

❐ refused

m4. **In the last two federal election campaigns, in 1984 and 1988, there were leaders debates on TV. Did you happen to watch any of them?**

❐ yes

❐ no

❐ don't know

❐ refused

m5. **[If yes (m4):] In deciding how to vote, did you find these debates *very* useful, *somewhat* useful, *not very* useful, or *not useful at all*?**

❐ very useful

❐ somewhat useful

❐ not very useful

❐ not useful at all

❐ don't know

❐ refused

m6a. **Do you think the law should require party leaders to participate in a televised debate at each election?**

❐ yes

❐ no

❐ don't know

❐ refused

m6. **Who do you think should organize the debates: the political parties, the TV stations, or the chief electoral officer?**

❐ political parties

❐ TV stations

❑ chief electoral officer

❑ combination of above

❑ don't know

❑ refused

m7. As you may know, in federal elections there are usually about 10 registered parties. Who do you think should participate in the debates: the leaders of the *three major* parties, the leaders of all *parties with members in Parliament,* or the leaders of *all 10 registered parties?*

❑ leaders of *three major* parties

❑ leaders of all *parties with members in Parliament*

❑ leaders of *all 10 registered parties*

❑ combination of above

❑ don't know

❑ refused

m8. *Basically,* do you *agree* or *disagree* with the following statement?

Debates give voters *the best* opportunity to compare the leaders' positions on the election issues.

(*Basically,* do you *agree* or *disagree?*)

❑ basically agree

❑ basically disagree

❑ don't know

❑ refused

m9. In your opinion, who usually wins the televised debates: the leader with the *best ideas or* the leader with the *most attractive image?*

❑ the best ideas

❑ the most attractive image

❑ don't know

❑ refused

m12a. Which of the following two statements comes closer to your own opinion?

We should limit spending on party advertising, otherwise parties with more money will have an unfair advantage.

or

Freedom of speech is such a fundamental right that parties should be allowed to advertise as much as they wish.

- ❐ limit spending
- ❐ freedom of speech
- ❐ don't know
- ❐ refused

m13a. And which of the following two statements:

We could do without party advertising, because it doesn't really inform us about what parties stand for.

or

We need party advertising because it is the only way that parties can get their message directly to the voter.

- ❐ do without advertising
- ❐ need advertising
- ❐ don't know
- ❐ refused

m12b. Which of the following two statements comes closer to your own opinion?

Freedom of speech is such a fundamental right that parties should be allowed to advertise as much as they wish.

or

We should limit spending on party advertising, otherwise parties with more money will have an unfair advantage.

- ❐ freedom of speech
- ❐ limit spending
- ❐ don't know
- ❐ refused

m13b. And which of the following two statements:

We need party advertising because it is the only way that parties can get their message directly to the voters.

or

We could do without party advertising, because it doesn't really inform us about what parties stand for.

- ❐ need advertising
- ❐ do without advertising

❏ don't know

❏ refused

Section D: Democracy

d1. Now we would like to get your views on the electoral system.

Under our present system, a party can win a majority of seats and form the government without winning a majority of votes. Do you find this *acceptable* or *unacceptable*, or *don't you have an opinion* on this?

❏ acceptable

❏ unacceptable

❏ don't have an opinion

❏ refused

d2. [If acceptable (d1):] Would you say it is *completely* or *somewhat* acceptable?

❏ completely acceptable

❏ somewhat acceptable

❏ don't know

❏ refused

d3. [If unacceptable (d1):] Would you say it is *completely* or *somewhat* unacceptable?

❏ completely unacceptable

❏ somewhat unacceptable

❏ don't know

❏ refused

d5. How about a system where you would have *two* votes, *one* to choose your local MP and *one* to choose which party forms the government? Would you be in *favour* of or *opposed* to such a system?

❏ in favour

❏ opposed

❏ don't know

❏ refused

d6. Some say that MPs who have been in Parliament for more than 12 years should not be allowed to run for Parliament again. Do you think this is a *good* idea, or a *poor* idea, or *don't you have an opinion* on this?

❏ good idea

❏ poor idea

❑ agree with the idea, but not 12 years

❑ don't have an opinion on this

❑ refused

d7a. What about MPs who want to change their party between elections: should they be *allowed to change* parties or should they be *required to resign* their seat in Parliament?

❑ allowed to change parties

❑ required to resign

❑ don't know

❑ refused

d7. When MPs vote on a controversial issue in Parliament such as the death penalty, should they follow what *they believe* to be *the public interest* or should they follow *the views of the people in their riding?*

❑ what they believe to be the public interest

❑ the views of the people in their riding

❑ don't know

❑ refused

d8. (version 1)

As you may know, there are many more men than women in the House of Commons. In your view is this a *very serious* problem, a *serious* problem, *not a very serious* problem, or *not a problem* at all?

❑ very serious problem

❑ serious problem

❑ not a very serious problem

❑ not a problem

❑ don't know

❑ refused

d8. (version 2)

As you may know, there are very few members of visible minorities in the House of Commons. In your view is this a *very serious* problem, a *serious* problem, *not a very serious* problem, or *not a problem* at all?

❑ very serious problem

❑ serious problem

❑ not a very serious problem

❑ not a problem

❑ don't know

❑ refused

d9. (version 1)

If there were as many women as men in the House of Commons, do you think we would have *much better* government, *better, worse* or *much worse* government, or do you think it *wouldn't really make a difference?*

❑ much better

❑ better

❑ worse

❑ much worse

❑ wouldn't really make a difference

❑ don't know

❑ refused

d9. (version 2)

If there were more members of visible minorities in the House of Commons, do you think we would have *much better* government, *better, worse* or *much worse* government, or do you think it *wouldn't really make a difference?*

❑ much better

❑ better

❑ worse

❑ much worse

❑ wouldn't really make a difference

❑ don't know

❑ refused

d10. (version 1)

Would you *favour* or *oppose* quotas requiring the parties to choose as many female as male candidates?

❑ favour

❑ oppose

❑ don't know

❑ refused

d10. (version 2)

> Would you *favour* or *oppose* quotas requiring the parties to choose more members of visible minorities as candidates?

> ❏ favour

> ❏ oppose

> ❏ don't know

> ❏ refused

d11. How strongly do you feel about this? *Very* strongly, *fairly* strongly, or *not very* strongly?

> ❏ very strongly

> ❏ fairly strongly

> ❏ not very strongly

> ❏ don't know

> ❏ refused

d12a. Now some questions about your political representatives.

> How good a job would you say your *federal* MP does of *keeping in touch* with the people in your riding: a *very good* job, a *good* job, a *poor* job, a *very poor* job, or *don't you have an opinion?*

> ❏ very good

> ❏ good

> ❏ poor

> ❏ very poor

> ❏ don't have an opinion

> ❏ refused

d13a. Have you ever contacted your present *federal* MP?

> ❏ yes

> ❏ no

> ❏ don't know

> ❏ refused

d14a. [If yes (d13a):] How satisfied were you with the contact: *very* satisfied, *somewhat* satisfied, *not very* satisfied, or *not at all* satisfied?

> ❏ very satisfied

> ❏ somewhat satisfied

> ❏ not very satisfied

❏ not at all satisfied

❏ don't know

❏ refused

d15a. How good a job would you say your *provincial* MHA, MLA or MNA does of *keeping in touch* with the people in your riding: a *very good* job, a *good* job, a *poor* job, a *very poor* job, or *don't you have an opinion?*

❏ very good

❏ good

❏ poor

❏ very poor

❏ don't have an opinion

❏ refused

> During the data collection period of this study, provincial elections were held in Ontario and Manitoba. Respondents from Ontario and Manitoba were asked questions d15i and d16i in place of d15a and d16a.

d16a. Have you ever contacted your present *provincial* MHA, MLA or MNA?

❏ yes

❏ no

❏ don't know

❏ refused

d15i. Thinking back *before* the recent provincial election, how good a job would you say your *provincial* MPP or MLA did of *keeping in touch* with the people in your riding: a *very good* job, a *good* job, a *poor* job, a *very poor* job, or *don't you have an opinion?*

❏ very good

❏ good

❏ poor

❏ very poor

❏ don't have an opinion

❏ refused

d16i. Did you contact that *provincial* MPP or MLA?

❏ yes

❏ no

❏   don't know

❏   refused

d17a.   [If yes (d16a, d16i):] How satisfied were you with the contact: *very* satisfied, *somewhat* satisfied, *not very* satisfied, or *not at all* satisfied?

❏   very satisfied

❏   somewhat satisfied

❏   not very satisfied

❏   not at all satisfied

❏   don't know

❏   refused

d12b.   Now we have some questions about your political representatives.

How good a job would you say your *provincial* MHA, MLA or MNA does of *keeping in touch* with the people in your riding: a *very good* job, a *good* job, a *poor* job, a *very poor* job, or *don't you have an opinion?*

❏   very good

❏   good

❏   poor

❏   very poor

❏   don't have an opinion

❏   refused

> During the data collection period of this study, provincial elections were held in Ontario and Manitoba. Respondents from Ontario and Manitoba were asked questions d12j and d13j in place of d12b and d13b.

d13b.   Have you ever contacted your present *provincial* MHA, MLA or MNA?

❏   yes

❏   no

❏   don't know

❏   refused

d12j.   Now we have some questions about your local representatives.

Thinking back to *before* the recent provincial election, how good a job would you say your *provincial* MPP or MLA did of *keeping in touch* with the people in your riding: a *very good* job, a *good* job, a *poor* job, a *very poor* job, or *don't you have an opinion?*

❏ very good

❏ good

❏ poor

❏ very poor

❏ don't have an opinion

❏ refused

d13j. Did you ever contact that *provincial* MPP or MLA?

❏ yes

❏ no

❏ don't know

❏ refused

d14b. [If yes (d13b, d13j):] How satisfied were you with the contact: *very* satisfied, *somewhat* satisfied, *not very* satisfied, or *not at all* satisfied?

❏ very satisfied

❏ somewhat satisfied

❏ not very satisfied

❏ not at all satisfied

❏ don't know

❏ refused

d15b. In general, how good a job would you say your *federal* MP does of *keeping in touch* with the people in your riding: a *very good* job, a *good* job, a *poor* job, a *very poor* job, or *don't you have an opinion*?

❏ very good

❏ good

❏ poor

❏ very poor

❏ don't know

❏ refused

d16b. Have you ever contacted your present *federal* MP?

❏ yes

❏ no

❏ don't know

❏ refused

d17b. [If yes (d16b):] How satisfied were you with the contact: *very* satisfied, *somewhat* satisfied, *not very* satisfied, or *not at all* satisfied?

❐ very satisfied

❐ somewhat satisfied

❐ not very satisfied

❐ not at all satisfied

❐ don't know

❐ refused

Section V: Values

v1.   Now we would like to get your views on some of the different opinions people have.

Basically, do you *agree* or *disagree* with each of the following statements.

The major issues of the day are too complicated for most voters.

(*Basically,* do you *agree* or *disagree?*)

❐ basically agree

❐ basically disagree

❐ don't know

❐ refused

v2.   Most people have enough sense to tell whether a government is doing a good job.

(*Basically,* do you *agree* or *disagree?*)

❐ basically agree

❐ basically disagree

❐ don't know

❐ refused

v3.   Most people who don't get ahead should not blame the system; they have only themselves to blame.

(*Basically,* do you *agree* or *disagree?*)

❐ basically agree

❐ basically disagree

❐ don't know

❐ refused

v4.   It's not up to the government to see to it that people have a job and a decent standard of living; the government should leave people to get ahead on their own.

(*Basically*, do you *agree* or *disagree?*)

☐ basically agree

☐ basically disagree

☐ don't know

☐ refused

v5. I'd rather put my trust in the down-to-earth thinking of ordinary people than the theories of experts and intellectuals.

(*Basically*, do you *agree* or *disagree?*)

☐ basically agree

☐ basically disagree

☐ don't know

☐ refused

v6. We would probably solve most of our big national problems if decisions could be brought back to the people at the grass roots.

(*Basically*, do you *agree* or *disagree?*)

☐ basically agree

☐ basically disagree

☐ don't know

☐ refused

v7. In times of crisis it doesn't really matter *what* the government does, what matters is that the government *does something.*

(*Basically*, do you *agree* or *disagree?*)

☐ basically agree

☐ basically disagree

☐ don't know

☐ refused

v8. This country would be better off if we worried less about how equal people are.

(*Basically*, do you *agree* or *disagree?*)

☐ basically agree

☐ basically disagree

☐ don't know

☐ refused

v9. (version 1)

> Discrimination makes it extremely difficult for women to get jobs equal to their abilities.
>
> (*Basically*, do you *agree* or *disagree?*)
>
> ❏ basically agree
>
> ❏ basically disagree
>
> ❏ don't know
>
> ❏ refused

v9. (version 2)

> Discrimination makes it extremely difficult for members of visible minorities to get jobs equal to their abilities.
>
> (*Basically*, do you *agree* or *disagree?*)
>
> ❏ basically agree
>
> ❏ basically disagree
>
> ❏ don't know
>
> ❏ refused

v10.
> Everyone would be better off if more women were satisfied to stay home and raise their children.
>
> (*Basically*, do you *agree* or *disagree?*)
>
> ❏ basically agree
>
> ❏ basically disagree
>
> ❏ don't know
>
> ❏ refused

v11.
> Reforms to improve society are worth trying even though they are risky.
>
> (*Basically*, do you *agree* or *disagree?*)
>
> ❏ basically agree
>
> ❏ basically disagree
>
> ❏ don't know
>
> ❏ refused

v12.
> Now I would like to know whether or not you have heard of the *Canadian Charter of Rights?*

❑ yes

❑ no

❑ don't know

❑ refused

v13.   [If yes (v12):] In general, do you think the Charter is a *good* thing or a *bad* thing for Canada, or *don't you have an opinion on this?*

❑ good thing

❑ bad thing

❑ don't have an opinion

❑ refused

v14.   If the courts say that a law conflicts with the Charter of Rights, who should have the final say? The *Courts*, because they are in the best position to decide what is just and unjust, or *Parliament*, because they are the representatives of the people?

❑ the Courts

❑ Parliament

❑ don't know

❑ refused

v15. (version 1)

Which is more important in a democratic society: letting the majority decide *or* protecting the needs and rights of minorities?

❑ let majority decide

❑ protecting the needs and rights of minorities

❑ both are equally important

❑ don't know

❑ refused

v15. (version 2)

Which is more important in a democratic society: protecting the needs and rights of minorities *or* letting the majority decide?

❑ protecting the needs and rights of minorities

❑ let majority decide

❑ both are equally important

❑ don't know

❑ refused

Section P: Political Parties

p1.   The next questions are about the way *federal* parties choose their
leaders. Are you *very* satisfied, *somewhat* satisfied, *not very* satisfied,
not at all satisfied with the way the parties choose their leaders, or
don't you have an opinion?

  ❏ very satisfied

  ❏ somewhat satisfied

  ❏ not very satisfied

  ❏ not at all satisfied

  ❏ don't have an opinion

  ❏ refused

p2.   Should there be a law controlling the way parties choose their
leaders or should it be up to the parties to decide?

  ❏ should be a law

  ❏ up to the parties to decide

  ❏ don't know

  ❏ refused

p3.   [If no opinion (p1):] How easy would you say it is in Canada for *new*
parties to get some of their candidates elected to the *federal*
Parliament? *Very easy, easy, difficult, or very difficult?*

  ❏ very easy

  ❏ easy

  ❏ difficult

  ❏ very difficult

  ❏ don't know

  ❏ refused

p4.   *Basically,* do you *agree* or *disagree* with each of the following
statements.

  I don't think that the government cares much what people like me
think.

  (*Basically,* do you *agree* or *disagree?*)

  ❏ basically agree

  ❏ basically disagree

❒ don't know

❒ refused

p5. Generally, those elected to Parliament soon lose touch with the people.

(*Basically,* do you *agree* or *disagree?*)

❒ basically agree

❒ basically disagree

❒ don't know

❒ refused

p6. People like me don't have any say about what the government does.

(*Basically,* do you *agree* or *disagree?*)

❒ basically agree

❒ basically disagree

❒ don't know

❒ refused

p7. We would have better laws if members of Parliament were allowed to vote freely rather than having to follow party lines.

(*Basically,* do you *agree* or *disagree?*)

❒ basically agree

❒ basically disagree

❒ don't know

❒ refused

p8. Without political parties, there can't be true democracy.

(*Basically,* do you *agree* or *disagree?*)

❒ basically agree

❒ basically disagree

❒ don't know

❒ refused

p9. All federal parties are basically the same; there isn't really a choice.

(*Basically,* do you *agree* or *disagree?*)

❒ basically agree

❒ basically disagree

❒ don't know

❒ refused

p11. Our system of government would work a lot better if the parties
weren't squabbling so much of the time.

(*Basically*, do you *agree* or *disagree?*)

☐ basically agree

☐ basically disagree

☐ don't know

☐ refused

p12. The parties confuse the issues rather than provide a clear choice on
them.

(*Basically*, do you *agree* or *disagree?*)

☐ basically agree

☐ basically disagree

☐ don't know

☐ refused

p12a. Politicians pay too much attention to public opinion polls.

(*Basically*, do you *agree* or *disagree?*)

☐ basically agree

☐ basically disagree

☐ don't know

☐ refused

p13. Most candidates in *federal* elections make campaign promises they
have no intention of fulfilling.

(*Basically*, do you *agree* or *disagree?*)

☐ basically agree

☐ basically disagree

☐ don't know

☐ refused

p14. Most members of Parliament care deeply about the problems of
ordinary people.

(*Basically*, do you *agree* or *disagree?*)

☐ basically agree

☐ basically disagree

☐ don't know

☐ refused

p15.   Most members of Parliament make a lot of money misusing public office.

(Basically, do you *agree* or *disagree?)*

❑ basically agree

❑ basically disagree

❑ don't know

❑ refused

p16.   On the whole, would you say that politicians are *more* honest, *less* honest, or *about as honest* as the average person?

❑ more honest

❑ less honest

❑ about as honest as average person

❑ don't know

❑ refused

p17.   Do you think there is *more, less,* or the *same amount* of corruption in government as in business?

❑ more

❑ less

❑ the same

❑ don't know

❑ refused

Section I: Interest and Information

i1.   We often find that people are so busy that they don't have much time to follow politics. How about you? Would you say that you follow politics: *very* closely, *fairly* closely, *not very* closely, or *not at all?*

❑ very closely

❑ fairly closely

❑ not very closely

❑ not at all

❑ don't know

❑ refused

i2.   Do you discuss politics with friends or relatives: *often, sometimes, rarely,* or *never?*

❑ often

❑ sometimes

❏ rarely

❏ never

❏ don't know

❏ refused

i3.   In every election, we find that a lot of people don't vote because they are sick, don't have time, or for some other reason. How about you, did you vote in the last federal election in 1988?

❏ yes

❏ no

❏ was not eligible to vote in 1988

❏ don't know

❏ refused

i4.   How about the *last provincial* election in [respondent's province]?

❏ yes

❏ no

❏ was not eligible to vote in last provincial election

❏ don't know

❏ refused

i5.   Have you ever been a member of a political party?

❏ yes

❏ no

❏ don't know

❏ refused

i6.   Have you ever given money to a political party or candidate?

❏ yes

❏ no

❏ don't know

❏ refused

Section S: Standard Demographics

s1.   Before we finish the interview, we would like to get a little more information about your background. We need this information to check that our sample is representative of all Canadians.

In what year were you born?

_____

☐ don't know

☐ refused

s2.   What is the highest level of education that you have completed?

☐ no schooling

☐ some elementary school

☐ completed elementary school

☐ some secondary/high school

☐ completed secondary/completed high school

☐ some technical, community college, CEGEP, Collège Classique

☐ completed technical, community college, CEGEP, Collège Classique

☐ some university

☐ completed bachelor's degree in arts, science, engineering, etc.

☐ master's degree (M.A., M.Sc., M.L.S., M.S.W., etc.)

☐ professional degree or "doctorate" (Ph.D., law, medicine, dentistry)

☐ refused

s3.   What is your religious affiliation? Is it Protestant, Catholic, Jewish, another religion or no religion?

☐ Protestant

☐ Catholic

☐ Jewish

☐ other religion (Non–Judeo-Christian)

☐ no religion

☐ don't know

☐ refused

s4.   [If Protestant (s3):] What church or denomination is that?

☐ Anglican

☐ United Church of Canada

☐ Presbyterian

☐ Baptist

❏ Lutheran

❏ Christian Reformed

❏ Pentecostal

❏ other

❏ don't know

❏ refused

s5.   In what country were you born?

❏ Canada

❏ British Isles	❏ Yugoslavia
❏ France	❏ Other European
❏ Germany	❏ India (incl. Pakistan, Sri Lanka, Bangladesh)
❏ Greece	
❏ Holland/Netherlands	❏ China/Hong Kong
❏ Hungary	❏ Other Asian
❏ Italy	❏ Latin America
❏ Poland	❏ Caribbean countries
❏ Russia/USSR	❏ African countries
❏ United States	❏ Oceania (Australia, New Zealand)
❏ other	

specify _____

❏ don't know

❏ refused

s6.   In what year did you come to live in Canada?

_____

❏ don't know

❏ refused

s7.   What is the first language you learned and still understand?

❏ French

❏ English

❏ other

specify_____

❏ don't know

❏ refused

s8.   What language do you usually speak at home?

❏ French

❏ English

❏ other

specify_____

❏ don't know

❏ refused

s9.   Including yourself, how many people live in your household?

_____

❏ don't know

❏ refused

s10.   Do you (or anyone in your household) belong to a labour union?

❏ yes

❏ no

❏ don't know

❏ refused

s10a.   Are you presently working for pay, or are you unemployed, retired, a student, a homemaker, or something else?

❏ working now (including on strike, maternity leave, etc.)

❏ laid off

❏ unemployed

❏ disabled

❏ retired

❏ student

❏ homemaker

❏ don't know

❏ refused

s11.   Are you the main income earner in your household?

❏ yes

❏ no

❐ don't know

❐ refused

s12a.   [If yes (s11):] What is your occupation?

_____

s12b.   [If no (s11):] What is the occupation of the main income earner in your household?

_____

s13.   How much income did you (and other members of your family living with you) receive *in total,* before deductions, in the last 12 months, not just from wages but from all sources, including pensions, unemployment insurance, interest from savings, and rental income?

We do not need the exact figure, just a broad category. Was it:

❐ less than $10 000

❐ between $10 000 and $19 000 (19 999)

❐ between $20 000 and $29 000 (29 999)

❐ between $30 000 and $39 000 (39 999)

❐ between $40 000 and $49 000 (49 999)

❐ between $50 000 and $59 000 (59 999)

❐ between $60 000 and $69 000 (69 999)

❐ between $70 000 and $79 000 (79 999)

❐ between $80 000 and $89 000 (89 999)

❐ between $90 000 and $99 000 (99 999)

❐ over $100 000

❐ don't know

❐ refused

s14.   Can you tell me the first three digits of your postal code?

_____

tst1.   Now we would like to know how well some political figures are known. Can you tell me who the Prime Minister of Canada is?

❐ Brian Mulroney

❐ Jean Chrétien

❐ George Bush

❐ Audrey McLaughlin

❑ other

specify _____

❑ don't know

❑ refused

tst2. The leader of the *federal* Liberal party?

❑ Brian Mulroney

❑ Jean Chrétien

❑ George Bush

❑ Audrey McLaughlin

❑ other

specify _____

❑ don't know

❑ refused

tst3. The leader of the *federal* New Democratic Party?

❑ Brian Mulroney

❑ Jean Chrétien

❑ George Bush

❑ Audrey McLaughlin

❑ other

specify _____

❑ don't know

❑ refused

tst4. If a federal election were held today, which party would you vote for?

❑ Conservative

❑ Liberal

❑ New Democratic Party

❑ Reform

❑ Bloc québécois

❑ Green

❑ other

specify _____

❑ don't know

❑ refused

tst5. Do you think having federal elections makes politicians pay *a good deal, some, a little,* or *very little* attention to what people think?

❑ a good deal

❑ some

❑ a little

❑ very little

❑ don't know

❑ refused

tst6. If a provincial election was held today which party would you vote for?

❑ Conservative

❑ Liberal

❑ New Democratic Party

❑ Reform

❑ Bloc québécois

❑ Green

❑ Confederation of Regions (COR)

❑ Social Credit

❑ Parti québécois (PQ)

❑ other

specify _____

❑ don't know

❑ refused

tst7. If we stopped having elections in Canada, do you think that things would be *much* better, *better, worse, much* worse, or *about the same?*

❑ much better

❑ better

❑ worse

❑ much worse

❏ about the same

❏ don't know

❏ refused

tele. How many different telephone numbers are in your household?

_____

❏ don't know

❏ refused

len1. In general would you say the questions were *very* interesting, *somewhat* interesting, or *not very* interesting?

❏ very interesting

❏ somewhat interesting

❏ not very interesting

❏ don't know

❏ refused

len2. Finally can you tell me how many minutes you think it took to complete this questionnaire?

_____

❏ don't know

❏ refused

APPENDIX C

CLUSTER ANALYSING POLITICAL VALUES AND BELIEFS

Cluster analysis provided us with an objective method for identifying groups of respondents who shared similar patterns of political values and beliefs. Since direct clustering is impractical with a large number of cases, we first cluster analysed a random subsample of 300 cases and then used the resulting cluster solution to classify the remaining cases. The random subsample was selected from those respondents with complete data on all of the questions relating to political values and beliefs.

Rather than relying on a single clustering criterion, we followed a two-step procedure recommended by Wishart (Wishart 1987; cf. Fleishman 1986). This procedure involved using Ward's hierarchical clustering method (1963) to obtain an initial part-optimum solution which was then optimized using Wishart's iterative relocation procedure.

As an agglomerative hierarchical method, Ward's method starts with as many clusters as there are cases (each case being considered a single cluster) and then successively merges the two clusters, at each stage, whose fusion yields the least increase in the Euclidean sum of squares. Fusion continues until all of the cases are combined into a single grand cluster. Wishart's iterative relocation procedure, on the other hand, starts with a classification of the cases into some prespecified number of clusters and then moves cases from cluster to cluster until an optimal solution is obtained.

Combining these two procedures enabled us to overcome the limitations of each. While Ward's method is generally judged to perform the best among the several hierarchical clustering methods (see Punj and Stewart 1987), it shares the major drawback of all such methods, namely that fusions, once made, are irrevocable. Wishart's iterative relocation procedure allowed for the reallocation of those cases that may have been poorly classified at an early stage of Ward's analysis. On the other hand, using Ward's solution as the initial configuration avoided the problems associated with starting Wishart's procedure from an arbitrary initial classification (Milligan 1980).

The number of clusters was determined on the basis of the results obtained from Ward's hierarchical clustering. Analysts have recommended that the agglomerative process be stopped when a significant increase, or discontinuity, occurs in the fusion coefficient. In the present case, the coefficient values obtained showed a sharp discontinuity between the 6-cluster (coefficient 4.07) and the 5-cluster (coefficient 5.32) levels. Accordingly, the 6-cluster solution was selected for iterative relocation.

The problem of "noise" in the data was resolved using Wishart's distance threshold to exclude outliers. This resulted in the exclusion of 37 cases from the iterative relocation procedure.

As an optimizing method, Wishart's iterative relocation procedure is vulnerable to the problem of local optima. To ensure that a global optimum had been achieved, the entire two-step clustering procedure was repeated on a second independent random subsample of 300 cases. With one exception (cluster 5 $r = .63$), the resulting cluster profiles correlated at the 0.95 level or higher. The distribution of cases among the clusters was also very similar.

The final stage of the cluster analysis involved using the QUICK CLUSTER routine in SPSS-X to classify the sample as a whole on a best-fit basis. Cases with missing data were included on a pairwise basis. A threshold was again used to exclude outlying cases. The resulting cluster profiles correlated with the profiles obtained from the initial two-step procedure at the 0.98 level or better for all six clusters and again the distribution of cases among the clusters was similar. We can be confident, then, that a robust solution was indeed obtained.

APPENDIX D

THE REGRESSIONS

As indicated in the introduction, we have chosen, for the sake of accessibility, to present our findings in the form of cross-tabulations. Our interpretation, however, is very much based on multivariate regressions. This appendix presents the results of these regressions.

In most regressions, the dependent variable is a dummy variable with scores of 0 and 1; the meanings of these two scores are indicated at the bottom of the tables. In a few instances, we also constructed scales, which are described in the tables and/or text. In a few other cases, the dependent variable has scores ranging from 0 to 2, 3 or 4, indicating the intensity as well as the direction of opinions; again, the exact meaning of each score is described at the bottom of the tables.

The regressions include as independent variables a set of nine socio-economic variables. Each variable has either been dichotomized or transformed into a set of dummy coded variables. The variables take the value of 1 in the following situations (and 0 in all others not listed):

1. Atlantic: resident of Newfoundland, Prince Edward Island, Nova Scotia or New Brunswick.
2. Quebec: resident of Quebec.
3. Man./Sask.: resident of Manitoba or Saskatchewan.
4. Alberta: resident of Alberta.
5. British Columbia: resident of British Columbia.
6. Gender: female.
7. Age: born before 1946.
8. Education – low: not completed secondary (high) school.
9. Education – high: having a university degree.
10. Income – low: total annual household income less than $30 000.
11. Income – high: total annual household income more than $60 000.
12. Blue collar: the occupation of the main earner in the household is manual (skilled or unskilled), farm labourer or skilled craft.
13. Union: someone in the household belongs to a labour union.
14. French: mother tongue is French.
15. Non-charter language: mother tongue is neither French nor English.
16. Catholic: religion is Catholic.
17. Protestant: religion is Protestant.

The reference category in all equations is thus: an Ontario male, born after 1945, who has completed high school but not university, with an annual household income between $30 000 and $60 000, a white-collar occupation, nonunionized, whose mother tongue is English and who is neither a Catholic nor a Protestant.

In all regressions, all individuals with missing data on any variable have been deleted. The regressions present the regression coefficient and, between parentheses, the value of the t statistic. The regression coefficient indicates the increased probability of an individual with a score of 1 on a given independent variable having a score of 1 on the dependent variable, controlling for all other factors, compared with an individual with a score of 0 for that same independent variable (the reference group). For example, in table 1.D18, the coefficient of 0.06 in column 1 indicates that, everything else being constant, an individual with a university degree is six percentage points more likely than a person of average education to think that there should be limits on party spending. The t statistic (between parentheses) indicates the level of statistical significance of the effect; with values of t greater than 1.96, the probability that the variable has an impact is greater than 95 percent. All such cases are marked by an asterisk. All regressions are estimated through ordinary least squares (OLS). Probit regressions are often recommended for dichotomous variables, but we have used OLS regressions because they are much simpler to compute, understand and interpret and because the results of OLS and Probit estimations are almost always very similar.

Some regressions include the political values and beliefs analysed in chapters 2 and 3. The operationalization of these variables is described in the tables presented in these chapters. It should be pointed out with respect to the typology of political values and beliefs that the technocratic liberals are the reference group in all equations. The coefficients for each of the types indicate how much higher (or lower) the probability is of having a score of 1 on the dependent variable for members of a given grouping compared with the technocratic liberals. For example, in column 3 of table 1.D18, the coefficient of 0.06 for the radical collectivists tells us that, everything else being equal, members of this grouping have a six percentage point greater probability of supporting limits on party spending. For a number of regressions, results are presented that show the effects of adding behavioural and attitudinal variables to the basic set of socio-economic variables. In these tables, Equation 1 presents the results of regressions based on the socio-economic variables (together with any experiments involving question wording or presentation). Equation 2 shows the effects of taking level of information (and party membership and/or contributions, where applicable) into account, while Equation 3 shows the effects of adding political values and beliefs.

Finally, all the results reported in this study are based on weighted data, that is, data adjusted for unequal probability of selection at the household level and corrected for disproportionate distribution of the sample among the provinces (see appendix A).

Table 1.D1
Determinants of typology membership

	Technocratic liberals	Populist liberals	Minoritarian individualists
1. Atlantic	-.01 (-.37)	.00 (.03)	.01 (.30)
2. Quebec	-.04 (-1.49)	.02 (.99)	.05 (1.81)
3. Man./Sask.	-.05 (-1.68)	.04 (1.16)	.01 (.33)
4. Alberta	-.02 (-.72)	.04 (1.29)	.02 (.92)
5. British Columbia	-.03 (-1.16)	.06 (2.30)*	-.01 (-.26)
6. Gender (female)	-.00 (-.20)	.01 (.65)	.01 (.63)
7. Age (45 and over)	-.02 (-.87)	-.07 (-3.96)*	.05 (3.04)*
8. Low education	-.05 (-2.36)*	-.04 (-2.00)*	.08 (4.39)*
9. High education	.13 (5.83)*	.00 (.06)	-.04 (-1.72)
10. Low income	-.04 (-2.05)*	-.02 (-.82)	.00 (.27)
11. High income	.03 (1.27)	-.03 (-1.66)	-.00 (-.05)
12. Blue collar	-.02 (-.86)	-.03 (-1.74)	-.01 (-.58)
13. Union	.00 (.18)	-.02 (-.89)	-.03 (-2.00)*
14. French	.01 (.25)	-.02 (-.80)	.03 (.97)
15. Non-charter language	-.05 (-1.90)	-.01 (-.51)	.05 (1.98)*
16. Catholic	-.01 (-.45)	-.01 (-.24)	-.02 (-.69)
17. Protestant	-.02 (-.82)	-.02 (-.73)	.01 (.30)
Constant	.22 (8.01)	.21 (7.98)	.08 (3.33)
N	2 200	2 200	2 200
R^2	.05	.02	.04

Table 1.D1 (cont'd)
Determinants of typology membership

	Majoritarian individualists	Radical collectivists	Party collectivists
1. Atlantic	-.00 (-.02)	.00 (.06)	.00 (.04)
2. Quebec	-.06 (-1.96)*	.03 (.96)	.00 (.08)
3. Man./Sask.	.02 (.57)	.07 (2.38)*	-.08 (-2.26)*
4. Alberta	.06 (1.81)	-.02 (-.93)	-.07 (-2.24)*
5. British Columbia	-.00 (-.01)	.00 (.16)	-.03 (-.88)
6. Gender (female)	-.08 (-4.98)*	.02 (1.38)	.05 (2.76)*
7. Age (45 and over)	.05 (2.64)*	-.02 (-1.09)	.00 (.13)
8. Low education	.01 (.58)	-.02 (-1.24)	.02 (.75)
9. High education	-.08 (-3.35)*	.04 (1.85)	-.06 (-2.22)*
10. Low income	.00 (.06)	.00 (.10)	.05 (2.23)*
11. High income	.03 (1.37)	-.02 (-1.10)	-.00 (-.07)
12. Blue collar	.04 (2.12)*	-.01 (-.40)	.02 (1.08)
13. Union	-.01 (-.48)	.05 (3.22)*	.00 (.11)
14. French	.00 (.14)	.00 (.16)	-.02 (-.59)
15. Non-charter language	.01 (.47)	-.01 (-.21)	.01 (.26)
16. Catholic	.02 (.63)	-.02 (-1.12)	.04 (1.49)
17. Protestant	.04 (1.70)	-.01 (-.52)	-.00 (-.07)
Constant	.20 (6.82)	.12 (4.76)	.17 (5.78)
N	2 200	2 200	2 200
R^2	.04	.02	.02

Table 1.D2
Determinants of political cynicism in Canada

1. Atlantic	.01 (.29)
2. Quebec	-.03 (-1.74)
3. Man./Sask.	.01 (.65)
4. Alberta	.08 (4.20)*
5. British Columbia	-.01 (-.74)
6. Gender (female)	.03 (3.25)*
7. Age (45 and over)	-.00 (-.20)
8. Low education	.02 (1.80)
9. High education	-.10 (-6.50)*
10. Low income	.04 (2.99)*
11. High income	.16 (1.14)
12. Blue collar	.03 (2.65)*
13. Union	.02 (1.54)
14. French	-.03 (-1.40)
15. Non-charter language	.06 (3.05)*
16. Catholic	-.02 (-1.56)
17. Protestant	-.02 (-1.31)
Constant	.69 (17.83)
N	1 921
R^2	.09

Note: The dependent variable is an index made up of responses to questions p4, p5, p13, p14, p15, p16 and p17. Those who disagreed with the statements presented in questions p4, p5, p13 and p15 were given a score of 0, as well as those who agreed with the statement presented in question p14. Those who said that politicians are more honest than the average person (p16) and that there is less corruption in government than in business (p17) were also given a score of 0. Those who said that politicians are as honest as the average person (p16) and that there is the same amount of corruption in government as in business (p17) were given a score of 0.5. All other responses were given a score of 1. Each respondent's total score was divided by 7 so that the net score in the index ranges from 0 to 1.

Table 1.D3
Determinants of attitudes about parties in Canada

	P7	P9	P11	P12
1. Atlantic	-.00 (-.07)	.08 (2.20)*	-.01 (-.27)	-.03 (-.99)
2. Quebec	-.08 (-2.34)*	.08 (2.04)*	-.14 (-4.69)*	-.10 (-3.99)*
3. Man./Sask.	.01 (.31)	.05 (1.31)	.02 (.66)	-.00 (-.02)
4. Alberta	.03 (.87)	.06 (1.55)	-.01 (-.49)	.01 (.30)
5. British Columbia	.00 (.90)	.00 (.09)	-.02 (-.84)	-.03 (-1.23)
6. Gender (female)	-.03 (-1.79)	.01 (.27)	.06 (3.90)*	-.02 (-.19)
7. Age (45 and over)	.04 (2.25)*	.04 (2.01)*	.02 (1.24)	.01 (.72)
8. Low education	.00 (.08)	.04 (1.75)	.07 (3.31)*	.02 (.86)
9. High education	-.02 (-.89)	-.06 (-2.17)*	-.11 (-4.83)*	-.08 (-3.90)*
10. Low income	.02 (1.10)	-.00 (-.09)	.02 (1.13)	.02 (1.01)
11. High income	.00 (.10)	-.04 (-1.42)	-.02 (-.86)	-.03 (-1.53)
12. Blue collar	.00 (.17)	.01 (.26)	.05 (2.64)*	.04 (2.29)*
13. Union	-.01 (-.46)	.01 (.61)	-.03 (-1.56)*	.02 (-1.34)
14. French	.08 (2.38)*	.13 (3.35)*	.03 (1.06)	-.04 (-1.33)
15. Non-charter language	.07 (2.19)*	.05 (1.27)	.09 (2.99)*	-.01 (-.36)
16. Catholic	.05 (1.73)*	-.01 (-.33)	.03 (1.22)	.04 (1.64)
17. Protestant	.01 (.29)	-.07 (-2.21)*	.05 (2.18)*	.02 (1.13)
Constant	.75 (25.40)	.40 (11.56)	.75 (27.90)	.89 (37.54)
N	2 239	2 331	2 347	2 316
R^2	.01	.04	.07	.04

Note: For each variable, those who agreed with the statement were given a score of 1 and those who disagreed a score of 0.

Table 1.D4
Determinants of attitudes about money in Canada

	F18	F19	F20
1. Atlantic	.02 (.39)	.03 (.99)	.09 (2.30)*
2. Quebec	-.04 (-1.00)	.01 (.54)	.10 (2.68)*
3. Man./Sask.	-.02 (-.50)	.08 (2.74)*	.04 (1.05)
4. Alberta	-.02 (-.61)	.07 (2.56)*	.12 (3.16)*
5. British Columbia	-.02 (-.58)	.04 (1.71)	.07 (1.91)
6. Gender (female)	-.02 (-.75)	-.01 (-.46)	-.00 (-.25)
7. Age (45 and over)	.03 (1.48)	-.00 (-.15)	.04 (2.08)*
8. Low education	-.04 (-1.59)	-.07 (-3.99)*	-.01 (-.58)
9. High education	-.09 (-3.03)*	-.05 (-2.24)*	.03 (1.09)
10. Low income	.03 (1.16)	-.01 (-.54)	.09 (3.74)*
11. High income	.03 (1.02)	-.00 (-.17)	.02 (.95)
12. Blue collar	.07 (2.82)*	.01 (.32)	.02 (1.00)
13. Union	.02 (1.11)	.03 (1.81)	.05 (2.27)*
14. French	-.04 (-1.01)	-.06 (-2.25)*	.01 (.21)
15. Non-charter language	-.03 (-.75)	-.10 (-3.68)*	.04 (1.01)
16. Catholic	-.03 (-.89)	.02 (.66)	-.00 (-.06)
17. Protestant	-.01 (-.37)	-.01 (-.28)	-.03 (-1.04)
Constant	.44 (13.09)	.87 (36.00)	.25 (7.53)
N	2 379	2 380	2 333
R^2	.01	.02	.02

Note: For each variable, those who agreed with the statement were given a score of 1 and those who disagreed a score of 0.

Table 1.D5
Determinants of opinions about the electoral system

	Equation 1	Equation 2	Equation 3
1. Atlantic	.03 (.33)	.03 (.33)	.01 (.07)
2. Quebec	-.31 (-3.58)*	-.32 (-3.60)*	-.39 (-4.21)*
3. Man./Sask.	-.03 (-.36)	-.03 (-.32)	-.04 (-.39)
4. Alberta	-.24 (-2.80)*	-.24 (-2.74)*	-.24 (-2.63)*
5. British Columbia	-.19 (-2.40)*	-.19 (-2.38)*	-.22 (-2.60)*
6. Gender (female)	-.15 (-3.12)*	-.15 (-3.15)*	-.12 (-2.27)*
7. Age (45 and over)	-.01 (-.20)	-.01 (-.13)	.01 (.27)
8. Low education	-.15 (-2.36)*	-.15 (-2.40)*	-.11 (-1.71)
9. High education	.16 (2.70)*	.17 (2.80)*	.21 (3.16)*
10. Low income	.03 (.45)	.02 (.42)	-.01 (-.11)
11. High income	.03 (.45)	-.02 (-.34)	-.06 (-1.04)
12. Blue collar	.13 (2.22)*	.12 (2.14)*	.09 (1.50)
13. Union	.01 (.21)	.01 (.25)	.03 (.48)
14. French	-.01 (-.07)	-.00 (-.00)	.08 (.84)
15. Non-charter language	-.05 (-.60)	-.05 (-.59)	-.05 (-.58)
16. Catholic	.08 (1.15)	.09 (1.21)	.08 (1.06)
17. Protestant	.10 (1.44)	.10 (1.53)	.09 (1.22)
18. Information	—	-.04 (-.49)	-.04 (-.46)
19. Party membership	—	-.02 (-.35)	-.03 (-.42)
20. Populist liberal	—	—	.00 (.05)
21. Minoritarian individualist	—	—	-.05 (-.55)
22. Majoritarian individualist	—	—	.03 (.41)
23. Radical collectivist	—	—	-.06 (-.63)
24. Party collectivist	—	—	.00 (.03)
Constant	1.41 (17.98)	1.44 (14.62)	1.44 (6.19)
N	1 619	1 617	1 481
R^2	.04	.04	.04

Note: The dependent variable is made up of a combination of questions d1, d2 and d3. The variable ranges in value from 0 for those who find the working of the electoral system completely unacceptable to 3 for those who find it completely acceptable.

Table 1.D6
Determinants of opinions about having two votes

	Equation 1	Equation 2	Equation 3
1. Atlantic	-.04 (-1.18)	-.04 (-1.07)	-.04 (-1.15)
2. Quebec	.17 (5.32)*	.18 (5.52)*	.17 (5.07)*
3. Man./Sask.	-.09 (-2.51)*	-.08 (-2.15)*	-.07 (-2.00)*
4. Alberta	.01 (.41)	.02 (.68)	.00 (.11)
5. British Columbia	-.04 (-1.23)	-.04 (-1.16)	-.04 (-1.25)
6. Gender (female)	.08 (4.45)*	.07 (3.79)*.	.08 (4.09)*
7. Age (45 and over)	-.13 (-6.93)*	-.12 (-5.95)*	-.12 (-5.72)*
8. Low education	.01 (.55)	-.00 (-.07)	.01 (.26)
9. High education	-.14 (-5.75)*	-.12 (-5.04)*	-.12 (-4.55)*
10. Low income	-.03 (-1.57)	-.04 (-1.90)	-.05 (-2.24)*
11. High income	-.02 (-1.11)	-.02 (-.95)	-.01 (-.51)
12. Blue collar	-.03 (-1.39)	-.04 (-1.71)	-.04 (-1.93)*
13. Union	-.02 (-1.16)	-.02 (-1.04)	-.03 (-1.31)
14. French	-.06 (-1.86)	-.06 (-1.88)	-.06 (-1.62)
15. Non-charter language	.06 (1.92)*	.06 (1.80)	.07 (2.02)*
16. Catholic	-.00 (-.00)	.00 (.08)	.00 (.10)
17. Protestant	.01 (.28)	.01 (.46)	.01 (.33)
18. Information	—	-.10 (-2.90)*	-.08 (-2.27)*
19. Party membership	—	-.05 (-2.21)*	-.05 (-2.10)*
20. Populist liberal	—	—	.06 (1.67)
21. Minoritarian individualist	—	—	.01 (.38)
22. Majoritarian individualist	—	—	.07 (2.42)*
23. Radical collectivist	—	—	.08 (2.30)*
24. Party collectivist	—	—	.13 (4.24)*
Constant	.80 (26.66)	.85 (23.46)	.80 (18.50)
N	2 280	2 278	2 087
R²	.07	.08	.09

Note: The dependent variable takes the value of 1 for those who favour having a two-vote system and 0 for those who are opposed (d5).

Table 1.D7
Determinants of opinions about limiting MPs' terms

	Equation 1	Equation 2	Equation 3
1. Atlantic	.10 (2.60)*	.11 (2.67)*	.11 (2.71)*
2. Quebec	.07 (1.76)	.08 (1.98)*	.10 (2.35)*
3. Man./Sask.	.08 (1.82)	.08 (1.98)*	.07 (1.61)
4. Alberta	.15 (3.84)*	.16 (3.95)*	.14 (3.32)*
5. British Columbia	.05 (1.46)	.06 (1.51)	.06 (1.65)
6. Gender (female)	.04 (1.74)	.03 (1.58)	.05 (2.03)*
7. Age (45 and over)	.06 (2.41)*	.06 (2.60)*	.06 (2.59)*
8. Low education	.02 (.71)	.02 (.56)	.01 (.32)
9. High education	-.12 (-4.15)*	-.12 (-3.98)*	-.10 (-3.17)*
10. Low income	-.00 (-.09)	-.00 (-.16)	-.01 (-.35)
11. High income	.00 (.13)	.01 (.24)	.02 (.67)
12. Blue collar	.01 (.47)	.01 (.41)	.02 (.73)
13. Union	-.01 (-.53)	-.01 (-.51)	-.04 (-1.43)
14. French	.01 (.15)	.00 (.09)	-.01 (-.29)
15. Non-charter language	.01 (.31)	.01 (.24)	.03 (.84)
16. Catholic	-.08 (-2.36)*	-.08 (-2.39)*	-.06 (-1.60)
17. Protestant	-.03 (-1.11)	-.04 (-1.12)	-.01 (-.41)
18. Information	—	-.01 (-.37)	.00 (.09)
19. Party membership	—	-.03 (-1.14)	-.04 (-1.39)
20. Populist liberal	—	—	.07 (1.87)
21. Minoritarian individualist	—	—	.07 (1.63)
22. Majoritarian individualist	—	—	.14 (3.71)*
23. Radical collectivist	—	—	.09 (2.06)*
24. Party collectivist	—	—	.09 (2.40)*
Constant	.36 (9.87)	.37 (8.34)	.26 (5.00)
N	2 060	2 058	1 881
R^2	.03	.03	.04

Note: The dependent variable takes the value of 1 for those who think that it is a good idea to limit MPs' terms and 0 for those who think that this is a poor idea (d6).

Table 1.D8
Determinants of opinions about MPs' role

	Equation 1	Equation 2	Equation 3
1. Atlantic	.05 (1.37)	.05 (1.47)	.05 (1.39)
2. Quebec	.08 (2.24)*	.09 (2.41)*	.10 (2.44)*
3. Man./Sask.	-.06 (-1.47)	-.05 (-1.37)	-.05 (-1.30)
4. Alberta	-.10 (-2.80)*	-.10 (-2.78)*	-.11 (-2.79)*
5. British Columbia	-.03 (-.94)	-.03 (-1.00)	-.04 (-.98)
6. Gender (female)	.02 (1.10)	.01 (.29)	.03 (1.28)
7. Age (45 and over)	.00 (.22)	.02 (1.14)	.02 (.83)
8. Low education	-.01 (-.44)	-.03 (-1.12)	-.03 (-1.05)
9. High education	-.06 (-2.25)*	-.04 (-1.60)	-.03 (-1.06)
10. Low income	.06 (2.25)*	.04 (1.86)	.04 (1.69)
11. High income	.03 (1.23)	.04 (1.38)	.03 (.99)
12. Blue collar	-.01 (-.61)	-.02 (-1.04)	-.03 (-1.10)
13. Union	.01 (.24)	.01 (.32)	.01 (.38)
14. French	.02 (.42)	.00 (.13)	-.00 (-.08)
15. Non-charter language	-.01 (-.20)	-.01 (-.36)	.00 (.00)
16. Catholic	-.02 (-.63)	-.02 (-.65)	-.02 (-.70)
17. Protestant	-.09 (-2.99)*	-.08 (-2.87)*	-.08 (-2.71)*
18. Information	—	-.16 (-4.49)*	-.17 (-4.37)*
19. Party membership	—	.01 (.25)	.02 (.55)
20. Populist liberal	—	—	-.04 (-1.13)
21. Minoritarian individualist	—	—	.01 (.36)
22. Majoritarian individualist	—	—	.02 (.57)
23. Radical collectivist	—	—	.05 (1.41)
24. Party collectivist	—	—	.02 (.67)
Constant	.36 (10.59)	.46 (11.29)	.45 (9.11)
N	2 316	2 315	2 119
R^2	.03	.04	.05

Note: The dependent variable takes the value of 1 for those who think that MPs should follow what they believe to be the public interest and 0 for those who believe that MPs should follow the views of the people in their riding (d7).

Table 1.D9
Determinants of opinions about allowing MPs to change parties

	Equation 1	Equation 2	Equation 3
1. Atlantic	-.01 (-.37)	-.01 (-.41)	-.02 (-.50)
2. Quebec	.01 (.35)	.01 (.32)	-.00 (-.11)
3. Man./Sask.	-.03 (-.73)	-.03 (-.82)	-.04 (-1.04)
4. Alberta	.06 (1.80)	.06 (1.72)	.08 (2.06)*
5. British Columbia	.03 (.92)	.03 (.90)	.04 (1.11)
6. Gender (female)	-.06 (-3.36)*	-.06 (-3.08)*	-.05 (-2.54)*
7. Age (45 and over)	-.02 (-1.20)	-.03 (-1.46)	-.02 (-1.04)
8. Low education	-.01 (-.59)	-.01 (-.37)	.01 (.48)
9. High education	.10 (3.88)*	.10 (3.57)*	.08 (2.92)*
10. Low income	-.00 (-.18)	-.00 (-.06)	-.00 (-.14)
11. High income	-.03 (-1.25)	-.03 (-1.28)	-.02 (-.84)
12. Blue collar	.02 (.82)	.02 (.95)	.02 (.93)
13. Union	.03 (1.30)	.03 (1.26)	.02 (1.12)
14. French	.09 (2.48)*	.09 (2.46)*	.11 (2.92)*
15. Non-charter language	-.01 (-.23)	-.01 (-.19)	-.00 (-.04)
16. Catholic	-.01 (-.43)	-.01 (-.47)	-.02 (-.60)
17. Protestant	.03 (1.01)	.03 (.92)	.02 (.54)
18. Information	—	.04 (1.22)	.07 (1.90)
19. Party membership	—	.01 (.56)	-.00 (-.07)
20. Populist liberal	—	—	-.02 (-.56)
21. Minoritarian individualist	—	—	-.06 (-1.74)
22. Majoritarian individualist	—	—	-.01 (-.37)
23. Radical collectivist	—	—	.03 (.81)
24. Party collectivist	—	—	-.02 (-.66)
Constant	.27 (8.36)	.24 (6.06)	.23 (4.90)
N	2 296	2 294	2 096
R^2	.02	.02	.03

Note: The dependent variable takes the value of 1 for those who think that MPs should be allowed to change parties and the value of 0 for those who think that they should be required to resign (d7a).

Table 1.D10

Determinants of opinions about the representation of women in the House of Commons

	Equation 1	Equation 2	Equation 3
1. Atlantic	.04 (.38)	-.03 (-.33)	-.06 (-.57)
2. Quebec	.14 (1.43)	.05 (.51)	-.00 (-.04)
3. Man./Sask.	-.07 (-.70)	-.10 (-.95)	-.12 (-1.09)
4. Alberta	-.02 (-.23)	-.08 (-.76)	-.08 (-.76)
5. British Columbia	-.05 (-.52)	-.07 (-.75)	-.07 (-.77)
6. Gender (female)	.32 (6.02)*	.28 (4.90)*	.23 (3.91)*
7. Age (45 and over)	-.05 (-.90)	-.08 (-1.25)	-.03 (-.47)
8. Low education	-.22 (-3.30)*	-.20 (-2.82)*	-.16 (-2.16)*
9. High education	.35 (4.80)*	.25 (3.11)*	.29 (3.51)*
10. Low income	.05 (.73)	.04 (.66)	.04 (.60)
11. High income	-.05 (-.70)	-.07 (-.95)	-.09 (-1.20)
12. Blue collar	.03 (.56)	.06 (.96)	.03 (.41)
13. Union	-.04 (-.70)	-.07 (-1.08)	-.07 (-1.14)
14. French	-.07 (-.71)	-.03 (-.29)	.02 (.24)
15. Non-charter language	-.14 (-1.49)	-.18 (-1.82)	-.19 (-1.86)
16. Catholic	-.20 (-2.50)*	-.24 (-2.75)*	-.21 (-2.41)*
17. Protestant	-.27 (-3.57)*	-.30 (-3.72)*	-.29 (-3.51)*
18. Information	—	.25 (2.35)*	.28 (2.68)*
19. Party membership	—	.10 (1.27)	.12 (1.60)
20. Populist liberal	—	.13 (1.41)	.11 (1.15)
21. Minoritarian individualist	—	-.02 (-.18)	-.01 (-.07)
22. Majoritarian individualist	—	-.12 (-1.29)	-.08 (-.87)
23. Radical collectivist	—	.17 (1.64)	.13 (1.26)
24. Party collectivist	—	.15 (1.57)	.13 (1.37)
25. Belief: discrimination (v9)	—	—	.47 (7.58)*
26. Belief: women's place (v10)	—	—	-.25 (-3.40)*
27. Interviewer's gender (female)	.19 (3.42)*	.19 (3.23)*	.18 (3.02)*
Constant	.99 (10.29)	.90 (6.46)	.62 (4.37)
N	1 153	1 040	975
R^2	.09	.10	.17

Note: The dependent variable ranges in value from 0 to 3. The higher the value, the more serious a problem one views there to be (question d8).

Table 1.D11

Determinants of opinions about the effects of increasing the number of women in the House of Commons

	Equation 1	Equation 2	Equation 3
1. Atlantic	-.06 (-.80)	-.09 (-1.26)	-.11 (-1.50)
2. Quebec	.07 (1.01)	.00 (.03)	-.03 (-.40)
3. Man./Sask.	-.03 (.64)	-.09 (-1.16)	-.11 (-1.45)
4. Alberta	.02 (.32)	-.03 (-.40)	-.01 (-.09)
5. British Columbia	-.03 (-.55)	-.07 (-1.04)	-.06 (-.83)
6. Gender (female)	.16 (4.27)*	.17 (4.15)*	.15 (3.77)*
7. Age (45 and over)	.06 (1.40)	.02 (.43)	.07 (1.58)
8. Low education	.05 (1.01)	.06 (1.18)	.05 (.96)
9. High education	.14 (2.72)*	.12 (2.17)*	.15 (2.63)*
10. Low income	.02 (.44)	.04 (.75)	.03 (.68)
11. High income	-.00 (-.06)	.00 (.05)	-.04 (-.69)
12. Blue collar	-.02 (-.44)	-.02 (-.44)	-.03 (-.58)
13. Union	.09 (2.15)*	.09 (2.13)*	.08 (1.90)
14. French	.01 (.12)	.01 (.07)	.03 (.45)
15. Non-charter language	-.10 (-1.49)	-.13 (-1.90)	-.15 (-2.13)*
16. Catholic	-.02 (-.27)	-.02 (-.31)	.00 (.08)
17. Protestant	-.03 (-.58)	-.05 (-.79)	-.06 (-.95)
18. Information	—	.07 (.92)	.04 (.60)
19. Party membership	—	.14 (2.67)*	.17 (3.16)*
20. Populist liberal	—	.19 (2.92)*	.19 (2.86)*
21. Minoritarian individualist	—	.15 (2.12)*	.14 (1.96)*
22. Majoritarian individualist	—	.12 (1.79)	.09 (1.40)
23. Radical collectivist	—	.16 (2.17)*	.12 (1.70)
24. Party collectivist	—	.11 (1.71)	.08 (1.18)
25. Belief: discrimination (v9)	—	—	.28 (6.27)*
26. Belief: women's place (v10)	—	—	-.13 (-2.41)*
27. Interviewer's gender (female)	-.02 (-.46)	.01 (.24)	-.02 (-.38)
Constant	.31 (4.59)	.16 (2.00)	.04 (.41)
N	1 104	992	934
R^2	.04	.05	.11

Note: The dependent variable ranges in value from 0 to 2. The higher the value, the more one thinks that better government would result (question d9). The small number of respondents who think that worse or much worse government would result have been excluded.

Table 1.D12
Determinants of opinions about quotas for women candidates

	Equation 1	Equation 2	Equation 3
1. Atlantic	.15 (.79)	.19 (.97)	.23 (1.15)
2. Quebec	.23 (1.23)	.26 (1.30)	.24 (1.21)
3. Man./Sask.	-.10 (-.52)	-.13 (-.63)	-.14 (-.66)
4. Alberta	-.03 (-.18)	-.02 (-.13)	.00 (.01)
5. British Columbia	-.11 (-.64)	-.03 (-.17)	.04 (.21)
6. Gender (female)	.52 (5.10)*	.41 (3.78)*	.33 (3.02)*
7. Age (45 and over)	-.05 (-.46)	.06 (.48)	.17 (1.36)
8. Low education	.39 (3.04)*	.27 (2.04)*	.23 (1.71)
9. High education	-.20 (-1.42)	-.06 (-.42)	.03 (.22)
10. Low income	.12 (.98)	.09 (.75)	.06 (.43)
11. High income	-.25 (-1.93)*	-.16 (-1.17)	-.23 (-1.67)
12. Blue collar	.19 (1.65)	.18 (1.48)	.17 (1.39)
13. Union	.28 (2.55)*	.27 (2.38)*	.28 (2.40)*
14. French	.16 (.85)	.08 (.39)	.08 (.39)
15. Non-charter language	.49 (2.83)*	.31 (1.70)	.37 (1.95)*
16. Catholic	-.04 (-.25)	-.05 (-.31)	-.01 (-.03)
17. Protestant	-.25 (-1.77)	-.22 (-1.44)	-.22 (-1.39)
18. Information	—	-.66 (-3.40)*	-.75 (-3.79)*
19. Party membership	—	-.13 (-.92)	-.18 (-1.24)
20. Populist liberal	—	.28 (1.60)	.25 (1.43)
21. Minoritarian individualist	—	.59 (3.03)*	.57 (2.83)*
22. Majoritarian individualist	—	.20 (1.15)	.20 (1.10)
23. Radical collectivist	—	.49 (2.56)*	.43 (2.28)*
24. Party collectivist	—	.45 (2.53)*	.41 (2.27)*
25. Belief: discrimination (v9)	—	—	.61 (5.18)*
26. Belief: women's place (v10)	—	—	-.14 (-.99)
27. Experiment (quotas)	-.20 (1.99)*	-.23 (2.21)*	-.26 (2.49)*
28. Interviewer's gender (female)	.06 (.62)	.05 (.43)	.01 (.06)
Constant	1.58 (8.45)	1.75 (6.72)	1.45 (5.34)
N	1 098	989	934
R^2	.10	.12	.15

Note: The dependent variable combines responses to questions d10 and d11. The variable ranges in value from 0 for those who are very strongly opposed to requiring the parties to choose as many female as male candidates to 5 for those who are very strongly in favour.

Table 1.D13

Determinants of opinions about the representation of visible minorities in the House of Commons

	Equation 1	Equation 2	Equation 3
1. Atlantic	.17 (1.76)	.22 (2.25)*	.14 (1.43)
2. Quebec	-.06 (-.69)	-.08 (-.79)	-.11 (-1.11)
3. Man./Sask.	-.17 (-1.64)	-.15 (-1.44)	-.20 (-1.94)*
4. Alberta	-.22 (-2.38)*	-.15 (-1.58)	-.11 (-1.17)
5. British Columbia	-.02 (-.20)	-.02 (-.25)	-.03 (-.32)
6. Gender (female)	.28 (5.36)*	.27 (5.05)*	.26 (4.85)*
7. Age (45 and over)	-.09 (-1.62)	-.06 (-1.07)	-.04 (-.73)
8. Low education	.12 (1.80)	.11 (1.70)	.11 (1.68)
9. High education	.10 (1.44)	.15 (2.05)*	.13 (1.80)
10. Low income	.12 (1.86)	.10 (1.56)	.12 (1.84)
11. High income	-.18 (-2.81)*	-.14 (-2.07)*	-.09 (-1.29)
12. Blue collar	-.07 (-1.13)	-.09 (-1.49)	-.08 (-1.35)
13. Union	.16 (2.83)*	.18 (3.08)*	.16 (2.73)*
14. French	.02 (.17)	.01 (.08)	-.01 (-.15)
15. Non-charter language	.21 (2.22)*	.25 (2.56)*	.18 (1.89)
16. Catholic	-.19 (-2.37)*	-.20 (-2.41)*	-.16 (-2.03)*
17. Protestant	-.30 (-3.98)*	-.32 (-4.14)*	-.32 (-4.18)*
18. Information	—	-.05 (-.54)	-.04 (-.45)
19. Party membership	—	-.02 (-.30)	.03 (.47)
20. Populist liberal	—	.41 (4.29)*	.33 (3.48)*
21. Minoritarian individualist	—	.22 (2.22)*	.10 (1.04)
22. Majoritarian individualist	—	.03 (.32)	.06 (.68)
23. Radical collectivist	—	.42 (4.36)*	.43 (4.51)*
24. Party collectivist	—	.38 (4.47)*	.23 (2.77)*
25. Belief: discrimination (v9)	—	—	.55 (9.48)*
Constant	1.31 (15.22)	1.10 (8.93)	.77 (6.19)
N	1 168	1 081	1 045
R^2	.09	.13	.21

Note: The dependent value ranges in value from 0 to 3. The higher the value, the more serious a problem one views there to be (question d8).

Table 1.D14

Determinants of opinions about the effects of increasing the number of visible minorities in the House of Commons

	Equation 1	Equation 2	Equation 3
1. Atlantic	.21 (3.07)*	.20 (2.83)*	.14 (2.06)*
2. Quebec	.06 (.88)	.05 (.79)	.03 (.43)
3. Man./Sask.	.03 (.36)	.03 (.38)	.02 (.28)
4. Alberta	-.08 (-1.13)	-.05 (-.64)	-.03 (-.42)
5. British Columbia	-.07 (-1.06)	-.05 (-.74)	-.05 (-.69)
6. Gender (female)	.11 (3.10)*	.12 (2.94)*	.12 (3.18)*
7. Age (45 and over)	.06 (1.49)	.08 (2.00)*	.09 (2.05)*
8. Low education	.03 (.68)	.03 (.67)	.00 (.08)
9. High education	.05 (.96)	.10 (1.88)	.11 (1.98)*
10. Low income	.03 (.60)	.02 (.37)	.01 (.26)
11. High income	-.11 (-2.27)*	-.11 (-2.19)*	-.07 (-1.49)
12. Blue collar	.03 (.69)	.00 (.00)	.00 (.04)
13. Union	-.00 (-.07)	.01 (.23)	.00 (.03)
14. French	-.15 (-2.18)*	-.16 (-2.22)*	-.14 (-2.07)*
15. Non-charter language	.10 (1.46)	.12 (1.65)	.10 (1.46)
16. Catholic	-.06 (-.99)	-.07 (-1.14)	-.06 (-.97)
17. Protestant	-.24 (-4.51)*	-.26 (-4.67)*	-.28 (-5.18)*
18. Information	—	-.13 (-1.80)	-.11 (-1.54)
19. Party membership	—	.03 (.52)	.02 (.51)
20. Populist liberal	—	.10 (1.46)	.06 (.86)
21. Minoritarian individualist	—	.10 (1.37)	.05 (.69)
22. Majoritarian individualist	—	.00 (.05)	.03 (.44)
23. Radical collectivist	—	.17 (2.36)*	.16 (2.28)*
24. Party collectivist	—	.20 (3.17)*	.13 (2.07)*
25. Belief: discrimination (v9)	—	—	.33 (7.80)*
Constant	.49 (8.04)	.48 (5.35)	.27 (2.99)
N	1 105	1 025	987
R^2	.06	.09	.15

Note: The dependent variable ranges in value from 0 to 2. The higher the value, the more one thinks that better government would result (question d9). The small number of respondents who think that worse or much worse government would result have been excluded.

Table 1.D15
Determinants of opinions about quotas for visible minority candidates

	Equation 1	Equation 2	Equation 3
1. Atlantic	.29 (1.53)	.30 (1.58)	.14 (.74)
2. Quebec	-.01 (-.06)	-.03 (-.18)	-.09 (-.49)
3. Man./Sask.	-.14 (-.72)	-.16 (-.77)	-.21 (-1.03)
4. Alberta	-.43 (-2.39)*	-.37 (-2.00)*	-.33 (-1.77)
5. British Columbia	-.22 (-1.25)	-.19 (-1.07)	-.19 (-1.08)
6. Gender (female)	.43 (4.24)*	.32 (3.01)*	.27 (2.57)*
7. Age (45 and over)	-.02 (-.20)	.04 (.41)	.12 (1.05)
8. Low education	.39 (3.04)*	.23 (1.78)	.18 (1.37)
9. High education	-.29 (-2.15)*	-.12 (-.82)	-.16 (-1.15)
10. Low income	.08 (.63)	.01 (.08)	.03 (.21)
11. High income	-.22 (-1.76)	-.19 (-1.46)	-.12 (-.93)
12. Blue collar	-.15 (-1.31)	-.24 (-1.99)*	-.22 (-1.86)
13. Union	-.03 (-.27)	.07 (.60)	.03 (.29)
14. French	.57 (3.06)*	.54 (2.81)*	.55 (2.95)*
15. Non-charter language	.31 (1.62)	.28 (1.44)	.16 (.79)
16. Catholic	-.13 (-.84)	-.15 (-.96)	-.12 (-.78)
17. Protestant	-.37 (-2.51)*	-.32 (-2.16)*	-.32 (-2.18)*
18. Information	—	-.53 (-2.81)*	-.52 (-2.79)*
19. Party membership	—	-.14 (-1.11)	-.07 (-.57)
20. Populist liberal	—	.37 (2.02)*	.22 (1.20)
21. Minoritarian individualist	—	.66 (3.42)*	.47 (2.48)*
22. Majoritarian individualist	—	-.12 (-.74)	.11 (-.66)
23. Radical collectivist	—	.39 (2.07)*	.38 (2.04)*
24. Party collectivist	—	.63 (3.84)*	.40 (2.45)*
25. Belief: discrimination (v9)	—	—	.91 (8.13)*
26. Experiment (quotas)	-.36 (3.68)*	-.39 (3.92)*	-.38 (3.81)*
Constant	2.01 (11.66)	2.14 (8.76)	1.62 (6.52)
N	1 103	1 022	992
R^2	.12	.16	.21

Note: The dependent variable combines responses to questions d10 and d11. The variable ranges in value from 0 for those who are very strongly opposed to requiring the parties to choose more members of visible minorities as candidates to 5 for those who are very strongly in favour.

Table 1.D16
Determinants of opinions about the way federal parties choose their leaders

	Equation 1	Equation 2	Equation 3
1. Atlantic	-.03 (-.45)	-.03 (-.37)	.01 (.07)
2. Quebec	-.42 (-6.08)*	-.40 (-5.88)*	-.34 (-4.78)*
3. Man./Sask.	-.07 (-.95)	-.05 (-.70)	-.04 (-.54)
4. Alberta	-.13 (-1.88)	-.12 (-1.69)	-.13 (-1.80)
5. British Columbia	-.06 (-.85)	-.05 (-.72)	-.06 (-.88)
6. Gender (female)	.07 (1.69)	.04 (1.05)	.06 (1.54)
7. Age (45 and over)	-.07 (-1.65)	-.03 (-.81)	-.05 (-1.06)
8. Low education	.08 (1.60)	.05 (1.02)	.08 (1.59)
9. High education	.02 (.31)	.05 (.99)	.04 (.75)
10. Low income	-.00 (-.03)	-.02 (-.47)	-.01 (-.14)
11. High income	-.09 (-1.92)*	-.08 (-1.70)	-.11 (-2.23)*
12. Blue collar	.07 (1.46)	.04 (.98)	.02 (.33)
13. Union	.04 (.92)	.04 (.96)	.06 (1.27)
14. French	-.07 (-1.04)	-.07 (-1.04)	-.12 (-1.64)
15. Non-charter language	.01 (.09)	-.01 (-.14)	-.01 (-.20)
16. Catholic	.06 (1.05)	.07 (1.22)	.07 (1.07)
17. Protestant	.11 (1.95)*	.13 (2.26)*	.13 (2.26)*
18. Information	—	-.30 (-4.10)*	-.35 (-4.65)*
19. Party membership	—	-.06 (-1.36)	-.04 (-.87)
20. Populist liberal	—	—	-.10 (-1.44)
21. Minoritarian individualist	—	—	-.16 (-2.06)*
22. Majoritarian individualist	—	—	-.12 (-1.78)
23. Radical collectivist	—	—	-.31 (-4.22)*
24. Party collectivist	—	—	-.12 (-1.79)
Constant	1.54 (22.99)	1.74 (21.06)	1.88 (19.53)
N	1 769	1 767	1 623
R^2	.07	.08	.10

Note: The dependent variable ranges in value from 0 to 3. The higher the value, the more satisfied one is with the way that the federal parties choose their leaders (question p1).

Table 1.D17

Determinants of opinions about having a law controlling the way that parties choose their leaders

	Equation 1	Equation 2	Equation 3
1. Atlantic	.07 (1.77)	.07 (1.74)	.08 (1.92)*
2. Quebec	.14 (3.42)*	.13 (3.34)*	.14 (3.24)*
3. Man./Sask.	-.07 (-1.70)	-.08 (-1.83)	-.09 (-1.91)
4. Alberta	.03 (.80)	.02 (.58)	.02 (.56)
5. British Columbia	-.08 (-2.03)*	-.08 (-2.15)*	-.07 (-1.78)
6. Gender (female)	.08 (3.53)*	.08 (3.38)*	.06 (2.56)*
7. Age (45 and over)	-.06 (-2.35)*	-.06 (-2.32)*	-.06 (-2.50)*
8. Low education	.04 (1.41)	.04 (1.40)	.04 (1.46)
9. High education	-.10 (-3.47)*	-.10 (-3.47)*	-.10 (-3.20)*
10. Low income	.02 (.65)	.02 (.56)	.01 (.47)
11. High income	.07 (2.69)*	.07 (2.63)*	.06 (2.05)*
12. Blue collar	.00 (.18)	.00 (.06)	.02 (.59)
13. Union	-.01 (-.32)	-.01 (-.38)	-.00 (-.09)
14. French	-.02 (-.44)	-.03 (-.63)	-.02 (-.56)
15. Non-charter language	.05 (1.16)	.04 (1.10)	.06 (1.34)
16. Catholic	-.02 (-.62)	-.02 (-.68)	-.03 (-.90)
17. Protestant	-.09 (-2.64)*	-.09 (-2.67)*	-.08 (-2.35)*
18. Information	—	-.04 (-1.06)	-.04 (-.91)
19. Party membership	—	.05 (1.87)	.05 (1.69)
20. Populist liberal	—	—	.07 (1.82)
21. Minoritarian individualist	—	—	.01 (.19)
22. Majoritarian individualist	—	—	.04 (1.12)
23. Radical collectivist	—	—	.10 (2.37)*
24. Party collectivist	—	—	.07 (1.84)
Constant	.29 (7.60)	.32 (6.71)	.27 (4.80)
N	1 724	1 722	1 577
R^2	.06	.06	.06

Note: The dependent variable takes the value of 1 for those who think that there should be a law controlling the way parties choose their leaders and the value of 0 for those who think that it is up to the parties to decide (question p2).

Table 1.D18
Determinants of opinions about party spending

	Equation 1	Equation 2	Equation 3
1. Atlantic	.01 (.36)	.01 (.42)	.04 (1.25)
2. Quebec	.04 (1.74)	.05 (1.81)	.07 (2.11)*
3. Man./Sask.	.04 (1.56)	.04 (1.57)	.03 (1.07)
4. Alberta	-.01 (-.37)	-.01 (-.31)	.01 (.39)
5. British Columbia	-.03 (-1.08)	-.02 (-1.07)	-.01 (-.44)
6. Gender (female)	.04 (2.75)*	.03 (1.93)*	.02 (1.02)
7. Age (45 and over)	.02 (1.10)	.02 (1.55)	.02 (.87)
8. Low education	.01 (.68)	.00 (.20)	.01 (.62)
9. High education	.06 (3.15)*	.07 (3.57)*	.11 (4.73)*
10. Low income	.04 (2.17)*	.03 (2.07)*	.03 (1.48)
11. High income	-.01 (-.46)	-.01 (-.29)	-.00 (-.20)
12. Blue collar	.00 (.20)	.00 (.46)	.00 (.11)
13. Union	.01 (.88)	-.01 (-.82)	-.01 (-.31)
14. French	-.00 (-.15)	-.01 (-.33)	-.02 (-.59)
15. Non-charter language	.02 (1.00)	.02 (.96)	.00 (.03)
16. Catholic	.03 (1.56)	.04 (1.75)	.07 (2.62)
17. Protestant	.01 (.58)	.02 (.88)	.03 (1.31)
18. Information	—	-.07 (-2.84)*	-.07 (-2.49)*
19. Contribution	—	.01 (.39)	.03 (1.36)
20. Cynicism	—	—	.07 (-1.78)
21. Belief: parties (p11)	—	—	.03 (1.47)
22. Money: motivations (f18)	—	—	-.04 (-2.32)*
23. Money: impact (f20)	—	—	.03 (1.66)
24. Populist liberal	—	—	-.04 (-1.46)
25. Minoritarian individualist	—	—	.03 (1.08)
26. Majoritarian individualist	—	—	-.02 (-.58)
27. Radical collectivist	—	—	.06 (2.05)*
28. Party collectivist	—	—	-.00 (-.08)
Constant	.82 (41.30)	.85 (29.27)	.73 (17.83)
N	2 218	2 187	1 652
R^2	.02	.02	.04

Note: The dependent variable takes the value of 1 for those who think there should be limits to party spending (question f1) and that limits are needed even if we know where the money is coming from (question f9) and the value of 0 otherwise.

Table 1.D19
Determinants of opinions about group advertising

	Equation 1	Equation 2	Equation 3
1. Atlantic	-.02 (-.77)	-.03 (-.85)	-.02 (-.46)
2. Quebec	-.04 (-1.25)	-.05 (-1.60)	-.07 (-1.88)
3. Man./Sask.	-.08 (-2.30)*	-.08 (-2.47)*	-.06 (-1.57)
4. Alberta	.02 (.72)	.02 (.67)	.03 (.72)
5. British Columbia	.00 (.77)	-.01 (-.17)	-.01 (-.43)
6. Gender (female)	-.03 (-1.72)	-.03 (-1.96)*	-.01 (-.70)
7. Age (45 and over)	-.05 (-2.92)*	-.05 (-2.63)*	-.01 (-.63)
8. Low education	.01 (.50)	.00 (.14)	.01 (.39)
9. High education	.09 (3.56)*	.09 (3.75)*	.06 (2.03)*
10. Low income	.07 (3.38)*	.07 (3.31)*	.07 (2.93)*
11. High income	.05 (2.11)*	.04 (2.04)*	.05 (2.18)*
12. Blue collar	-.06 (-3.00)*	-.06 (-3.07)*	-.03 (-1.23)
13. Union	.02 (.81)	.01 (.81)	.03 (1.34)
14. French	-.01 (-.28)	-.01 (-.21)	.03 (.92)
15. Non-charter language	.00 (.11)	.00 (.12)	.02 (.50)
16. Catholic	-.02 (-.92)	-.02 (-.76)	-.06 (-1.91)
17. Protestant	-.03 (-1.11)	-.01 (-.98)	-.05 (-1.79)
18. Information	—	-.07 (-2.23)*	-.07 (-2.00)*
19. Contribution	—	.05 (2.25)*	.01 (.34)
20. Cynicism	—	—	-.14 (3.18)*
21. Belief: parties (p11)	—	—	-.11 (-4.22)*
22. Money: motivations (f18)	—	—	-.04 (-2.18)*
23. Money: impact (f20)	—	—	-.06 (-2.96)*
24. Populist liberal	—	—	.01 (.43)
25. Minoritarian individualist	—	—	-.05 (-1.29)
26. Majoritarian individualist	—	—	.00 (.03)
27. Radical collectivist	—	—	.00 (.09)
28. Party collectivist	—	—	-.01 (-.32)
29. Experiment	.27 (16.01)*	.27 (15.91)*	.27 (13.95)*
Constant	.35 (11.95)	.39 (10.59)	.62 (8.53)
N	2 210	2 082	1 600
R^2	.12	.13	.14

Note: The dependent variable is a scale made up of responses to question f12 to f15. The higher the score, the more favourable one is to allowing group advertising.

Table 1.D20
Determinants of opinions about contribution ceilings

	Equation 1	Equation 2	Equation 3
1. Atlantic	.04 (1.10)	.05 (1.20)	.02 (.45)
2. Quebec	-.03 (-.85)	-.02 (-.59)	-.07 (-1.60)
3. Man./Sask.	.04 (1.01)	.06 (1.42)	.05 (1.11)
4. Alberta	.06 (1.48)	.07 (1.74)	.06 (1.33)
5. British Columbia	.07 (2.02)*	.08 (2.24)*	.06 (1.38)
6. Gender (female)	.05 (2.50)*	.03 (1.47)	.02 (1.00)
7. Age (45 and over)	-.12 (-5.42)*	-.09 (-4.00)*	-.10 (-3.58)*
8. Low education	.01 (.56)	-.01 (-.34)	.00 (.12)
9. High education	-.04 (-1.36)	-.01 (-.33)	-.03 (-.79)
10. Low income	-.00 (-.08)	-.01 (-.43)	.01 (.34)
11. High income	-.06 (-2.23)*	-.05 (-1.86)	-.03 (-.89)
12. Blue collar	-.00 (-.13)	-.01 (-.46)*	-.01 (-.26)
13. Union	.04 (1.77)	.04 (1.86)	.06 (2.42)
14. French	.00 (.10)	-.00 (-.74)	.05 (1.02)
15. Non-charter language	.04 (1.00)	.04 (.96)	.06 (1.31)
16. Catholic	.05 (1.41)	.06 (1.71)	.05 (1.46)
17. Protestant	.08 (2.59)*	.10 (3.15)*	.11 (3.16)*
18. Information	—	-.20 (-5.07)*	-.17 (-3.82)*
19. Contribution	—	-.04 (-1.57)	-.09 (-2.97)*
20. Cynicism	—	—	-.06 (-1.04)
21. Belief: parties (p11)	—	—	-.08 (-2.43)*
22. Money: motivations (f18)	—	—	-.03 (-1.07)
23. Money: impact (f20)	—	—	-.17 (-6.58)*
24. Populist liberal	—	—	.01 (.34)
25. Minoritarian individualist	—	—	.04 (.89)
26. Majoritarian individualist	—	—	.02 (.58)
27. Radical collectivist	—	—	-.02 (-.40)
28. Party collectivist	—	—	.08 (1.94)
Constant	.37 (10.57)	.49 (11.05)	.62 (8.32)
N	2 158	2 130	1 621
R^2	.02	.04	.07

Note: The dependent variable takes the value of 1 for those opposed to ceilings on donations and the value of 0 for those in favour.

Table 1.D21

Determinants of opinions about the appropriate amount for contribution ceilings (level)

	Equation 1	Equation 2	Equation 3
1. Atlantic	256.92 (.56)	266.14 (.58)	390.81 (.76)
2. Quebec	354.21 (.82)	388.84 (.88)	672.76 (1.25)
3. Man./Sask.	1 199.60 (2.44)*	1 222.14 (2.45)*	1 519.50 (2.75)*
4. Alberta	1 139.69 (2.52)*	1 134.42 (2.49)*	1 274.14 (2.47)*
5. British Columbia	1 268.28 (2.98)*	1 287.26 (3.00)*	1 693.48 (3.42)
6. Gender (female)	-19.52 (-.08)	-5.92 (-.02)	62.54 (.22)
7. Age (45 and over)	-523.63 (-2.04)*	-519.14 (-1.96)*	-560.62 (-1.83)*
8. Low education	-310.79 (-1.02)	-320.95 (-1.03)	-127.49 (-.35)
9. High education	779.19 (2.39)*	751.04 (2.26)*	701.86 (1.84)
10. Low income	-410.34 (-1.37)	-448.78 (-1.49)	-279.03 (-.80)
11. High income	156.24 (.51)	137.29 (.45)	-120.82 (-.34)
12. Blue collar	-322.68 (-1.12)	-338.39 (-1.17)	-471.23 (-1.44)
13. Union	183.29 (.68)	180.94 (.67)	296.17 (.96)
14. French	-683.07 (-1.56)	-689.84 (-1.55)	-809.87 (-1.50)
15. Non-charter language	-515.74 (-1.17)	-527.93 (-1.19)	-662.75 (-1.26)
16. Catholic	97.47 (.27)	39.41 (.11)	-165.93 (-.40)
17. Protestant	-124.16 (-.36)	-172.49 (-.49)	-352.93 (-.89)
18. Information	—	82.69 (.19)	-149.78 (-.30)
19. Contribution	—	-169.77 (-.57)	-416.34 (-1.24)
20. Cynicism	—	—	-1 800.39 (2.82)*
21. Belief: parties (p11)	—	—	-518.82 (-1.36)*
22. Money: motivations (f18)	—	—	-138.08 (-.48)
23. Money: impact (f20)	—	—	-496.95 (-1.75)
24. Populist liberal	—	—	-1 175.63 (-2.47)*
25. Minoritarian individualist	—	—	-1 549.03 (-2.87)*
26. Majoritarian individualist	—	—	-601.27 (-1.29)
27. Radical collectivist	—	—	-2 325.43 (-4.65)*
28. Party collectivist	—	—	-1 543.49 (-3.30)*
Constant	2 412.28 (6.26)	2 462.00 (4.91)	5 854.23 (5.16)
N	1 055	1 048	826
R²	.03	.03	.08

Note: The dependent variable is the amount of money deemed appropriate as a ceiling on contribution (question f2b). Those choosing a "more than $10 000" target were put at $20 000 and "other" responses were left out. The regression excludes all those opposed to ceilings.

Table 1.D22
Determinants of opinions about disclosure

	Equation 1	Equation 2	Equation 3
1. Atlantic	.00 (.01)	-.01 (-.19)	.02 (.42)
2. Quebec	-.02 (-.81)	-.03 (-1.00)	-.02 (-.39)
3. Man./Sask.	.00 (.11)	.00 (.42)	.01 (.36)
4. Alberta	.01 (.43)	.01 (.31)	.03 (.71)
5. British Columbia	.03 (1.03)	.03 (1.00)	.03 (.83)
6. Gender (female)	-.04 (-2.52)*	-.02 (-1.05)	-.01 (-.47)
7. Age (45 and over)	.02 (1.04)	-.00 (-.16)	.01 (.24)
8. Low education	-.04 (-2.06)*	-.02 (-1.12)	-.04 (-1.39)
9. High education	.07 (2.88)*	.04 (1.81)	.04 (1.39)
10. Low income	-.05 (-2.36)*	-.04 (-2.04)*	-.04 (-1.58)
11. High income	.00 (.16)	-.00 (-.08)	-.00 (-.17)
12. Blue collar	-.02 (-.77)	-.01 (-.33)	.02 (.68)
13. Union	.02 (1.11)	.02 (1.01)	.01 (.55)
14. French	-.03 (-.90)	-.02 (-.55)	-.01 (-.29)
15. Non-charter language	-.03 (-.81)	-.02 (-.70)	-.02 (-.59)
16. Catholic	-.05 (-1.80)	-.06 (-2.07)*	-.05 (-1.72)
17. Protestant	-.07 (-2.76)*	-.08 (-3.29)*	-.08 (-2.81)*
18. Information	—	.22 (6.73)*	.22 (5.88)*
19. Contribution	—	-.02 (-.97)	-.04 (-1.73)
20. Cynicism	—	—	.08 (1.65)
21. Belief: parties (p11)	—	—	-.07 (-2.50)*
22. Money: motivations (f18)	—	—	.10 (4.66)*
23. Money: impact (f20)	—	—	.00 (.06)
24. Populist liberal	—	—	-.01 (-.41)
25. Minoritarian individualist	—	—	-.03 (-.71)
26. Majoritarian individualist	——	—	.00 (.11)
27. Radical collectivist	—	—	-.04 (-1.01)
28. Party collectivist	—	—	-.03 (-.80)
Constant	.88 (30.37)	.75 (20.48)	.69 (13.76)
N	2 151	2 121	1 622
R^2	.02	.05	.05

Note: The dependent variable takes the value of 1 for those in favour of disclosure of contribution and the value of 0 for those opposed (question f8).

Table 1.D23
Determinants of opinions about group contributions

	Equation 1	Equation 2	Equation 3
1. Atlantic	.05 (1.38)	.05 (1.32)	.06 (1.57)
2. Quebec	.01 (.35)	-.01 (-.16)	-.02 (-.50)
3. Man./Sask.	-.07 (-1.77)	-.09 (-2.23)	-.09 (-2.03)*
4. Alberta	-.02 (-.52)	-.03 (-.74)	-.01 (-.28)
5. British Columbia	-.05 (-1.63)	-.06 (-1.79)	-.05 (-1.34)
6. Gender (female)	.04 (1.97)*	.03 (1.46)	.04 (1.70)
7. Age (45 and over)	-.06 (-2.76)*	-.06 (-2.64)*	-.05 (-2.01)*
8. Low education	-.01 (-.44)	-.02 (-.70)	-.00 (-.73)
9. High education	.03 (1.12)	.04 (1.30)	.00 (.10)
10. Low income	-.01 (-.21)	.00 (.01)	-.00 (-.12)
11. High income	-.00 (-.01)	-.00 (-.18)	-.02 (-.57)
12. Blue collar	-.00 (-.37)	-.00 (-.22)	.01 (.44)
13. Union	.01 (.38)	.01 (.54)	.02 (1.03)
14. French	-.01 (-.24)	-.01 (-.16)	-.00 (-.42)
15. Non-charter language	.08 (2.26)*	.08 (2.20)*	.10 (2.30)*
16. Catholic	.00 (.05)	.01 (.28)	-.00 (-.10)
17. Protestant	.00 (.16)	.01 (.32)	.00 (.03)
18. Information	—	-.09 (-2.59)*	-.06 (-1.58)
19. Contribution	—	.09 (3.61)*	.06 (2.04)*
20. Cynicism	—	—	-.14 (-2.83)*
21. Belief: parties (p11)	—	—	-.04 (-1.28)
22. Money: motivations (f18)	—	—	-.06 (-2.72)*
23. Money: impact (f20)	—	—	-.09 (-3.94)*
24. Populist liberal	—	—	-.04 (-1.10)
25. Minoritarian individualist	—	—	-.06 (-1.32)
26. Majoritarian individualist	—	—	-.03 (-.89)
27. Radical collectivist	—	—	-.02 (-.58)
28. Party collectivist	—	—	-.02 (-.55)
Constant	.57 (17.65)	.61 (15.17)	.81 (10.91)
N	2 007	1 984	1 541
R^2	.01	.01	.04

Note: The dependent variable is a scale made up of responses to questions f4 to f6. The higher the score, the more favourable one is to allow group contribution.

Table 1.D24
Determinants of opinions about direct public funding for parties and candidates

	Equation 1	Equation 2	Equation 3
1. Atlantic	.03 (.76)	.03 (.75)	.02 (.43)
2. Quebec	.06 (1.67)*	.05 (1.19)	.02 (.42)
3. Man./Sask.	-.01 (-.26)	-.01 (-.29)	-.03 (-.75)
4. Alberta	-.09 (-2.39)*	-.09 (-2.35)*	-.06 (-1.42)
5. British Columbia	-.08 (-2.30)	-.09 (-2.42)*	-.08 (-1.92)
6. Gender (female)	.04 (1.70)	.02 (.72)	-.01 (-.31)
7. Age (45 and over)	-.07 (-2.97)*	-.04 (-1.96)*	-.06 (-2.21)*
8. Low education	.02 (.86)	.00 (.12)	.03 (.86)
9. High education	-.01 (-.28)	.02 (.56)	.03 (.81)
10. Low income	.02 (.80)	.02 (.70)	.05 (1.70)
11. High income	-.06 (-2.12)*	-.05 (-1.88)	-.05 (-1.77)
12. Blue collar	.03 (1.13)	.02 (.83)	.03 (1.04)
13. Union	-.05 (-2.22)*	-.05 (-2.01)*	-.05 (-1.95)
14. French	.06 (1.56)	.07 (1.71)	.09 (2.05)*
15. Non-charter language	.05 (1.32)	.05 (1.30)	.08 (1.67)
16. Catholic	.00 (.17)	.02 (.53)	.03 (.71)
17. Protestant	-.09 (-2.84)*	-.07 (-2.21)*	-.04 (-1.25)
18. Information	—	-.17 (-4.46)*	-.17 (-3.87)*
19. Contribution	—	.01 (.27)	.02 (.81)
20. Cynicism	—	—	.01 (.19)
21. Belief: parties (p11)	—	—	.00 (.13)
22. Money: motivations (f18)	—	—	-.01 (-.21)
23. Money: impact (f20)	—	—	-.04 (-1.48)
24. Populist liberal	—	—	-.04 (-1.01)
25. Minoritarian individualist	—	—	-.01 (-.29)
26. Majoritarian individualist	—	—	-.08 (-2.08)*
27. Radical collectivist	—	—	.08 (1.82)
28. Party collectivist	—	—	.04 (1.08)
Constant	.38 (11.11)	.48 (11.07)	.48 (7.33)
N	2 094	2 071	1 592
R^2	.05	.05	.06

Note: The dependent variable takes the value of 1 for those who think the government should reimburse all or some of the money spent by parties and candidates during an election campaign and the value of 0 for those who think the government should reimburse none of it (question f10).

Table 1.D25
Determinants of opinions about tax credits for contributions

	Equation 1	Equation 2	Equation 3
1. Atlantic	.08 (2.11)*	.08 (2.11)*	.09 (2.02)*
2. Quebec	.08 (2.07)*	.06 (1.43)	.10 (2.16)*
3. Man./Sask.	.06 (1.55)	.04 (.95)	.05 (1.09)
4. Alberta	-.04 (-1.10)	-.05 (-1.38)	-.02 (-.51)
5. British Columbia	-.05 (-1.44)	-.07 (-1.80)	-.06 (-1.53)
6. Gender (female)	-.02 (-.91)	-.03 (-1.51)	-.03 (-1.33)
7. Age (45 and over)	-.00 (-.21)	-.01 (-.29)	-.01 (-.48)
8. Low education	.06 (2.16)*	.05 (1.79)	.04 (1.42)
9. High education	.03 (1.03)	-.04 (1.27)	.07 (1.97)*
10. Low income	-.01 (-.37)	-.01 (-.26)	-.01 (-.23)
11. High income	.04 (1.52)	.03 (1.25)	.04 (1.23)
12. Blue collar	.04 (1.58)	.03 (1.34)	.04 (1.43)
13. Union	-.03 (-1.11)	-.02 (-.94)	-.01 (-.42)
14. French	.09 (2.16)*	.08 (2.12)*	.06 (1.38)
15. Non-charter language	.07 (1.87)	.07 (1.75)	.06 (1.35)
16. Catholic	.04 (1.23)	.05 (1.53)	.00 (.07)
17. Protestant	.01 (.48)	.02 (.72)	.02 (.47)
18. Information	—	-.16 (-4.18)*	-.15 (-3.42)*
19. Contribution	—	.19 (7.06)*	.16 (5.10)*
20. Cynicism	—	—	-.09 (-1.63)
21. Belief: parties (p11)	—	—	.00 (.05)
22. Money: motivations (f18)	—	—	-.13 (-5.32)*
23. Money: impact (f20)	—	—	-.03 (-1.09)
24. Populist liberal	—	—	.01 (.24)
25. Minoritarian individualist	—	—	.07 (1.48)
26. Majoritarian individualist	—	—	.14 (3.32)*
27. Radical collectivist	—	—	.11 (2.42)*
28. Party collectivist	—	—	.15 (3.77)*
Constant	.35 (9.97)	.43 (9.72)	.48 (5.77)
N	2 160	2 132	1 626
R^2	.03	.06	.08

Note: The dependent variable takes the value of 1 for those who are favourable to tax credits and the value of 0 for those opposed (question f3).

Table 1.D26
Determinants of opinions about eligibility for public funding

	Equation 1	Equation 2	Equation 3
1. Atlantic	-.07 (-1.02)	-.07 (-1.00)	-.09 (-1.15)
2. Quebec	-.10 (-1.39)	-.09 (-1.13)	-.12 (-1.38)
3. Man./Sask.	-.12 (-1.58)	-.12 (-1.52)	-.10 (-1.09)
4. Alberta	.02 (-.23)	.02 (.19)	.06 (.69)
5. British Columbia	-.02 (-.30)	-.02 (-.28)	.04 (.43)
6. Gender (female)	.11 (2.99)*	.12 (2.97)*	.09 (1.93)
7. Age (45 and over)	-.04 (-.97)	-.05 (-1.18)	-.02 (-.42)
8. Low education	.07 (1.44)	.08 (1.56)	-.00 (-.09)
9. High education	-.03 (-.53)	-.04 (-.75)	-.10 (-1.47)
10. Low income	-.06 (-1.33)	-.06 (-1.34)	-.02 (-.37)
11. High income	-.05 (-.90)	-.06 (-1.03)	.00 (.06)
12. Blue collar	-.00 (-.08)	-.00 (-.08)	.04 (.75)
13. Union	.00 (.11)	.00 (.04)	.02 (.55)
14. French	-.07 (-.98)	-.08 (-1.08)	-.08 (-.92)
15. Non-charter language	-.07 (-1.07)	-.08 (-1.10)	-.25 (-3.16)*
16. Catholic	-.04 (-.71)	-.05 (-.90)	-.08 (-1.21)
17. Protestant	.06 (.92)	.04 (.68)	.01 (.18)
18. Information	—	.03 (.48)	.10 (1.26)
19. Contribution	—	.02 (.44)	.05 (.81)
20. Cynicism	—	—	.02 (.15)
21. Belief: parties (p11)	—	—	.07 (1.12)
22. Money: motivations (f18)	—	—	-.01 (-.17)
23. Money: impact (f20)	—	—	-.02 (-.49)
24. Populist liberal	—	—	-.08 (-.94)
25. Minoritarian individualist	—	—	.04 (.46)
26. Majoritarian individualist	—	—	-.17 (-2.18)*
27. Radical collectivist	—	—	-.10 (-1.30)
28. Party collectivist	—	—	-.04 (-.57)
Constant	.51 (8.17)	.50 (6.32)	.48 (4.02)
N	683	674	541
R^2	.04	.04	.05

Note: The dependent variable takes the value of 1 for those who think all parties and candidates should be eligible for public funding and the value of 0 for those who think that only those who obtain a certain percentage of the vote should be eligible (question f11).

Table 1.D27

Determinants of opinions about the feasibility of controls for party electoral spending

	Equation 1	Equation 2	Equation 3
1. Atlantic	.05 (2.00)*	.05 (1.93)	.05 (1.93)
2. Quebec	-.00 (-.11)	.00 (.04)	.02 (.51)
3. Man./Sask.	.03 (1.15)	.04 (1.42)	.04 (1.22)
4. Alberta	.04 (1.61)	.04 (1.56)	.04 (1.35)
5. British Columbia	.06 (2.39)*	.06 (2.38)*	.07 (2.66)*
6. Gender (female)	.02 (1.40)	.01 (1.06)	.01 (.44)
7. Age (45 and over)	.02 (1.70)	.04 (2.40)*	.01 (.82)
8. Low education	.01 (.31)	-.00 (-.04)	-.01 (-.25)
9. High education	-.08 (-3.99)*	-.07 (-3.41)*	-.06 (-2.79)*
10. Low income	.01 (.44)	.00 (.13)	-.01 (-.56)
11. High income	-.01 (-.43)	-.00 (-.26)	-.00 (-.11)
12. Blue collar	.02 (1.54)	.02 (1.35)	.01 (.72)
13. Union	-.00 (-.14)	-.00 (-.16)	-.00 (-.13)
14. French	.01 (.38)	.01 (.32)	.01 (.37)
15. Non-charter language	.02 (1.01)	.02 (.97)	.02 (.63)
16. Catholic	-.02 (-.76)	-.02 (-.78)	-.01 (-.61)
17. Protestant	-.00 (.14)	-.00 (-.00)	-.00 (-.17)
18. Information	—	-.05 (-1.89)	-.03 (-1.00)
19. Contribution	—	-.05 (-2.78)*	-.03 (-1.60)
20. Cynicism	—	—	.14 (3.82)*
21. Belief: parties (p11)	—	—	.05 (2.62)*
22. Money: motivations (f18)	—	—	.04 (2.32)*
23. Money: impact (f20)	—	—	.01 (.79)
24. Populist liberal	—	—	-.06 (-2.11)*
25. Minoritarian individualist	—	—	.06 (1.87)
26. Majoritarian individualist	—	—	-.01 (-.56)
27. Radical collectivist	—	—	-.01 (-.40)
28. Party collectivist	—	—	.02 (.63)
Constant	.31 (13.61)	.35 (12.11)	.18 (7.27)
N	2 213	2 086	1 611
R^2	.02	.02	.05

Note: The dependent variable takes the value of 1 for those who think it is impossible to really control electoral finances and who think controls are a waste of energy, the value 0.5 for those who think it is impossible to really control but still worth trying and the value of 0 for those who do not think that it is impossible to really control (questions f21 and f22).

Table 1.D28
Determinants of opinions about party advertising

	Equation 1	Equation 2	Equation 3
1. Atlantic	.04 (1.32)	.04 (1.26)	.04 (1.12)
2. Quebec	.05 (1.66)	.05 (1.44)	.08 (2.19)*
3. Man./Sask.	.02 (.65)	.01 (.38)	.02 (.51)
4. Alberta	-.03 (-.99)	-.03 (-.94)	-.01 (-.35)
5. British Columbia	.01 (.44)	.02 (.61)	.02 (.50)
6. Gender (female)	.02 (1.39)	.03 (1.53)	.02 (1.06)
7. Age (45 and over)	-.04 (-2.11)*	-.05 (-2.37)*	-.05 (-2.29)*
8. Low education	-.04 (-1.61)	-.03 (-1.19)	-.03 (-1.23)
9. High education	.08 (3.12)*	.06 (2.44)*	.10 (3.48)*
10. Low income	-.02 (-.94)	-.02 (-.81)	-.02 (-.72)
11. High income	.02 (1.02)	.02 (.93)	.02 (.97)
12. Blue collar	.04 (1.91)	.04 (2.18)*	.04 (1.96)*
13. Union	.00 (.19)	-.00 (-.04)	.01 (.23)
14. French	.02 (.54)	.02 (.64)	-.03 (-.75)
15. Non-charter language	.03 (.82)	.03 (.93)	.03 (.79)
16. Catholic	.01 (.34)	.01 (.28)	.07 (2.22)*
17. Protestant	.02 (.75)	.02 (.58)	.05 (1.71)
18. Information	—	.07 (2.19)*	.08 (2.22)*
19. Member	—	-.00 (-.20)	.01 (.47)
20. Cynicism	—	—	.10 (2.29)*
21. Belief: parties (p11)	—	—	-.03 (-.96)
22. Ad: need (m13)	—	—	.05 (2.50)*
23. Experiment	-.14 (-8.10)*	-.13 (-7.68)*	-.12 (-5.93)*
24. Populist liberal	—	-.02 (-.82)	-.07 (-1.99)*
25. Minoritarian individualist	—	-.01 (-.32)	-.01 (-.16)
26. Majoritarian individualist	—	-.04 (-1.56)	-.05 (-1.42)
27. Radical collectivist	—	.04 (1.29)	.01 (.34)
28. Party collectivist	—	-.01 (-.33)	-.02 (-.62)
Constant	.80 (26.74)	.77 (18.35)	.66 (13.39)
N	2 160	2 135	1 656
R^2	.04	.04	.05

Note: The dependent variable is the combination of questions m12a and m12b. The variable takes the value of 1 when the individual believes that we should limit spending on party advertising and the value of 0 when one thinks that parties should be allowed to advertise as much as they wish.

Table 1.D29
Determinants of opinions about media coverage of election campaigns

	Equation 1	Equation 2	Equation 3
1. Atlantic	.05 (1.45)	.05 (1.67)	.05 (1.66)
2. Quebec	.07 (2.19)*	.08 (2.58)*	.08 (2.46)*
3. Man./Sask.	-.01 (-.26)	.00 (.12)	.01 (.17)
4. Alberta	-.03 (-.80)	-.01 (-.42)	-.01 (-.27)
5. British Columbia	-.04 (-1.28)	-.03 (-1.04)	-.03 (-1.05)
6. Gender (female)	.07 (4.11)*	.06 (3.37)*	.06 (3.02)*
7. Age (45 and over)	.04 (2.15)*	.06 (3.19)*	.06 (3.32)*
8. Low education	.03 (1.58)	.02 (.77)	.02 (.81)
9. High education	-.08 (-3.08)*	-.06 (-2.28)*	-.06 (-2.31)*
10. Low income	-.00 (-.23)	-.01 (-.54)	-.01 (-.63)
11. High income	-.07 (-3.00)*	-.06 (-2.65)*	-.06 (-2.57)*
12. Blue collar	-.04 (-1.77)	-.04 (-2.03)*	-.04 (-1.97)*
13. Union	.03 (1.82)	.04 (1.90)	.04 (1.85)
14. French	-.01 (-.31)	-.02 (-.46)	-.01 (-.43)
15. Non-charter language	.04 (1.44)	.04 (1.36)	.04 (1.37)
16. Catholic	-.02 (-.87)	-.02 (-.67)	-.02 (-.70)
17. Protestant	-.03 (-1.13)	-.02 (-.79)	-.02 (-.71)
18. Information	—	-.11 (-3.49)*	-.11 (-3.48)*
19. Member	—	-.07 (-2.92)*	-.06 (-2.76)*
20. Populist liberal	—	—	.02 (.69)
21. Minoritarian individualist	—	—	.00 (.12)
22. Majoritarian individualist	—	—	-.04 (-1.32)
23. Radical collectivist	—	—	.02 (.49)
24. Party collectivist	—	—	.04 (1.63)
Constant	.64 (22.46)	.71 (19.76)	.70 (17.42)
N	2 218	2 190	2 190
R^2	.03	.04	.04

Note: The dependent variable is made out of responses to questions m1 and m2. The higher the score on the scale, the more positive the evaluation of media coverage.

Table 1.D30
Determinants of opinions about mandatory leaders debates

	Equation 1	Equation 2	Equation 3
1. Atlantic	.05 (1.35)	.06 (1.53)	.02 (.51)
2. Quebec	-.02 (-.63)	.00 (.02)	.02 (.52)
3. Man./Sask.	-.13 (-3.25)*	-.12 (-2.98)*	-.06 (-1.31)
4. Alberta	-.07 (-1.84)	-.06 (-1.59)	-.07 (-1.68)
5. British Columbia	-.02 (-.44)	-.01 (-1.79)	-.01 (-.39)
6. Gender (female)	.03 (1.21)	.01 (.40)	-.01 (-.44)
7. Age (45 and over)	-.08 (-3.50)*	-.06 (-2.71)*	-.04 (-1.35)
8. Low education	.04 (1.39)	.00 (.13)	.02 (.58)
9. High education	-.13 (-4.27)*	-.09 (-2.95)*	-.03 (-.89)
10. Low income	.08 (3.22)*	.06 (2.25)*	.04 (1.54)
11. High income	-.02 (-.68)	-.02 (-.59)	-.01 (-.38)
12. Blue collar	-.01 (-.50)	-.03 (-1.08)	-.05 (-2.00)*
13. Union	.03 (1.15)	.02 (1.12)	.04 (1.49)
14. French	.03 (.88)	.01 (.24)	.02 (.54)
15. Non-charter language	.20 (5.34)*	.19 (4.91)*	.15 (3.40)*
16. Catholic	.02 (.67)	.01 (.36)	.01 (.20)
17. Protestant	-.04 (-1.21)	-.04 (-1.38)	-.04 (-1.30)
18. Information	—	-.16 (-4.22)*	-.10 (-2.31)*
19. Member	—	-.05 (-1.79)	-.03 (-.91)
20. Cynicism	—	—	.18 (3.48)*
21. Belief: parties (p11)	—	—	.03 (.83)
22. Media coverage	—	—	-.03 (-.83)
23. Debate: useful	—	—	.05 (1.72)
24. Debate: not useful	—	—	-.13 (-3.97)*
25. Debate: compare	—	—	.27 (9.73)*
26. Debate: ideas	—	—	.05 (1.93)
27. Populist liberal	—	.09 (2.38)*	.07 (1.76)
28. Minoritarian individualist	—	.15 (3.99)*	.12 (2.61)*
29. Majoritarian individualist	—	.11 (3.12)*	.05 (1.34)
30. Radical collectivist	—	.13 (3.55)*	.10 (2.25)*
31. Party collectivist	—	.18 (5.36)*	.14 (3.81)*
Constant	.59 (16.91)	.61 (12.45)	.27 (6.31)
N	2 166	2 139	1 544
R^2	.05	.07	.19

Note: The dependent variable takes the value of 1 for those who believe there should be a law requiring party leaders to participate in a debate (question m6a) and the value of 0 for those opposed to such a law.

Table 1.D31
Determinants of satisfaction with existing electoral procedures

	Equation 1	Equation 2	Equation 3
1. Atlantic	.12 (1.77)	.12 (1.78)	.11 (1.20)
2. Quebec	-.12 (-1.86)	-.12 (-1.85)	-.01 (-.10)
3. Man./Sask.	-.16 (-2.30)*	-.15 (-2.19)*	-.17 (-1.78)
4. Alberta	-.17 (-2.61)*	-.18 (-2.72)*	-.11 (-1.17)
5. British Columbia	-.15 (-2.47)*	-.15 (-2.44)*	-.15 (-1.71)
6. Gender (female)	-.07 (-2.02)*	-.07 (-1.87)	.05 (.92)
7. Age (45 and over)	-.03 (-.81)	-.03 (-.87)	-.01 (-.17)
8. Low education	-.10 (-2.10)*	-.10 (-2.16)*	.04 (.58)
9. High education	-.04 (-.79)	-.04 (-.92)	-.12 (-1.86)
10. Low income	-.06 (-1.38)	-.05 (-1.20)	-.02 (-.34)
11. High income	.04 (.86)	.04 (.77)	.03 (.49)
12. Blue collar	-.05 (-1.24)	-.05 (-1.19)	-.06 (-.94)
13. Union	.03 (.66)	.03 (.80)	.03 (.61)
14. French	.17 (2.54)*	.17 (2.52)*	.16 (1.64)
15. Non-charter language	.15 (2.31)*	.15 (2.34)*	.17 (1.76)
16. Catholic	.05 (.93)	.06 (1.06)	-.04 (-.51)
17. Protestant	.11 (2.16)*	.11 (2.22)*	.07 (1.03)
18. F18	—	—	-.10 (-1.99)*
19. F20	—	—	-.11 (-2.02)*
20. Cynicism	—	—	-.62 (-5.45)*
21. Belief: parties (p11)	—	—	-.02 (-0.29)
22. Electoral system	—	—	.23 (4.37)*
23. Quotas	—	—	-.05 (-.86)
24. Mand. debates	—	—	.08 (1.45)
25. Public funding	—	—	.07 (1.22)
26. Ceilings	—	—	.04 (.81)
27. Spending limits	—	—	-.15 (-1.82)
28. Spending	—	—	-.00 (-.07)
29. Group contrib.	—	—	.14 (2.38)*
30. Populist liberal	—	-.08 (-1.29)	.08 (.97)
31. Minoritarian individualist	—	-.03 (-.44)	-.07 (-.74)
32. Majoritarian individualist	—	-.08 (-1.27)	-.03 (-.41)
33. Radical collectivist	—	-.18 (-2.72)*	-.13 (-1.45)
34. Party collectivist	—	-.13 (-2.28)*	-.05 (-.57)
Constant	1.69 (28.30)	1.76 (25.41)	2.06 (9.36)
N	1 884	1 884	933
R^2	.02	.02	.11

Note: The dependent variable is overall satisfaction with the way federal elections work in Canada (question e1). The variable takes the value of 0 for those not at all satisfied, 1 for those not very satisfied, 2 for those somewhat satisfied and 3 for the very satisfied.

Table 1.D32
Determinants of comparative evaluation of Canadian and American electoral procedures

1. Atlantic	.00 (.09)
2. Quebec	-.11 (-3.29)*
3. Man./Sask.	.02 (.72)
4. Alberta	-.09 (-2.78)*
5. British Columbia	-.04 (-1.30)
6. Gender (female)	.04 (2.27)*
7. Age (45 and over)	.01 (.75)
8. Low education	.01 (.53)
9. High education	.12 (4.73)*
10. Low income	.01 (.54)
11. High income	-.03 (-1.26)
12. Blue collar	-.00 (-.15)
13. Union	-.01 (-.78)
14. French	.03 (1.07)
15. Non-charter language	.03 (.93)
16. Catholic	-.01 (-.28)
17. Protestant	-.03 (-1.03)
Constant	.56 (18.94)
N	1 523
R^2	.03

Note: The dependent variable takes the value of 1 for those who think Canadian elections work better, 0 for those who think American elections work better, and 0.5 for those who think neither works better.

Table 1.D33
Determinants of comparative evaluation of federal and provincial electoral procedures

1. Atlantic	-.03 (-1.25)
2. Quebec	-.08 (-3.61)*
3. Man./Sask.	.09 (3.75)*
4. Alberta	.08 (3.65)*
5. British Columbia	.04 (1.69)
6. Gender (female)	-.00 (-.36)
7. Age (45 and over)	.00 (.26)
8. Low education	-.02 (-1.09)
9. High education	.00 (.19)
10. Low income	-.02 (-1.28)
11. High income	-.05 (-2.89)*
12. Blue collar	.00 (.02)
13. Union	.02 (1.22)
14. French	.02 (1.09)
15. Non-charter language	.01 (.59)
16. Catholic	.03 (1.76)
17. Protestant	.01 (.65)
Constant	.57 (27.72)
N	1 762
R^2	.03

Note: The dependent variable takes the value of 1 for those who think provincial elections work better, 0 for those who think federal elections work better, and 0.5 for those who think neither works better.

BIBLIOGRAPHY

ABBREVIATIONS

c.	chapter
Pub. L.	Public Law
R.S.C.	Revised Statutes of Canada
s(s).	sections

This study was completed in October 1991.

Abramson, Paul R. 1983. *Political Attitudes in America: Formation and Change.* San Francisco: W.H. Freeman.

Almond, Gabriel, and Sydney Verba. 1963. *The Civic Culture: Political Attitudes and Democracy in Five Nations.* Princeton: Princeton University Press.

American Political Science Association. 1950. *Towards a More Responsible Two-Party System.* New York: Rinehart.

Archer, Keith. 1985. "The Failure of the New Democratic Party: Unions, Unionists and Politics in Canada." *Canadian Journal of Political Science* 18:353–66.

Bachrach, Peter. 1967. *The Theory of Democratic Elitism: A Critique.* Boston: Little, Brown.

Bashevkin, Sylvia B. 1989. "Political Parties and the Representation of Women." In *Canadian Parties in Transition,* ed. Alain G. Gagnon and Brian Tanguay. Scarborough: Nelson.

———. 1990. "Women's Participation in Political Parties." Paper presented at Symposium on the Active Participation of Women in Politics, Royal Commission on Electoral Reform and Party Financing. Ottawa.

Bates, D. 1984. "Attitudes Towards Smoking By-Law Legislation Sample Report." Toronto: York University, Institute for Social Research.

Bernier, Robert, and Denis Monière. 1991. "The Organization of Televised Leaders Debates in the United States, Europe, Australia and Canada." In *Media and Voters in Canadian Election Campaigns,* ed. Frederick J. Fletcher. Vol. 18 of the research studies of the Royal Commission on Electoral Reform and Party Financing. Ottawa and Toronto: RCERPF/Dundurn.

Birch, A.H. 1971. *Representation.* New York: Praeger.

Blais, André. 1990. "Issue Voting: The Utility of Tapping Introspective Judgements." Proceedings of the Conference on Analyzing Democracy. York University.

———. 1991. "The Debate over Electoral Systems." *International Journal of Political Science* 12:239–60.

Blais, André, and Kenneth Carty. 1991. "The Psychological Impact of Electoral Laws: Measuring Duverger's Elusive Factor." *British Journal of Political Science* 21:79–93.

Blais, André, and Stéphane Dion. 1987. "Trop d'État? Un baromètre de l'opinion." *Politique* 11:43–73.

Blais, André, and Elisabeth Gidengil. 1990. "A Survey of Attitudes About Electoral Reform." Study prepared for the Royal Commission on Electoral Reform and Party Financing. Toronto: York University, Institute for Social Research.

Blake, Donald E. 1985. *Two Political Worlds: Parties and Voting in British Columbia.* Vancouver: University of British Columbia Press.

Blishen, B., B. Carroll and D. Moore. 1987. "The 1981 Socio-economic Index for Occupations in Canada." *Canadian Review of Sociology and Anthropology* 24:465–88.

Bollen, Kenneth A. 1979. "Political Democracy and the Timing of Development." *American Sociological Review* 44:572–87.

Brady, Henry E., and Richard Johnston. 1988. "Conventions Versus Primaries: A Canadian–American Comparison." In *Party Democracy in Canada: The Politics of National Party Conventions,* ed. George Perlin. Scarborough: Prentice-Hall.

Brennan, Geoffrey, and Philip Pettit. 1990. "Unveiling the Vote." *British Journal of Political Science* 20:311–33.

Breton, Raymond. 1986. "Multiculturalism and Canadian Nation-Building." In *The Politics of Gender, Ethnicity and Language in Canada,* ed. Alan Cairns and Cynthia Williams. Vol. 34 of the research studies of the Royal Commission on the Economic Union and Development Prospects for Canada. Toronto: University of Toronto Press.

Brodie, Janine. 1985. *Women and Politics in Canada.* Toronto: McGraw-Hill Ryerson.

———. 1988. "The Gender Factor and National Leadership Conventions in Canada." In *Party Democracy in Canada: The Politics of National Party Conventions,* ed. George Perlin. Scarborough: Prentice-Hall.

———. 1991. "Women and the Electoral Process in Canada." In *Women in Canadian Politics: Toward Equity in Representation,* ed. Kathy Megyery. Vol. 6 of the research studies of the Royal Commission on Electoral Reform and Party Financing. Ottawa and Toronto: RCERPF/Dundurn.

Bryant, A., M. Gold, D. Northrup and M. Stevenson. 1990. "Public Attitudes Toward the Exclusion of Evidence: Section 24(2) of the *Canadian Charter of Rights and Freedoms.*" *Canadian Bar Review* 69:1–45.

Butler, David, Howard R. Penniman and Austin Ranney. 1981. "Introduction: Democratic and Undemocratic Elections." In *Democracy at the Polls: A Comparative Study of Competitive National Elections*, ed. David Butler, Howard R. Penniman and Austin Ranney. Washington, DC: American Enterprise Institute for Public Policy Research.

Cairns, Alan C. 1973. "The Electoral System and the Party System in Canada, 1921–1965." In *The Canadian Political Process: A Reader*, ed. O.M. Kruhlak, R. Schultz and S.I. Pobihushchy. Toronto: Holt, Rinehart and Winston.

———. 1988. "The Canadian Constitutional Experiment." In *Constitution, Government, and Society in Canada: Selected Essays by Alan C. Cairns*, ed. Douglas E. Williams. Toronto: McClelland and Stewart.

———. 1989. "Ritual, Taboo and Bias in Constitutional Controversies in Canada, or Constitutional Talk Canadian Style." The Timlin Lecture. Saskatchewan: University of Saskatchewan. Reprinted in Alan C. Cairns, *Disruptions: Constitutional Struggles, from the Charter to Meech Lake*, ed. Douglas E. Williams. Toronto: McClelland and Stewart, 1991.

———. 1991. "Constitutional Minoritarianism in Canada." In *Canada: The State of the Federation 1990*, ed. Ronald L. Watts and Douglas M. Brown. Kingston: Queen's University, Institute of Intergovernmental Relations.

Campbell, Angus. 1981. *The Sense of Well-Being in America: Recent Patterns and Trends*. New York: McGraw-Hill.

Canada. *Canada Elections Act*, R.S.C. 1985, c. E-2.

———. *Canadian Charter of Rights and Freedoms*, ss. 1, 2, Part I of the *Constitution Act, 1982*, being Schedule B of the *Canada Act 1982 (U.K.)*, 1982, c. 11.

Canada. Statistics Canada. 1985. *Telephone Statistics*. Catalogue 56-203. Ottawa: Minister of Supply and Services Canada.

Castles, Francis G. 1981. "Female Legislative Representation and the Electoral System." *Politics* 1:21–27.

Chi, N.H. 1972. "The Regression Model of Regionalism: A Critique." *Canadian Journal of Political Science* 5:291–97.

Christian, William, and Colin Campbell. 1990. *Political Parties and Ideologies in Canada*. 3d ed. Toronto: McGraw-Hill Ryerson.

Clarke, Harold D., and Allan Kornberg. 1979. "Moving Up the Political Escalator: Women Party Officials in the United States and Canada." *Journal of Politics* 41:442–76.

Conover, Pamela Johnston. 1988. "Feminists and the Gender Gap." *Journal of Politics* 50:985–1010.

Converse, Philip E. 1964. "The Nature of Belief Systems in Mass Publics." In *Ideology and Discontent*, ed. David E. Apter. New York: Free Press.

————. 1970. "Attitudes and Non-Attitudes: Continuation of a Dialogue." In *The Quantitative Analysis of Social Problems,* ed. Edward R. Tufte. Reading: Addison-Wesley.

————. 1974. "Some Priority Variables in Comparative Research." In *Electoral Behavior: A Comparative Handbook,* ed. Richard Rose. New York: Free Press.

Courtney, John C. 1986. "Leadership Conventions and the Development of the National Political Community in Canada." In *National Politics and Community in Canada,* ed. R. Kenneth Carty and W. Peter Ward. Vancouver: University of British Columbia Press.

Dahl, Robert A. 1956. *A Preface to Democratic Theory.* Chicago: University of Chicago Press.

————. 1989. *Democracy and Its Critics.* New Haven: Yale University Press.

Dennis, Jack. 1966. "Support of the Party System by the Mass Public." *American Political Science Review* 60:600–15.

————. 1975. "Trends in Public Support for the American Party System." *British Journal of Political Science* 5:187–230.

Dicey, Albert Venn. 1960. *Introduction to the Study of the Law of the Constitution.* 10th ed. with an introduction by E.C.S. Wade. London: Macmillan.

Dillman, D.A. 1978. *Mail and Telephone Surveys: The Total Design Method.* New York: John Wiley and Sons.

Downs, Anthony. 1957. *An American Theory of Democracy.* New York: Harper.

Dunkelberg, W.C., and G.S. Day. 1973. "Nonresponse Bias and Callbacks in Sample Surveys." *Journal of Marketing Research* 10:160–68.

Elkins, David J. 1985. "British Columbia as a State of Mind." In *Two Political Worlds: Parties and Voting in British Columbia,* ed. Donald E. Blake. Vancouver: University of British Columbia Press.

Elkins, David, and Richard Simeon, eds. 1980. *Small Worlds: Provinces and Party in Canadian Political Life.* Toronto: Methuen.

Elster, Jon. 1986. "The Market and the Forum: Three Varieties of Political Theory." In *Foundations of Social Choice Theory,* ed. Jon Elster and Aanund Hylland. Cambridge: Cambridge University Press.

Elton, David, and Roger Gibbins. 1979. "Western Alienation and Political Culture." In *The Canadian Political Process,* ed. Richard Schultz, Orest M. Kruhlak and John C. Terry. Toronto: Holt, Rinehart and Winston.

Erickson, Lynda. 1991. "Women and Candidacies for the House of Commons." In *Women in Canadian Politics: Toward Equity in Representation,* ed. Kathy Megyery. Vol. 6 of the research studies of the

Royal Commission on Electoral Reform and Party Financing. Ottawa and Toronto: RCERPF/Dundurn.

Feldman, Stanley. 1982. "Economic Self-Interest and Political Behavior." *American Journal of Political Science* 26:446–66.

———. 1988. "Structure and Consistency in Public Opinion: The Role of Core Beliefs and Values." *American Journal of Political Science* 32:416–40.

Fenno, Richard F., Jr. 1975. "If, as Ralph Nader Says, Congress Is the Broken Branch, How Come We Love Our Congressmen So Much?" In *Congress in Change*, ed. Norman J. Ornstein. New York: Praeger.

Ferguson, K. 1984. *The Feminist Case against Bureaucracy.* Philadelphia: Temple University Press.

Fiorina, Morris P. 1981. *Retrospective Voting in American Elections.* New Haven: Yale University Press.

Fishkin, James. 1992. *Democracy and Deliberation.* New Haven: Yale University Press.

Fitzgerald, R., and L. Fuller. 1982. "I Hear You Knocking But You Can't Come In: The Effects of Reluctant Respondents and Refusers on Sample Survey Estimates." *Sociological Methods and Research* 11 (1): 3–32.

Fleishman, John A. 1986. "Types of Political Attitude Structure: Results of a Cluster Analysis." *Public Opinion Quarterly* 50:371–86.

Fletcher, Frederick J. 1981. *The Newspaper and Public Affairs.* Vol. 7 of the research studies of the Royal Commission on Newspapers. Ottawa: Minister of Supply and Services Canada.

———. 1988. "The Mass Media and the Selection of National Party Leaders: Some Explorations." In *Party Democracy in Canada: The Politics of National Party Conventions,* ed. George Perlin. Scarborough: Prentice-Hall.

Franks, C.E.S. 1987. *The Parliament of Canada.* Toronto: University of Toronto Press.

Frey, J.H. 1983. *Survey Research by Telephone.* Beverly Hills: Sage Publications.

Galeotti, Gianluigi, and Albert Breton. 1986. "An Economic Theory of Political Parties." *Kyklos* 39:47–65.

Gibbins, Roger. 1985. *Conflict and Unity: An Introduction to Canadian Political Life.* Toronto: Methuen.

Gidengil, Elisabeth. 1989. "Class and Region in Canadian Voting: A Dependency Interpretation." *Canadian Journal of Political Science* 22:563–87.

Ginsberg, Benjamin. 1982. *The Consequences of Consent: Elections, Citizen Control and Popular Acquiescence.* New York: Random House.

Groves, R.M. 1989. *Survey Errors and Survey Costs.* New York: John Wiley and Sons.

Groves, R.M., and L.E. Lyberg. 1988. "An Overview of Nonresponse Issues in Telephone Surveys." In *Telephone Survey Methodology,* ed. Robert M. Groves, Paul P. Biemer, Lars E. Lyberg, James T. Massey, William L. Nicholls II and Joseph Waksberg. New York: John Wiley and Sons.

Horowitz, Gad. 1966. "Conservatism, Liberalism and Socialism in Canada: An Interpretation." *Canadian Journal of Economics and Political Science* 32:143–71.

Inglehart, Ronald. 1977. *The Silent Revolution.* Princeton: Princeton University Press.

———. 1990. *Culture Shift in Advanced Industrial Society.* Princeton: Princeton University Press.

Ionescu, Ghita, and Ernest Gellner, eds. 1967. *Populism: Its Meanings and National Characteristics.* London: Weidenfeld and Nicolson.

Ippolito, Dennis S., Thomas G. Walker and Kenneth L. Kolson. 1976. *Public Opinion and Responsible Democracy.* Englewood Cliffs: Prentice-Hall.

Irvine, William P. 1979. *Does Canada Need a New Electoral System?* Kingston: Queen's University, Institute of Intergovernmental Relations.

Johnston, Richard. 1986. *Public Opinion and Public Policy in Canada.* Vol. 35 of the research studies of the Royal Commission on the Economic Union and Development Prospects for Canada. Toronto: University of Toronto Press.

Kaase, Max. 1988. "Political Alienation and Protest." In *Comparing Pluralist Democracies: Strains in Legitimacy,* ed. Mattei Dogan. Boulder: Westview Press.

Katz, Richard S. 1980. *A Theory of Parties and Electoral Systems.* Baltimore: Johns Hopkins University Press.

Kinder, Donald R. 1983. "Diversity and Complexity in American Public Opinion." In *Political Science: The State of the Discipline,* ed. Ada W. Finifter. Washington, DC: American Political Science Association.

King, Anthony. 1981. "What Do Elections Decide?" In *Democracy at the Polls: A Comparative Study of Competitive National Elections,* ed. David Butler, Howard R. Penniman and Austin Ranney. Washington, DC: American Enterprise Institute for Public Policy Research.

King, William Lyon Mackenzie. 1918. *Industry and Humanity.* New York: Houghton Mifflin.

Koole, Ruud. 1989. "The 'Modesty' of Dutch Party Finance." In *Comparative Political Finance in the 1980's,* ed. Herbert E. Alexander. Cambridge: Cambridge University Press.

Kornberg, Allan, William Mishler and Harold D. Clarke. 1982. *Representative Democracy in the Canadian Provinces.* Scarborough: Prentice-Hall.

Kraus, Sydney. 1988. *Televised Presidential Debates and Public Policy.* Hillsdale: Lawrence Erlbaum.

Krukones, Michael G. 1984. *Promises and Performances: Presidential Campaigns as Policy Prediction.* Lanham: University Press of America.

Laycock, David. 1990. *Populism and Democratic Thought in the Canadian Prairies, 1910 to 1945.* Toronto: University of Toronto Press.

LeDuc, Lawrence. 1984. "Canada: The Politics of Stable Dealignment." In *Electoral Change in Advanced Industrial Democracies,* ed. R.J. Dalton, S.C. Flanagan and P.A. Beck. Princeton: Princeton University Press.

LeDuc, Lawrence, and Richard Price. 1990. "Campaign Debates and Party Leader Images: The Encounter '88 Case." Paper presented at the Canadian Political Science Association annual meeting, Victoria.

Levesque, Terrence J. 1983. "On the Outcome of the 1983 Conservative Leadership Convention: How They Shot Themselves in the Other Foot." *Canadian Journal of Political Science* 16:779–84.

Lijphart, Arend. 1985. "The Field of Electoral System Research: A Critical Survey." *Electoral Studies* 4:3–14.

Lipset, Seymour M. 1983. *Political Man: The Social Basis of Politics.* London: Heinemann.

———. 1990. *Continental Divide: The Values and Institutions of the United States and Canada.* New York: Routledge.

Massie, Michele. 1990. "Study of Canadians' Attitudes Toward the Electoral System." Presented to the Royal Commission on Electoral Reform and Party Financing. Ottawa.

McClosky, Herbert, and John Zaller. 1984. *The American Ethos: Public Attitudes Toward Capitalism and Democracy.* Cambridge: Harvard University Press.

Meisel, John, and Richard Van Loon. 1966. "Canadian Attitudes to Election Expenses 1965–66." In Canada. Committee on Election Expenses. *Studies in Canadian Party Finance.* Ottawa: Queen's Printer.

Milbrath, Lester W. 1965. *Political Participation: How and Why Do People Get Involved in Politics.* Chicago: Rand McNally.

Miller, Arthur H., and Ola Listhaug. 1990. "Political Parties and Confidence in Government: A Comparison of Norway, Sweden and the United States." *British Journal of Political Science* 29:357–86.

Milligan, G.W. 1980. "An Examination of the Effect of Six Types of Error Perturbation on Fifteen Clustering Algorithms." *Psychometrika* 45:325–42.

Monière, Denis. 1988. *Le discours electoral: les politiciens sont-ils fiables?* Montreal: Québec/Amérique.

Nadeau, Richard, and André Blais. 1990. "Do Canadians Distinguish Between Parties? Perception of Party Competence." *Canadian Journal of Political Science* 23:317–35.

Nevitte, Neil, Herman Bakvis and Roger Gibbins. 1989. "The Ideological Contours of 'New Politics' in Canada: Policy, Mobilization and Partisan Support." *Canadian Journal of Political Science* 22:475–503.

Norris, Pippa. 1985a. "The Gender Gap in Britain and America." *Parliamentary Affairs* 38:192–201.

———. 1985b. "Women's Legislative Participation in Western Europe." *Western European Politics* 8:90–101.

Northrup, D. 1985. "Survey of RRAP Renters: Methodological Report." Report prepared for Canada Mortgage and Housing Corporation. Toronto: York University, Institute for Social Research.

———. 1989. *The 1988 Canadian National Election Study: Technical Documentation.* Toronto: York University, Institute for Social Research.

Olsen, Dennis. 1980. *The State Elite.* Toronto: McClelland and Stewart.

Ontario. Commission on Election Contributions and Expenses. 1986. *Political Financing, Studies on Election Spending Limits and Party Leadership Campaigns.* Toronto: Government of Ontario.

Ornstein, Michael D., H. Michael Stevenson and A. Paul Williams. 1980. "Region, Class and Political Culture in Canada." *Canadian Journal of Political Science* 13:227–71.

O'Rourke, D., and J. Blair. 1983. "Improving Random Respondent Selection in Telephone Surveys." *Journal of Marketing Research* 20:428–32.

Paltiel, Khayyam Z. 1989. "Canadian Election Expense Legislation, 1963–85: A Critical Appraisal or Was the Effort Worth It?" In *Comparative Political Finance in the 1980's,* ed. Herbert E. Alexander. Cambridge: Cambridge University Press.

Pateman, Carole. 1970. *Participation and Democratic Theory.* Cambridge: Cambridge University Press.

———. 1980. "The Civic Culture: A Philosophic Critique." In *The Civic Culture Revisited,* ed. Gabriel A. Almond and Sydney Verba. Boston: Little, Brown.

Pelletier, Alain. 1991. "Politics and Ethnicity: Representation of Ethnic and Visible-Minority Groups in the House of Commons." In *Ethno-cultural Groups and Visible Minorities in Canadian Politics: The Question of Access,* ed. Kathy Megyery. Vol. 7 of the research studies of the Royal

Commission on Electoral Reform and Party Financing. Ottawa and Toronto: RCERPF/Dundurn.

Pennock, J. Roland. 1968. "Political Representation: An Overview." In *Representation*, ed. J. Roland Pennock and John W. Chapman. New York: Atherton Press.

———. 1979. *Democratic Political Theory*. Princeton: Princeton University Press.

Perlin, George, ed. 1988. *Party Democracy in Canada: The Politics of National Party Conventions*. Scarborough: Prentice-Hall.

Pitkin, Hannah F. 1967. *The Concept of Representation*. Berkeley: University of California Press.

Porter, J., P. Pineo and H. McRoberts. 1985. "Revisions of the Pineo-Porter-McRoberts Socio-economic Classification of Occupations for the 1981 Census." In *Program for Quantitative Studies in Economics and Population*. Report No. 125. Hamilton: McMaster University.

Powell, G. Bingham, Jr. 1982. *Contemporary Democracies: Participation, Stability and Violence*. Cambridge: Harvard University Press.

Public Opinion. 1984. "Opinion Roundup." 7:31.

Punj, Girish, and David W. Stewart. 1987. "Cluster Analysis in Marketing Research: Review and Suggestions for Application." In *Multivariate Data Analysis*, ed. Joseph F. Hair, Jr., Rolph E. Anderson and Ronald L. Tatham. 2d ed. New York: Macmillan.

Richards, John. 1981. "Populism: A Qualified Defense." *Studies in Political Economy* 5:5–27.

Riker, William H. 1982. *Liberalism Against Populism*. San Francisco: W.H. Freeman.

Robinson, John P., and Mark R. Levy. 1986. *The Main Source: Learning from Television News*. Beverly Hills: Sage Publications.

Rokeach, Milton. 1973. *The Nature of Human Values*. New York: Free Press.

Rollings, Colin. 1987. "The Influence of Election Programmes: Britain and Canada, 1945–1979." In *Ideology, Strategy and Party Change*, ed. Ian Budge et al. Cambridge: Cambridge University Press.

Rule, Wilma. 1987. "Electoral Systems, Contextual Factors and Women's Opportunity for Election to Parliament in Twenty-Three Democracies." *Western Political Quarterly* 40:477–98.

Sartori, Giovanni. 1977. *Parties and Party Systems: A Framework for Analysis*. Cambridge: Cambridge University Press.

Scarbrough, Elinor. 1984. *Political Ideology and Voting: An Exploratory Study*. Oxford: Clarendon Press.

Scheibe, Karl E. 1970. *Beliefs and Values.* New York: Holt, Rinehart and Winston.

Schneider, William, and I.A. Lewis. 1985. "Views on the News." *Public Opinion* 8 (4): 6–12.

Schumpeter, Joseph A. 1943. *Capitalism, Socialism, and Democracy.* New York: Harpers.

Schwartz, Mildred A. 1967. *Public Opinion and Canadian Identity.* Berkeley: University of California Press.

————. 1974. *Politics and Territory: The Sociology of Regional Persistence in Canada.* Montreal: McGill-Queen's University Press.

Searing, Donald D. 1979. "A Study of Values in the British House of Commons." In *Understanding Human Values: Individual and Societal,* ed. Milton Rokeach. New York: Free Press.

Sears, D., and S. Chaffee. 1978. "Uses and Effects of the 1976 Debates: An Overview of Empirical Studies." In *The Great Debates: Carter vs. Ford, 1976,* ed. S. Kraus. Bloomington: Indiana University Press.

Seidle, F. Leslie. 1985. "The Election Expenses Act: The House of Commons and the Parties." In *The Canadian House of Commons: Essays in Honour of Norman Ward,* ed. John Courtney. Calgary: University of Calgary Press.

Shils, Edward. 1956. *The Torment of Secrecy: The Background and Consequences of American Security Policies.* London: Heinemann.

Simard, Carolle. 1991. "Visible Minorities and the Canadian Political System." In *Ethno-cultural Groups and Visible Minorities in Canadian Politics: The Question of Access,* ed. Kathy Megyery. Vol. 7 of the research studies of the Royal Commission on Electoral Reform and Party Financing. Ottawa and Toronto: RCERPF/Dundurn.

Simeon, Richard, and David J. Elkins. 1980. "Provincial Political Cultures." In *Small Worlds: Provinces and Party in Canadian Political Life,* ed. David J. Elkins and Richard Simeon. Toronto: Methuen.

Sorauf, Frank J. 1988. *Money in American Elections.* Boston: Little, Brown.

Stasiulis, Daiva, and Yasmeen Abu-Laban. 1990. "Ethnic Minorities and the Politics of Limited Inclusion in Canada." In *Canadian Politics: An Introduction to the Discipline,* ed. Alain G. Gagnon and James P. Bickerton. Peterborough: Broadview Press.

————. 1991. "The House the Parties Built: (Re)constructing Ethnic Representation in Canadian Politics." In *Ethno-cultural Groups and Visible Minorities in Canadian Politics: The Question of Access,* ed. Kathy Megyery. Vol. 7 of the research studies of the Royal Commission on Electoral Reform and Party Financing. Ottawa and Toronto: RCERPF/Dundurn.

Steech, C.G. 1981. "Trends in Nonresponse Rates, 1952–1979."
Public Opinion Quarterly 45 (1): 40–57.

Stewart, Angus. 1967. "The Social Roots." In *Populism: Its Meanings and
National Characteristics,* ed. Ghita Ionescu and Ernest Gellner. London:
Weidenfeld and Nicolson.

Stewart, Ian. 1988. "The Brass Versus the Grass: Party Insiders and Outsiders
at Canadian Leadership Conventions, and Class Politics at Canadian
Leadership Conventions." In *Party Democracy in Canada: The Politics of
National Party Conventions,* ed. George Perlin. Scarborough: Prentice-Hall.

Stoetzel, Jean. 1983. *Les valeurs du temps present: une enquête.* Paris: Presses
universitaires de France.

Struble, Robert, Jr., and Z.W. Jahre. 1991. "Rotation in Office: Rapid but
Restricted to the House." *PS: Political Science & Politics* 24 (March): 34–37.

Swerdlow, Joel. 1984. *Beyond Debate: A Paper on Televised Presidential Debates.*
New York: Twentieth Century Fund.

Tibert, J. 1987. "Attitudes Towards Civil Liberties and the Canadian Charter
of Rights Technical Documentation." Toronto: York University,
Institute for Social Research.

Tremblay, V., and H. Hofmann. 1983. "The Random Generation of
Telephone Numbers." Montreal: Université de Montréal, Centre de
sondage.

United States. *Federal Election Campaign Act of 1971,* Pub. L. 92-225,
Feb. 7, 1972.

Verba, Sydney, and Gary R. Orben. 1985. *Equality in America: The View from
the Top.* Cambridge: Harvard University Press.

Ward, J.H. 1963. "Hierarchical Grouping to Optimize an Objective
Function." *Journal of the American Statistical Association* 58:236–44.

Wattenberg, Martin P. 1986. *The Decline of American Political Parties,
1952–1980.* Cambridge: Harvard University Press.

Wearing, Joseph. 1988. "The High Cost of High Tech: Financing the Modern
Leadership Campaign." In *Party Democracy in Canada: The Politics of
National Party Conventions,* ed. George Perlin. Scarborough: Prentice-Hall.

Wearing, Peter, and Joseph Wearing. 1991. "Does Gender Make a Difference
in Voting Behaviour?" In *The Ballot and Its Message: Voting in Canada,*
ed. Joseph Wearing. Mississauga: Copp Clark Pitman.

Wiles, Peter. 1967. "A Syndrome, not a Doctrine: Some Elementary Theses
on Populism." In *Populism: Its Meanings and National Characteristics,* ed.
Ghita Ionescu and Ernest Gellner. London: Weidenfeld and Nicolson.

Williams, R.M., Jr. 1968. "The Concept of Values." In *International Encyclopedia of the Social Sciences*, Vol. 16, ed. D.L. Shils. New York: Macmillan and Free Press.

Wiseman, F., and P. McDonald. 1979. "Noncontact and Refusal Rates in Consumer Telephone Surveys." *Journal of Marketing Research* 16:478–84.

Wishart, David. 1987. *CLUSTAN User Manual.* 4th ed. St. Andrews: University of St. Andrews.

Worsley, Peter. 1967. "The Concept of Pluralism." In *Populism: Its Meanings and National Characteristics*, ed. Ghita Ionescu and Ernest Gellner. London: Weidenfeld and Nicolson.

Young, Lisa. 1991. "Legislative Turnover and the Election of Women to the Canadian House of Commons." In *Women in Canadian Politics: Toward Equity in Representation*, ed. Kathy Megyery. Vol. 6 of the research studies of the Royal Commission on Electoral Reform and Party Financing. Ottawa and Toronto: RCERPF/Dundurn.

ACKNOWLEDGEMENTS

Care has been taken to trace the ownership of copyright material used in the text, including the tables and figures. The authors and publishers welcome any information enabling them to rectify any reference or credit in subsequent editions.

Consistent with the Commission's objective of promoting full participation in the electoral system by all segments of Canadian society, gender neutrality has been used wherever possible in the editing of the research studies.

THE COLLECTED RESEARCH STUDIES*

_____

* The titles of studies may not be final in all cases.

SYLVIA BASHEVKIN	Women's Participation in Political Parties
LISA YOUNG	Legislative Turnover and the Election of Women to the Canadian House of Commons
LYNDA ERICKSON	Women and Candidacies for the House of Commons
GERTRUDE J. ROBINSON AND ARMANDE SAINT-JEAN, WITH THE ASSISTANCE OF CHRISTINE RIOUX	Women Politicians and Their Media Coverage: A Generational Analysis

VOLUME 7

Ethno-cultural Groups and Visible Minorities in Canadian Politics: The Question of Access
Kathy Megyery, Editor

DAIVA K. STASIULIS AND YASMEEN ABU-LABAN	The House the Parties Built: (Re)constructing Ethnic Representation in Canadian Politics
ALAIN PELLETIER	Politics and Ethnicity: Representation of Ethnic and Visible-Minority Groups in the House of Commons
CAROLLE SIMARD, WITH THE ASSISTANCE OF SYLVIE BÉLANGER, NATHALIE LAVOIE, ANNE-LISE POLO AND SERGE TURMEL	Visible Minorities and the Canadian Political System

VOLUME 8

Youth in Canadian Politics: Participation and Involvement
Kathy Megyery, Editor

RAYMOND HUDON, BERNARD FOURNIER AND LOUIS MÉTIVIER, WITH THE ASSISTANCE OF BENOÎT-PAUL HÉBERT	To What Extent Are Today's Young People Interested in Politics? Inquiries among 16- to 24-Year-Olds
PATRICE GARANT	Revisiting the Voting Age Issue under the *Canadian Charter of Rights and Freedoms*

Commission Organization

Chairman
Pierre Lortie

Commissioners
Pierre Fortier
Robert Gabor
William Knight
Lucie Pépin

Senior Officers

Executive Director
Guy Goulard

Director of Research
Peter Aucoin

Special Adviser to the Chairman
Jean-Marc Hamel

Research
F. Leslie Seidle,
  Senior Research Coordinator

Legislation
Jules Brière, Senior Adviser
Gérard Bertrand
Patrick Orr

Coordinators
Herman Bakvis
Michael Cassidy
Frederick J. Fletcher
Janet Hiebert
Kathy Megyery
Robert A. Milen
David Small

Communications and Publishing
Richard Rochefort, Director
Hélène Papineau, Assistant
  Director
Paul Morisset, Editor
Kathryn Randle, Editor

Assistant Coordinators
David Mac Donald
Cheryl D. Mitchell

Finance and Administration
Maurice R. Lacasse, Director

Contracts and Personnel
Thérèse Lacasse, Chief

Editorial, Design and Production Services

Printed and bound in Canada by
Best Gagné Book Manufacturers